THEISM OR ATHEISM

Theism or Atheism
The Eternal Debate

F.F. CENTORE

LONDON AND NEW YORK

First published 2004 by Ashgate Publishing

Reissued 2018 by Routledge
2 Park Square, Milton Park, Abingdon, Oxon OX14 4RN
605 Third Avenue, New York, NY 10017

First issued in paperback 2021

Routledge is an imprint of the Taylor & Francis Group, an informa business

© F.F. Centore 2004

F.F. Centore has asserted his moral right under the Copyright, Designs and Patents Act, 1988, to be identified as the author of this work.

Typeset in Times Roman by J.L. & G.A. Wheatley Design, Aldershot.

All rights reserved. No part of this book may be reprinted or reproduced or utilised in any form or by any electronic, mechanical, or other means, now known or hereafter invented, including photocopying and recording, or in any information storage or retrieval system, without permission in writing from the publishers.

A Library of Congress record exists under LC control number: 2003043682

Notice:
Product or corporate names may be trademarks or registered trademarks, and are used only for identification and explanation without intent to infringe.

Publisher's Note
The publisher has gone to great lengths to ensure the quality of this reprint but points out that some imperfections in the original copies may be apparent.

Disclaimer
The publisher has made every effort to trace copyright holders and welcomes correspondence from those they have been unable to contact.

ISBN 13: 978-0-815-39841-7 (hbk)
ISBN 13: 978-1-351-14476-6 (ebk)
ISBN 13: 978-1-138-35844-7 (pbk)

DOI: 10.4324/9781351144766

Contents

Preface	vii
Acknowledgements	xi
About the Author	xiii

1. The Reach of Reason — 1
2. The Problem of Evil — 11
3. Naturalistic Theism — 25
4. Supernaturalistic Theism — 35
5. The As-if Approach to God — 45
6. The For-real Approach to God: The A Priori Method — 69
7. The For-real Approach: A Posteriori Internal Experience Method — 75
8. The For-real Approach: A Posteriori External Experience Method Based on Essence — 117
9. The For-real Approach: A Posteriori External Experience Method Based on Existence — 159

Bibliography	191
Index	197

Preface

In this work I examine what can be said about the existence and nature of God without the direct aid of scripture. Doing this is called philosophical or natural theology, an undertaking just as valuable today as it was centuries ago. It depends upon the use of our native rational powers, our ability to reason logically, open debate, and our capacity to use appropriate life experiences. In conformity with proper rational procedure, it means sticking to the facts. But which facts?

Some facts are more pertinent than others to natural theology. Irrelevant facts would include information about the number of people belonging to religion R. In order to know the number we must meet at least two conditions. First, R must have a well-defined set of doctrines. Saying, for instance, that the members of R do not agree on anything is the same as saying that all we have is a name with nothing behind it. Second, the membership must really believe in those doctrines. In many cases there is no set of core teachings defining R. And even if there is, as in the case of the Roman Catholic Church, many 'members' do not follow the core teachings. Many 'members' are only 'cafeteria' members, picking and choosing this or that part of R as they see fit. Consequently, specifying numbers is misleading and thus best avoided.

In addition, as they say in the social sciences, the plural of anecdote is data. Clever people can play with numbers. For example, if organization R is short on members, all its leaders need do is reduce the requirements for membership and thereby immediately realize an increase in membership. Whether with respect to university admissions or to the priesthood, one way to increase the number of recruits is by decreasing the conditions required to join. The shorter the creed, the longer the membership list.

Also misleading is the notion that we can take someone's word for membership in R. You cannot bear witness to yourself in such matters. Can you be a Muslim, a Jew, or a Hindu simply because you claim to be? If you could get away with making such a claim on your own authority, you could also get away with awarding yourself a Harvard MD degree or issuing yourself a Canadian passport. Are you a loyal and devoted member of R? Am I? That is not for me to say and it is not for you to say. Deciding who is and who is not a loyal and devoted member of R requires a standard drawn from the real world outside of one's own peculiar psychological condition. If there is no objective measure, then there is no R (no church), only a collection of Rs (churches), each with a grand total membership of one.

Avoiding these dead ends, my plan of presentation is, in chapters 1 and 2, to clear the ground of various superficial arguments raised against religion and the existence of God. Discussions in this area are sometimes sidetracked by useless objections. To be meaningful, all sides must be willing to consider the evidence in a serious way. If they are not, then there is really no discussion at all, but only trench warfare, with each side hurling verbal abuse at the other. In this regard, all forms of extremism must be avoided. Some people, for example, refuse to spell God with a capital letter, as if doing so would show a commitment to God's existence. Forgetting that the use of capitals is dictated by the rules of grammar, not by religious beliefs, they may as well refuse to spell Bambi, Mickey Mouse, or Popeye with capital letters.

Appropriately, since it is the argument against the existence of God that is most often raised, chapter 2 pays special attention to this problem. I discuss the problem with particular reference to moral evil. Why, for instance, is it wrong for you and me not to care for the poor? Thinking of the economically poor as a class of people deserving attention originated among the ancient Jews. Going back to about 600 BC, according to Deuteronomy 15, the Israelites were under direct orders from God to care for the poor. However, if the God of Abraham, Isaac, and Jacob is dead, why bother?

Chapters 3 and 4 are devoted to outlining the main ways in which God or The Divine have been defined throughout the many years of human thinking on the subject. In these chapters some attention is paid to various forms of religion found in places such as China, India, and the Near East. I also look at the main variations found within the monotheistic supernaturalistic view of God.

The remainder of the work, chapters 5 through 9, sets out a sampling of the basic arguments for the existence of God. There are at least two ways of doing this: one way is to follow the chronological order of the thinkers; another way is to look at the types of argument used. My approach is the latter. I take at least one sample from each of the different types. As it turns out, contemporary writers have not really added any significant content to the basic arguments. Examples, illustrations, and forms of expression change, but the basic arguments remain the same.

The presentation of each argument follows a certain pattern. First, the argument is outlined according to the mind of the thinker most noted for using the argument. This outline is then followed by a critique of the argument, again as much as possible adhering to the thinking of the critic. Sometimes the critique is short and sometimes lengthy. In many cases, the critique of one thinker's position is the whole position of another thinker. For example, Hegel's view is an attempt to correct the view previously defended by Kant.

In another case, all those who elevate essences to the highest rank in their approach to reality are critics of someone such as Aquinas, a thinker who regards existence as the pinnacle of reality and human thought. By the same token, Aquinas is the major critic of all those following the path of essences. Those who concentrate on essence are concerned primarily with the question

'What is it?' rather than 'Is it?' This is the typical way of proceeding in the sciences. Knowing the formula, the definition of the thing or process, the idea of the thing, is of greatest significance, so much so that whether or not the thing exists is something we can ignore. Can there be a science of dinosaurs? Textbooks in science are always written in a generalized, abstract way. Science always aims at attaining universal and necessary knowledge of the material world. In contrast, without denying the importance of definitions and concepts, Aquinas regards the existential question as the most important of all possible questions.

Finally, throughout all the presentations I devote some time to the life-history of the thinker primarily responsible for the position under discussion. Knowing about the thinker's intellectual strengths, lifestyle, and personal problems goes a long way in throwing light on the thinker's arguments for or against the existence of God.

Acknowledgements

I wish to thank Ayli Raphaela Lapkoff and Jennifer Lee for alerting me to various refinements required in order to make the work more understandable. My son, Paul Matthew, also deserves thanks for doing the same. In addition, I wish to thank Larry Azar, who earned his doctorate at Saint Michael's College, University of Toronto, for introducing me to Aquinas-the-existentialist. In this regard, it is not too much to say that Gilson begot Owens, who begot Azar, who begot Centore. In chapter 9, for instance, the subsection entitled 'Aquinas' Unique Philosophy' is an expanded version of a talk originally given by Professor Azar to the philosophy department of C.W. Post College in Brookeville, Long Island, in the Autumn of 1964. He was kind enough to take me along, thus beginning my enlightenment. Finally, I must take responsibility for any translations of Aquinas' Latin into English.

About the Author

F.F. Centore was born on 29 August 1938, in Brooklyn, NY, the oldest child of Paul and Jenny Centore. While still an infant, his family moved to Buffalo, NY, where he received his early education.

His post-secondary work was done at Canisius College, Buffalo, NY; the University of Maryland, College Park, Maryland; and St John's University, New York, NY, where he received his PhD in Philosophy.

Shortly after completing his academic work, he started teaching philosophy at St Jerome's University, Waterloo, Canada in July 1969.

His love of teaching and interaction with his students, both formally and informally, was to become his whole life, second only to his family. He married Helen Angela Rizzo, on 6 August 1966. They had three children: Helen, Paul Matthew, and Laura.

Many of his students saw him as a life-long mentor, keeping him informed of the many vicissitudes in their lives. Although he belonged to several professional organizations, nothing pleased him more than face-to-face contact for sheer enjoyment. He participated in some administrative duties, at St Jerome's, but students were his main joy.

This work is being published posthumously, since Floyd died on 24 August 2003. He is sorely missed, and deeply mourned by many colleagues, friends, and family.

Chapter 1

The Reach of Reason

Religion and Science

Philosophical or natural theology is a venerable undertaking, beginning among the ancient Greeks, as illustrated in the dialogue *The Laws* by Plato (427–347 BC) and in the *Metaphysics* by Aristotle (384–22 BC). As we will see, over the centuries the basic questions concerning our relationship to God have remained the same (Plato, 1963; Aristotle, 1941).

To illustrate, in modern times, according to Samuel Beckett (1906–89) in his play *Waiting for Godot* (1952), everyone is waiting for God to show up so that God can give us instructions about what to do. However, God does not show up and so we are thrown back on our own devices. Should we commit suicide or invent busy-work for ourselves?

Yet the question remains: Why doesn't God talk to us in a direct physical way? But then we can also ask: Is this a reasonable expectation? Assuming that God is a spiritual being, is it reasonable to expect that we would experience God in the same way as a material thing? Perhaps the proper way to experience God is by means of conscience or through the love we have for other human beings. Whereas things of the body grow and decay, things of the spirit live forever. If true lovers are to experience love in an everlasting way, maybe it can only be in heaven.

Furthermore, is religion opposed to science, which prides itself on physical observations and material experiments? Some people interested in defending religion seem to think that by degrading science the value of religion must rise. This attitude, though, is a mistake. When considering the relationship of science and religion, there are four possible positions.

1. Science can increase while religion decreases.
2. Science can decrease while religion increases.
3. Both science and religion can decrease.
4. Both science and religion can increase.

Even assuming that science is evil or that it has done more harm than good over the past 400 years, those advocating the denigration of science overlook the third possibility. As we see in the case of David Hume, for instance, one's scepticism can extend to everything, including science. In contrast, for someone such as Thomas Aquinas, the human intellect is capable of knowing the truth in both science and religion. There is no need to deny knowledge in order to make room for faith.

The next obvious issue, then, concerns how we go about actually achieving such a balance. Certainly, being negative will not do. To be reasonable we must be affirmative; we must offer positive arguments. In order to be useful in natural theology, any argument for the existence of God must meet certain positive conditions.

1. It must be accessible to anyone with a basic education and basic reasoning powers. It should not be restricted to only a few people with specialized training in science, philosophy, or theology. It should not require that someone be a specialist in all of the fine points of either humanistic or computer logic. Consequently, saying that you have a perfect proof for the existence of God, but that you are the only one who can understand it, will not do.
2. It must be in conformity with the available evidence, even while being free of any particular scientific theory of the universe. The natural sciences keep advancing in their discovery of more and more certainties about nature. When the sciences enter upon the philosophy of nature, however, they are not at all certain. For example, what are the ultimate constituents of nature? Matter and form? Atoms? History is full of discarded relics. Plotinus (205–70), with his universe full of many layers of gods, magic, and mysticism, all coming from the great non-being by a fatalistic process, represented theoretical science at its best. We have also seen the scientific theories of Plato, Aristotle, Descartes, Néwton, and Darwin come and go. Any argument that is bound to the latest scientific theory is sure to die as soon as the scientific theory dies. How long will Einstein's view last? From the perspective of natural theology, for instance, it seems odd that God's power to move something should be limited to the speed of light.
3. In order to be useful in a religious context, the argument must show an agreement between reason and whatever revelation is significant within a given religious context. Such a convergence must not be forced. At each stage it should be possible to check the argument against the available evidence and the rules of ordinary logic. In this way, if there is a convergence of the God of reason with the God of religion, it will not be the result of propaganda or indoctrination.

Some Non-arguments

Style versus Content

Should all statements concerning the existence of God be taken seriously? Consider, for instance, the following: 'You do not really believe in God, do you! You must accept the fact that you are a mistake of nature regurgitated up out of the primeval slime with no purpose whatsoever!' The first rule of rational discourse is to avoid emotional outbursts. Statements such as the above say something about someone's state of mind, but not something about the state of things outside the mind. It is as useless as asking, I wonder why people in the newspaper always die in alphabetical order? I wonder why hospitals always seem to have so many sick people? Or, I wonder what the world would be like if all the men were women and all the women were men? Emotional statements are statements of fact about someone's psychological condition. But what is emotionally embraced by one person can be emotionally rejected by another person. We must not confuse the cognitive with the affective, knowledge with feelings.

By the same token, merely asserting that the earth is cube-shaped does not tell us anything about the real earth. In parallel fashion, denying the existence of God because someone was taught to believe in God at a young age is no argument at all. The same line could be used to hassle the atheist. The only reason you (the atheist) disbelieve in God is that you were raised in an atheistic family. Is the truth always the opposite of what you were taught at home or in school?

Neither should we think that someone's manner of speaking, physical appearance, or lifestyle is relevant to the truth or falsity of the statements being made. Someone, for instance, can tell you in the nicest way that two and two make five. However, regardless of the person's good looks, beautiful speech, fine clothes, and charming personality, the answer is wrong. On the other hand, someone might punch you in the mouth, throw you down on the ground, and hurl insults at you, all the while telling you that two and two make four. The fact that someone is attractive does not guarantee that the person is saying something true. Neither is there any necessary connection between being attractive and being moral.

We must beware of attempting to judge something on the basis of something else that happens to be close to it. Similar to the situation wherein someone's personality is used as a basis for deciding what is true or false, deciding which of two or more propositions is true or false by association is a good way to often be mistaken. For instance, the fact that someone is very prejudiced against Whites does not mean that he is unable to solve some very thorny problem in mathematics. The reason for this is simple. When you have a conjunction of two propositions (P and Q), one can be true while the other one is false, or both can be true, or both can be false. For instance, in the case of 'the moon is made of green cheese and all hydrogen is combustible', there is no need to assume that the latter is false because the former is false.

This becomes significant when dealing with arguments for the existence of God made by people who lived in times when the level of scientific knowledge was far below that of ours today. Does this mean that anything they have to say must be inferior to what we have today? Certainly not. To assert that what they have to say is unfit for modern ears would itself be a form of prejudice. Instead, each statement made by the older thinker must be judged on its own merits.

Similarly, we must be careful about our initial assumptions. Over the years, for example, many people have criticized Pope Pius XII (1876–1958) for not speaking out louder and more constantly against the Nazis. The critics, though, usually begin with the false assumption that the best way to control the actions of a vicious dictator is to publicly condemn him loudly and often. Those who tried this approach with Hitler soon learned that it did more harm than good; constantly slapping the vicious dog on the nose will not make the beast less vicious. The proper approach in Hitler's case was to work behind the scenes in order to save as many of the intended victims as possible, which is exactly what Pope Pius XII did.

In other words, appearances can be deceiving. The spoon in the water is not really broken and the person seen from a distance walking across campus is not really only three inches tall. What is up-front and what is behind the scenes can be quite different. Style and outward appearance can be one thing while the actual content can be something else.

Yes, but does not having any sort of commitment, whether internal or external, make a discussion of religion impossible? No, because it is possible to be committed and tolerant at the same time. As a matter of fact, neutrality in religious matters is impossible. Everyone must maintain some view with respect to God. Even the agnostic is maintaining a definite position. Nevertheless, although neutrality in the area of religion is neither possible nor necessary, getting to the roots of the issues is both possible and necessary in philosophy. For example, if someone should lament the fact that a young boy committed suicide rather than go through life as a homosexual, the philosopher would not say: 'Oh, how terrible,' and leave it at that. He would become obnoxious and ask: 'So what's wrong with suicide?'

As we will see, real philosophers are in the business of radical thinking. They love cutting through propaganda and outward appearances. Their main tool for doing this is the embarrassing question. They question what others take for granted. This is a good way not to be popular at parties, especially if you are dealing with politicians. Nevertheless, it is something that must be done if we are to make any progress in our discussion of the existence of God.

The Crutch Theory

Another non-argument is the crutch theory of religion, which says that religion is really only a way of overcoming our many fears concerning the precariousness of life. Our fear creates the gods. According to this view, the more a creature is likely to suffer the more religious it is.

However, it is easy enough to see that being dependent on something for comfort does not disprove the existence of the thing. A child, for instance, can depend upon a blanket for comfort. Also, why are animals, which suffer as much if not more than humans, not just as religious?

In addition, the argument can be turned against the critic. It is the critic who fears the existence of God because of what taking God seriously means for his immoral lifestyle. If God can come into his life, his whole sense of security would be upset. Taking God seriously means that tonight God might demand his life. His fear of punishment creates the atheist.

A variation on the crutch theory is the old Marxist view that religion is a tool of the capitalist oppressors, the opium of the people, used to keep the workers tranquilized. The old Marxist sings:

> You will eat, bye and bye
> In that glorious land above the sky;
> Work and pray, live on hay,
> You'll get pie in the sky when you die.
>
> Joe Hill (Joseph Hillstrom, 1879–1915),
> *The Preacher and the Slave*

Following in the footsteps of Ludwig Feuerbach (1804–72), who said that God did not create us, but rather we created God, Marx believed that theology is really anthropology. Saying that the will of God should be done is really saying that the will of man should be done. For the Marxist, humanity is God. The Church must now be replaced with secular government central planning. According to Marxist theory, physically comfortable people are naturally atheists; radically reorganize the material basis of human life and religion will simply fade away. Unfortunately, this is another case of trying to make the facts fit the theory. In fact, physically comfortable people do not act like well-kept animals. As self-conscious, rational beings we become bored, restless, and suffer in mind from existential angst.

Cultural Relativism

One of the most current pseudo-arguments against the existence of God is cultural relativism. If the theory is right, the most we could have would be as-if (subjective) arguments for the existence of God. It would be impossible to say anything for-real (objectively true) about God.

Modernism refers to the rise of science, with its objective explanation of the world. For the enlightened scientific person, everything is nature and nothing is culture. The emphasis is on reason and how reason discovers the fixed natures (essences) of things. Pushed too far, though, this has some serious anti-humanistic consequences. If scientific determinism is the truth, what becomes of our human dignity? If we have a natural constitution that determines our every move, how can we determine our own personal and social destinies? Obviously, something must be done to neutralize the influence of science. Somehow or other we must free ourselves from the suffocating oppression of the inexorable laws of nature. How can man's will power be restored to its rightful place at the centre of the universe?

The answer given by post-modernists is that everything must be constantly constructed, deconstructed, and reconstructed. There is no truth, only 'truth'. All basic world-views are only cultural prejudices. There is no methodology, scientific or otherwise, capable of providing us with the truth. Everything is nurture (culture) and nothing is nature. Perspective is everything. Religious stories, for example, are not just failed attempts to do good science. Contrary to Freud's view, religion is not a rival to science. Rather, religious myths serve a social function, which is to provide cohesiveness for the people. Something can be true, but only within a given belief system. There is no truth that cuts across all times, places, and societies. Cultural relativism begins with the basic assumption that nothing at all, even science, is essentially real, true, and good. In a word, philosophical renewal is essence removal.

Whence, then, the appearance of something essentially fixed? The answer is man-the-maker. Temporary stability is the result of the human will creating the nature and function of things. The enlightened post-modern person is always asking: Whose reality? Why was it constructed? What social function is served? For instance, when the Aryans invaded India they set up the caste system in order to make themselves feel good about their superior position. Likewise, the early Christians, who were persecuted for so many years, invented stories about a suffering Jesus Christ in order to make themselves feel good about their inferior position. Over time, the main ingredient of all man-made social constructs is language.

This is why tradition, especially linguistic tradition, is so important to Hans-Georg Gadamer (1900–2002), someone following in the footsteps of Martin Heidegger (1889–1976). For Gadamer, tradition is the great flywheel of society, keeping things stable through many changes. It restrains arbitrariness. Even though we are free to take everything apart and put it back together in any way we wish, our traditions give us stability. When Gadamer died in March 2002, even Pope John-Paul II praised him for his emphasis on tradition.

As emphasized by Gadamer, the hermeneutical phenomenon can be illuminated only in light of the fundamental finitude of being, which is wholly verbal in character. Furthermore, he wants to go beyond the concept of method held by modern science and envisage in a fundamentally universal way what always happens, which is that all understanding is determined by man-made culture. Instead of our language being a reflection of reality, reality is a reflection of our language (Gadamer, 1989, pp. 458, 512, 555).

Without a doubt, cultural relativism, in the sense that some aspects of human life are the result of social conditioning, is partially true. However, the basic principle of cultural relativism, when stated universally, is false. It is a truism that everything in life is part of a context. We are all children of our times. However, saying, rightly, that there is no going back to the past does not mean that there are no principles of moral human behaviour persisting through the past, present, and future. In real life we are not free to act in any way we want or to pass any law we feel like. In the social and political realm, for instance, the state cannot, without dire consequences, pass a law saying that women must drive on the right side of the road and men must drive on the left, or a law encouraging married women not to have children. Unless our purpose is to deliberately throw everything into chaos, neither can we pass a law saying that two and two make five.

Likewise in the sciences. Science seeks the universal and necessary causes for things in the physical world. Where there is a fixed nature (essence) inherent in something, there is a law. Where there is a law, there is science. Where there is science, there is predictability. And where there is predictability, there is the possibility of technology. Unsurprisingly, those in mathematics and science do not take seriously the deconstructionist brand of relativism.

Consider, for instance, feminism. No biologist is surprised when a teenage girl becomes pregnant. That is what she is supposed to do. Biologically speaking, females are baby-making machines. How, then, can feminism get started – that is, how can anyone justify ignoring nature? Enter Jean-Paul Sartre (1905–80), another Heidegger student, who figured out a way of rendering science irrelevant to human life. He told us in his *Being and Nothingness* and *Existentialism is a Humanism*, that man is freedom, which cannot be based on being. Being is the in-itself, the world of nature that is fixed and determined. Being is completely lacking in freedom and as such is anti-human. Freedom, therefore, must be based on the opposite of being, which can only be non-being (nothingness). Thus freed from nature, man can do whatever he wishes.

It is no accident that the bible of modern feminism was written by Sartre's loyal disciple, Simone de Beauvoir (1908–86). The divorce of man from nature allows her to declare in her work *The Second Sex* (1947) that everything feminine is the result of highly variable culture. If everything is the result of social history, then certainly some thing, such as what makes a male or female, is also. Cut loose from nature, females are given a licence to become the same as males in every way; anyone saying otherwise is guilty of oppressing women. She differs from her master in so far as her womanly instinct for the importance of interpersonal relationships causes her to place a greater emphasis on society and togetherness. In such a context, language is important. Everyone must use 'inclusive' language in order to show 'his or her' devotion to the new doctrine. For instance, words such as 'chairman' must be replaced with 'chairperson'. And anyone daring to say 'God the Father' is anathema.

In rebuttal we can say that both appealing to nothingness to explain something and ignoring the laws of nature are irrational moves. Concerning nothingness, Sartre's sense of absence can be explained rationally in terms of Aristotle's potency, namely, that which can be but which in fact now is not. There is no need to invoke the unthinkable nothingness.

Concerning nature, the facts must dictate to the theory, not vice versa. Claiming that the only thing holding back egalitarianism is paternalism ignores the facts. Let us assume that everything feminine is the result of historical circumstances. The theory is that, from their earliest days, all human beings are blank sheets of paper to be written on by the culture. The theory claims that so far the script has been dictated by males. What, though, are the facts? In fact, even if we gave dolls to every little boy to play with and guns to every little girl, they would still grow up to be different. In a marathon race, the fastest male will come in 15 minutes ahead of the fastest female, and so forth. The facts of nature cannot be denied.

We live in curious times, when lawmakers and judges foolishly think that they can make pigs fly and rocks float on water by writing down a few words on a piece of paper. Such foolishness leads to sheer arbitrariness in social matters, such as demanding that every slate of candidates for a university teaching position include at least one female. Why one? Why not 20? Why not demand that the group include at least one 400-pound, dark-skinned man in a wheelchair? Today we have judges who see nothing wrong with one male marrying another male. They say that defining marriage as possible only between one male and one female is unfair discrimination. Alright, but why continue with one male and one female? Why not one male and four females, one female and four males, three males, five females, and so on? And let's not forget the woman who really loves her dog. Divorced from nature, we can legalize anything.

The destruction of society is sure to follow from such a divorce. Having a genuine democracy, for instance, requires that certain dogmas be accepted as absolute and unchanging. We must know that, in the sight of God, each and every human being is of infinite worth, that each and every human being possesses an eternal destiny, and so forth. Under the sway of cultural relativism, however, none of the propositions required in order to justify an authentic democracy can be maintained with certainty. The most we can say is that a certain mythology is prevalent at this time.

Not only does cultural relativism ignore the facts, it is also self-refuting. It is so eager to devour everything in sight that it eats up even itself. If it is true that everything concerning human thinking and behaving is the consequence of cultural conditioning, then the theory itself must also be an unnecessary and temporary social construct. It can no more claim to be absolutely true than any other scientific, philosophical, or theological doctrine. The sword that the relativist swung in order to cut off the head of the absolutist has swung back, cutting off his own head.

As a consequence, if the cultural relativism doctrine were true, we could never know that it is true. We would be forever trapped within the cocoon of social conditioning, unable to view ourselves in relationship to anything else. It would be like someone who was born and lived forever in a submarine and who never saw or heard or knew anything about the fact that she was in a submarine. She could never step outside of her situation and compare herself with anything else.

We know, though, that this is not the case. We can stand outside of our situations and make comparisons with other situations. If we could not, we would be trapped in a perpetual propaganda situation. Said otherwise, we know the difference between fact and fiction and between the 'is' and the 'ought'. Can society change the laws of nature? Can we treat stones as soft? Can we jump off a tall building and fly by flapping our arms? We all know that anyone taking the route of illusion is not long for this world. By the same token, how could we ever work for something better if we cannot know the difference between what is the case and the ideal situation? The doctrine that everything is a prejudice is supposed to make us more tolerant. In fact, the result is just the opposite. Since nothing is really right or wrong, anything goes.

For example, what sort of twisted thinking allowed Hitler to enlist the aid of so many outstanding minds? In philosophy, for instance, Heidegger endorsed Hitler, calling him the epitome of German culture. David H. Hirsch reports that, after the war, in response to Herbert Marcuse's complaint that Heidegger was a Nazi, Heidegger said that he was no prophet and so could not see the consequences of Nazism. This, says Hirsch, is nothing short of a lie. Hirsch wonders why, in 1938, a supposedly backward Catholic thinker like Jacques Maritain (1882–1973) could see the consequences of Nazism while the avant-garde Heidegger could not (Hirsch, 1991).

Moreover, David Lehman claims that the whole emphasis on deconstructionism in literature is an effort to hide the Nazi roots of thinkers such as Heidegger and Paul de Man (1919–83), the Yale University professor of literature who had emigrated from Belgium to America after the war and who championed the deconstructionist doctrine in literature courses (Lehman, 1991).

Gadamer's attempt to get over these hurdles only confirms the rebuttal. When told by the German philosopher Leo Strauss (1899–1973) that cultural relativism is self-defeating, Gadamer answered by saying that believing in the existence of objective truth is itself the result of social conditioning. Even an unhistorical belief system is the result of historical conditioning. An absolutist is really a relativist who has been culturally conditioned to be an absolutist. This must be so in any given particular case because everything is historically conditioned. For instance, knowing that all people are mortal tells us that some people, such as Sally and Sam, are mortal. Similarly, according to Gadamer, knowing that all world-views are temporary social constructs tells us that some world-views, such as that God is eternally real and that He created a world with unchanging physical and moral laws, are temporary social constructs (Gadamer, 1989, Supplement I).

This, though, begs the question and must be rejected for what it is, namely, a fundamental error in logical reasoning. We do not know by definition that all world-views are social conventions. There is nothing in the nature of a world-view to make it such. The most we can say from the study of history and the social sciences is that some are. The only way to justify saying that all are is by forcing the issue. The person making the assertion must begin with the assumption that all are and then proceed to make the particular facts fit the theory. Neither is there anything in the definition of law making it inherently unstable. If anything, the nature of law favours its stability.

Consequently, the claim that, because everything is culture-bound, we cannot say anything objectively true concerning God is without merit. The truth of the matter lies between the two extremes of nurture and nature. There must be a balance between existence and essence, becoming and permanence, freedom and science, freedom and authority, novelty and tradition, diversity and identity, love and law, and so forth (Centore, 1991, pp. 217–18).

Chapter 2

The Problem of Evil

The Three Positions on Evil

One of the most popular arguments against the existence of God is called the problem of evil. How can you reconcile the existence of evil with the existence of a loving God possessing the attributes of omnipotence, omniscience, and providence? Everyone admits that we experience physical pain and mental anguish. Even while suffering, though, we distinguish between matters of lesser and greater significance. Is getting a parking ticket evil? What about assassinating your philosophy professor? Usually we reserve the title of evil for those things that involve something of momentous significance. Something can be a civil crime without being a great evil.

The possible relationships between God and evil can be spelled out using a simple matrix. We could have:

1 evil without God,
2 neither evil nor God,
3 God without evil, or
4 both evil and God.

The naive atheistic view upholds the first possibility. The sophisticated atheistic view maintains the second of the four possible combinations. The traditional theistic view covers the last two possibilities.

Agnosticism

What is the difference between ignorance and indifference? I don't know and I don't care. Agnosticism, because it neither affirms nor denies anything about the existence of God and/or evil, does not count as part of the matrix of combinations with respect to God and/or evil. Agnosticism is an ambiguous position, which can be used for either affirming or denying the existence of God and the need for absolute moral values. As a matter fact, 95 per cent of the time it is not used as a preparation for the arguments of Pascal, Kant, and James. The term agnosticism (not-knowing) was coined by Thomas Henry Huxley (1825–95), known as Darwin's bulldog because of his dogged defense of Darwin. Like his master, Huxley did not want to come out absolutely against the existence of God. The typical agnostic finds the issues of God's existence and the foundations of morality very opaque. Our intellects are much too weak to unravel such mysteries.

However, if not used to support the existence of God, agnosticism is in effect a practical atheism. This in turn necessarily leads to moral relativism. This means that, objectively speaking, we must always suspend judgment concerning good and evil. We can never seriously say either that something is evil or good. This is often the position taken in the social sciences, especially in sociology, psychology, and political science, where evil exists only in the mind of the beholder.

A modern example of this attitude is found in the thought of the English philosopher Alfred Jules Ayer (1910–89). Because he refused to debate the issue at all, Ayer claimed that he was not a theist, atheist, or agnostic. He claimed that, because God's existence could not be verified in a scientific way, the question of God's existence is meaningless and so there is no reason to discuss it at all.

In practice, though, Ayer could not avoid the moral implications of his view. Since the God question is meaningless, so is anything attached to it, such as the whole set of moral questions. All moral judgments, he insisted, are nothing more than expressions of subjective feelings. Even those who claim an absolute morality transcending all times and places are doing no more than expressing their own emotional state. This must be so in any given particular case because all moral preferences are no more than an expression of one's personal perspective and emotional state of mind.

Why someone here and now has a particular subjective emotional feeling is a matter for investigation by the social sciences. There cannot be any such thing as a science of ethics itself. Parallel to aesthetics, in so far as ethics is a branch of knowledge at all, it falls entirely within the social sciences, especially psychology and sociology. In this regard, Ayer's view is in keeping with the denial of free choice by thinkers such as Hume, Freud, and Skinner (Ayer, 1946, pp. 111–13).

The question, though, is whether or not anyone can really live with such an impersonal doctrine. If either evil or God or both are only ideas in my mind, then nothing is really good or evil, and so the problem of evil vanishes. If someone you love is killed by a drunk driver, you would not say: 'Oh well, even though I feel badly about it, there is no real evil here. Objectively speaking, you know, one event is no more significant than any other event.'

Atheism

Naive Atheism: Evil without God

Unlike agnosticism, atheism takes a hard line on evil. Atheists do not mince their words or pull their punches. Even though not a real being like Satan, evil is real. Children born with syphilis, volcanic eruptions burying people alive, people starving to death or being rounded up and slaughtered like animals are real things and events that should not be there. There is nothing feeble here; evil must be taken seriously.

Assuming that we can know about evil according to the ordinary meaning of the term 'real', such as saying that the tree outside in the yard is real or that the book really is resting on top of the table, how do we go about using evil to argue against the existence of God? Very simply, if evil is real then the perfect supreme being is unreal. There is a disjunction in which a God who is all-knowing, all-powerful, and all-loving stands in stark opposition to the presence of evil. The two parts are incompatible; if one exists then the other cannot exist. Now it is obvious that evil exists and therefore God is eliminated.

Bertrand Russell (1872–1970), for instance, never tired of pointing this out to theists. He did not say: 'So who knows for sure if X is really evil?' He knew evil when he saw it. According to Russell:

> When you come to look into this argument from design, it is a most astonishing thing that people can believe that his world, with all the things that are in it, with all its defects, should be the best that omnipotence and omniscience has been able to produce in millions of years. I really cannot believe it. Do you think that, if you were granted omnipotence and omniscience and millions of years in which to perfect your world, you could produce nothing better than the Ku-Klux-Klan or the Fascists? (see Russell, 1967, p. 18)

> Then there is another point which I consider excellent. You will remember that Christ said: 'Judge not lest ye be judged.' ... Then Christ says: 'Give to him that asketh thee, and from him that would borrow of thee turn not thou away.' ... Then there is one other maxim of Christ which I think has a great deal in it, but I do not find that it is very popular among some of our Christian friends. He says: 'If thou wilt be perfect, go and sell that thou hast, and give to the poor.' That is a very excellent maxim, but, as I say, it is not much practised. (Russell, 1967, p. 21)

> A good world needs knowledge, kindliness, and courage; it does not need a regretful hankering after the past, or a fettering of the free intelligence by the words uttered long ago by ignorant men. It needs a fearless outlook and a free intelligence. It needs hope for the future, not looking back all the time towards a past that is dead, which we trust will be far surpassed by the future that our intelligence can create. (Russell, 1967, pp. 26–27)

Russell's recommendations, though, are naive. He wants to draw interest on a non-existent bank account. How can Russell assert that anything, whether a political philosophy, a social organization, or a religious war, is really evil? How can moral values be peremptory and absolute if there is no peremptory and absolute standard to distinguish good from evil? Russell thinks that we should develop our minds and change the world for the better. But what is better, and best?

It might also be pointed out that it was Russell who asserted that believing something on faith means believing something on the basis of nothing. He delighted in condemning 'blind faith' as unreasonable and unscientific. However, this is also naive. Faith means accepting something because it is told to you by a trustworthy witness. We all do this kind of thing all the time – even scientists. How often does one scientist repeat the experimental work of another scientist? Should we abandon all criminal trials and legal proceedings that depend upon the information provided by credible witnesses?

Moreover, Russell never did catch on to reality in other important ways. The last 20 years or so of his life were devoted to preaching world peace, which he insisted would be achieved by means of scientific reason. He failed to realize that peace depends upon love much more than knowledge. The basic cause of war is sin, not a lack of scientific knowledge. Indeed, scientific knowledge and technology, if not controlled by a proper morality, only serves to make war more inevitable and horrible. How can we have evil without good? How do we know that some things, such as intelligence, kindness, and courage, are good and that their opposites are evil? Russell wants to kill God while keeping Satan alive. This will not do.

Sophisticated Atheism: Neither Evil nor God

In recent philosophical history, the best example of sophisticated atheism is Friedrich Wilhelm Nietzsche. He was born in 1844 in the little town of Roecken, located near Leipzig, Prussia, into a family whose grandfather and father were Lutheran clergymen. He was named after the current king of Prussia, Friedrich Wilhelm IV (1795–1861), who went insane in 1857. Nietzsche's family was composed mostly of clergymen and women. When Nietzsche was not yet five years old, his father died; a short time later his younger brother died. He then lived with his grandmother, mother, two unmarried aunts, and his sister. He went on to study theology and classical philology at the Universities of Bonn and Leipzig, at which time he completely lost his family faith.

His university studies were interrupted, however, when, in October 1867, Nietzsche began his obligatory military service, serving in the artillery. In March of the following year he was injured by a horse, went on sick leave, and returned to Leipzig in October 1868. At 24, in 1869, even before he finished his PhD, he was given a temporary professorship of classical studies at the University of Basel, Switzerland. In the same year he was awarded an honorary PhD by Leipzig. He became a Swiss citizen in 1870 and soon after obtained a regular teaching appointment. With the outbreak of the Franco-Prussian War, Nietzsche signed up as a volunteer medical orderly. However, within a month he developed a long-lasting illness and returned to Basel in October 1871.

While in Basel, he met Richard Wagner (1813–83), who at the time was living in the vicinity of Basel. At first he loved Wagner because, in his early works (for example, *Tannhäuser*, 1845), Wagner was ready to declare that human beings, even though they will suffer because of their audacity, should live independently of God. At the time, Nietzsche looked upon Wagner as the wonderful father figure he so desperately desired to have in his life. The period

1876 to 1880, however, saw the writing of Nietzsche's work *Human, All Too Human*, marking the beginning of an attack on Wagner and others for their incipient religiosity and sentimental emotionalism. About this same time, in 1879, he resigned his teaching position due to a nervous disturbance and eye problems that had begun in 1876. He spent the next nine years in various parts of Switzerland, France, and Italy at different health resorts, all the while composing his critiques of religion and culture. His main source of income was not from his writings, which did not sell at all, but from a small pension awarded to him by the University of Basel.

Nietzsche wrote intensely between 1880 and 1888. Earlier, at the same time Ivy League football was getting started in New England, Nietzsche had written *The Birth of Tragedy and the Spirit of Music* (1872), *Untimely Meditations* (1873–76), and *Human, All Too Human* mentioned above. Following these writings there appeared *Dawn* (1881), *The Gay Science* (1882, 1887), *Thus Spoke Zarathustra* (1883–85), *Beyond Good and Evil* (1886, an explanation of *Zarathustra*), *The Genealogy of Morals* (1887), *The Corruption of Wagner* (1888), *The Decline of the Gods* (1888), *The Anti-Christ* (1888), and *Ecce Homo* (1888, an autobiographical work). Also, he left behind an extensive set of notes for *The Will to Power*. In many ways, much of what Nietzsche had to say is presented as a report card on the state of religion in Europe in the 1800s. He saw religion as being on its last legs, leaving a vacuum to be filled in with his own version of salvation.

At the end of January 1889 he collapsed on a street in Turin, Italy, most likely from the effects of syphilis. After that he was considered insane and was forced to spend the rest of his life in the care of institutions, his mother, or his sister. He died on 25 August 1900 and was buried, ironically, because he thought that Judao-Christianity was the greatest obstacle to progress in the world, in the churchyard in his little home town near Leipzig.

From 1895 to 1901, at first while Nietzsche was still alive but mentally incapacitated, and then following his death, a more or less complete edition of his works appeared. *The Complete Works*, in English, edited by Oscar Levy, was published in 1914. Nietzsche's younger sister, Elisabeth (1846–1935), released her brother's *Ecce Homo* for publication in 1908. There were also editions of his many letters. Elisabeth wrote his biography, *The Life of Nietzsche*, in several volumes, from 1895 to 1904. She included in her biography parts of *The Will to Power*. An expanded edition of *The Will to Power* was published in 1906. Unfortunately for future scholarship, her versions of the work were contaminated by containing fraudulent and rewritten passages seeming to support the notion of a one superior Aryan race.

After World War II, when the true import of Nietzsche's philosophy had become evident to everyone, a new version of *The Will to Power*, based on the original notes, was edited by Walter Arnold Kaufmann (1921–76) (Nietzsche, 1968). As a devotee of Nietzsche, Kaufmann was at pains to knock down the idea of Nietzsche as a proto-Nazi. In his introduction to *The Gay Science*, Kaufmann explains that being a Nazi means that you are devoted to exterminating the Jews (Nietzsche, 1974). This, though, was not Nietzsche's position and so Nietzsche was not a Nazi, or even a proto-Nazi. However, the procedure of redefining something to suit yourself, although typical of the master himself, is ineffective. Arbitrarily restricting the definition of Nazism to violent anti-Semitism is revisionist history.

More objectively, even if Elisabeth's elaborations are extracted from her brother's works, it is still clear that the editors of the early editions of Nietzsche's works, even without *The Will to Power*, regarded their master as what we today would call a proto-Nazi, in the sense that Hitler best matched the picture of what it takes to be a superman. The superman believes in living life to the fullest in his own way. Courageously, Hitler felt good about himself as an anti-intellectual believing in government by instinct. He lived by his own rules and made his own choices. He was what he was and nobody was going to change him. He showed leadership and did not fear change.

One of the features most distinctive of Nietzsche is his writing style. He wrote largely in aphorisms, that is, short, punchy passages that made his point in a very graphic, unhesitating, and dogmatic manner. His acid tongue never hesitated to offend those whom he hated. In a way similar to some modern obnoxious talk-show hosts, his style may help to explain his continuing popularity. Moreover, since his works were hardly read during his own lifetime, they were not critiqued by other philosophers. Consequently, we do not know how Nietzsche would have answered his critics.

As a sophisticated atheist Nietzsche knew that only if evil is real is there a problem of reconciling evil and God. Therefore, instead of using evil to disprove God, he took it for granted that science had killed God. This then ushered in the age of nihilism, defined as the radical repudiation of all value, meaning, and desirability. (See Nietzsche, 1968, section 1. Also Nietzsche, 1987, 1974; Kaufmann, 1982.)

This radicalness is often overlooked. To illustrate, imagine that someone writes a play ridiculing God. Then the playwright is killed by a theist. All of his supporters then condemn the assassin as an evil person. According to Nietzsche's view, though, this is sheer foolishness on their part. They fail to see the meaning of atheism, which includes the right of the assassin to do his own thing. The best way to see Nietzsche's radicalness is to see him as he saw himself, as an Anti-Christ.

Jesus Christ actively embraced suffering, not for its own sake, but as a means to an end. Suffering is a sign of real commitment. Also, Christ's suffering shows that innocent people often suffer because of the evil deeds of others. Bless those who torture you for affirming the Messiah, do not seek revenge, give generously to those in need, remain a virgin until marriage, remain faithful to your spouse no matter what happens, and do not cheat on your taxes. This is not something most people want to hear. Hollywood is certainly against it. It is also opposed by the many watered-down versions of Christianity, which can be defined as Christianity without the crucifixion.

However, encouraging suffering did not mean that Jesus Christ condemned all pleasure as evil. Quite the contrary, he enjoyed wedding feasts and music, the conversation of friends and relatives, good food and fine wine, being clean and well-groomed, a comfortable place to sleep, and telling humorous stories. He certainly delighted in exciting teaching techniques and debating societies. (See Knox, 1955, pp. 132–41, 1963a, pp. 380–87. See also Kreeft, 1986.)

Imitating Jesus Christ means avoiding two extremes. One is the Puritan extreme of regarding all personal pleasure as evil. The other is the playboy extreme of regarding all suffering and self-sacrifice as evil. For the playboy, self-gratification and pleasure, both bodily and aesthetic, are the only worthwhile things in life. For the suffering-phobic egotist, the ideal world is the world of roses without thorns, whitewall tyres that never get dirty, gourmet meals all the time, and top-heavy hairless pornography prostitutes engaging in endless sex. An infinite amount of pleasure and zero amount of responsibility is the playboy's ideal. As we are taught by the overpowering pornography business, the best way to achieve this ideal is for every female to be a whore, thus maximizing the size of the herd from which fresh meat can be selected.

In actual daily life, of course, neither extreme can be achieved. The Puritan finds himself enjoying something in spite of himself, while the egotist is forced to make some sacrifices in order to stay out of jail. Such compromises, though, must always be minimized. What makes the extremist so extreme is that he is constantly pushing the limits of his position. If someone at one extreme finds himself gravitating toward the other extreme, he feels guilty about it and tries to move back.

The Christian, however, is different. He willingly makes sacrifices in order to please God and help others. Very often this means denying himself some earthly pleasures and maybe even earthly life itself. For example, a young man cannot remain a carefree bachelor; he must suffer either as a celibate priest or as a family man. Women are in the same situation: the religious life or a husband and children. Likewise, given the choice between abandoning his family and death, the man chooses death. By the same token, a Christian wife, abandoned by her faithless husband, nevertheless remains faithful (like God) even in the face of faithlessness. This does not mean that the saintly Christian regards earthly pleasures as evil. It means that he will deliberately sacrifice his own personal pleasure in order to help others and please God. Words are cheap, but real commitment is shown by life-long deeds, for instance, celibacy.

Nietzsche understood his enemy very well. Writing as if he were delivering a revelation from above, he knew that in order to finish off Judao-Christianity once and for all he also had to avoid both extremes. The overman is neither a Puritan denying himself all pleasure nor a playboy maximizing his own physical pleasure. Instead, his superman is someone who happily accepts suffering in order to work for the ignorant masses in a purely secular way. And the masses do need help. Everywhere the weeds dominate over the roses. The ordinary person is weak and deficient, the female more than the male. Nietzsche had little respect for women, who are useful only for sex. And to be beautiful a woman had to be the tall, long-legged type (Nietzsche, 1974, section 75). He even says that any woman interested in philosophy must have something wrong with her womb and that all women wish to be beaten (Nietzsche, 1987, sections 144, 147).

Ordinary people possess the herd (slave) mentality attributed to Apollo, the later Greek god of light, poetry, learning, and health. Like Apollo, their outlook is optimistic. They crave compromise and fair play. They are the shopkeepers of the world, outer-directed by public opinion and religion. The herd members suppress their passions and extol self-control. They use reason to justify mediocrity. They love their priests and demand democracy, which is based on the ridiculous notion that all souls are equal before God. Overall, they have a cowardly resistance to change.

For Nietzsche, freedom and equality are incompatible. In contrast to the herd stands nature's aristocrat, the new god. He is true-to-himself, inner-directed, startling, bold, a man of powerful passions, an actor, not a speculator. He is the cultured one who desires to be young and spontaneous forever. He believes in the gratuitous deed, justified simply because he wills it. He is the only one who is really alive. While the heard is bogged down in the cement of contentment, the elite overman follows a special morality. He regards democracy and welfare programmes with contempt. Not only must the superman himself suffer, he must also be ready to inflict suffering on others.

> This universal love of men is in practice the *preference* for the suffering, underprivileged, degenerate: it has in fact lowered and weakened the strength, the responsibility, the lofty duty to sacrifice men. ... The species requires that the ill-constituted, weak, degenerate, perish; but it was precisely to them that Christianity turned as a conserving force; it further enhanced that instinct in the weak, already so powerful, to take care of and preserve themselves and to sustain one another. What is 'virtue' and 'charity' in Christianity if not this mutual preservation, this solidarity of the weak, this hampering of selection? (Nietzsche, 1968, section 246)

Nietzsche realizes that without the support of Judao-Christian theology the whole Judao-Christian moral system collapses. In the new age, the greatest immorality is following the old religious morality. The superman is therefore forced to create his own new morality. Anything else would not be authentic. The only sin is not being honest with himself (Nietzsche, 1987, sections 62, 195, 261; *The Decline of the Gods* (in Nietzsche, 1982) sections X, 5; 1968, sections 246, 253, 266, 400, 464, 727–28, 859).

The superman is a Dionysian character, named after Dionysus, the later Greek god of sex, fertility, wine, and emotional abandonment, who underwent a mythical process of death and rebirth (Winter and Spring) in order to bring life to mankind. He joyously accepts the ugly, dirty, and destructive aspects of life, especially as he finds them in himself. Excessiveness is part of his lifestyle. He combines the ruthlessness of Julius Caesar with the compassion of Jesus Christ, brutality with an appreciation of sublime art and music. Destruction and creation go together. The Dionysian drive, says Nietzsche, is the great pantheistic combination of joy and sorrow that sanctifies and calls good even the most terrible qualities of life (Nietzsche, 1968, section 1050). It follows that the superman is the tragic man. Soon enough he will be absorbed back into an impersonal nature that is completely indifferent to both his defeats and triumphs.

Nietzsche thought that atheism was the great irony of Judao-Christianity, which was largely responsible for the rise of science in the first place. It was then destroyed by its own offspring (rational science), which plunged Europe into a moral crisis. Modern science, with its mechanistic universe, killed God. Kant and Hegel tried to replace God, but to no avail. Neither is the deistic humanism of someone such as Voltaire worth anything. Now we must realize, concludes Nietzsche, that along with the death of God goes the death of Satan. Without God, nothing is really evil (Nietzsche, 1974, sections 125, 357; 1987, section 37).

Nietzsche was the mentor to many thinkers, some of whom were peaceful and some of whom were not. Camus and Sartre wanted to be among the peaceful ones. The old theologians offered us the God-or-suicide dichotomy. The deists offered us the God-or-absurdity (anti-science) dichotomy. In both cases the recommendation was to choose God. With Heidegger and Gadamer it is God-or-culture and we are told to choose culture. With Camus and Sartre we once again face the God-or-absurdity dichotomy, but this time around we are told to choose the absurdity (anti-science) alternative. The aim of the twentieth-century atheists was to do away with Nietzsche's elitism by making nihilism democratic, by extending the special morality of the superman to everyone.

Albert Camus (1913–60), for instance, stoutly refused to make the leap of faith to God in order to avoid despair and suicide. Parallel to Darwin, survival (efficiency) must become an end in itself. For the atheistic existentialist, the individual is a lonely consciousness detached from God, nature, and other people. Suicide is wrong because it would deprive you of your consciousness, the only really valuable thing you have. For Camus, being self-conscious makes you a god, but being a god nowadays is a rather mundane affair. In the old days a conqueror-god wanted to rule the world. Nowadays, though, Camus' absurd man is expected to do no more than conquer himself. In contrast to Nietzsche's elitism, Camus is very democratic.

> Yes, man is his own end. And he is his only end. If he aims to be something, it is in this life. Conquerors sometimes talk of vanquishing and overcoming. But it is always 'overcoming oneself' that they mean. You are well aware of what that means. Every man has felt himself to be the equal of a god at certain moments. At least, this is the way it is expressed. But this comes from the fact that in a flash he felt the amazing grandeur of the human mind. The conquerors are merely those among men who are conscious enough of their strength to be sure of living constantly on those heights and fully aware of that grandeur. (Camus, 1955, p. 65)

For his part, Sartre admitted that without God all actions are morally permissible. Sartre, in the theoretical sphere, knew nothing of the gods, and so, in the practical sphere, man is the highest plane of existence. Man then becomes a god, the measure of right and wrong. In 1945 Sartre gave a lecture in Paris, directed mainly to Marxists, outlining his philosophy. The central point of his whole effort, he said, was to draw out the full moral consequences of atheism. Atheism was the very starting point of his existentialism. Earlier, after the publication of his *Being and Nothingness*, a French reporter had dubbed this view 'existentialism', a title that Sartre quickly adopted as his own.

The important thing for Sartre is realizing that we are on our own in moral matters. Man is freedom. And if I am free, then everyone is free. In the new true humanism, freedom must become an end in itself. The only sin is the lack of authenticity. As long as we are authentic, that is, as long as we make no excuses for ourselves, as long as we accept full responsibility for our actions, we are free to do as we wish within the situation in which we find ourselves. The situation is important. Because each of us is situated in a real world with real limitations, our absolute freedom does not produce absolute chaos. When we choose for ourselves, says Sartre, we also choose for the whole of humanity. A husband is not obliged to beat his wife. A young man can stay home and care for his mother. A woman is not required to be childless. In general, we can choose to treat others with respect. Thus, community is possible and despair is avoided.

> Existentialism is not atheist in the sense that it would exhaust itself in demonstrations of the non-existence of God. It declares, rather, that even if God existed that would make no difference from its point of view. Not that we believe God does exist, but we think that the real problem is not that of His existence; what man needs is to find himself again and to understand that nothing can save him from himself, not even a valid proof of the existence of God. In this sense existentialism is optimistic, it is a doctrine of action, and it is only by self-deception, by confusing their own despair with ours that Christians can describe us as without hope. (Sartre, 1982, p. 56)

Nevertheless, closer to Nietzsche's ideal are the warrior disciples, such as Mussolini, Stalin, Hitler, Mao Tse-tung, Castro, and Idi Amin. Adolf Hitler (1889–1945), for instance, saw himself as a bold, sincere, lucid, loving, hard-working, servant-figure, committed to beauty, especially in architecture. He was an honest man, answering the call of his evolutionary destiny. Thinking like Nietzsche, he was free to use his instincts and work his will on other people. His only regret at the time of his death was that he had not carried out his passionate feelings, especially against the Jews, sooner and more vigorously.

In the world of nihilism, any restriction, such as saying that you can do anything you wish just as long as you do not hurt anyone or just as long as the action is between consenting adults, is sure to limit your style. Hitler did his own thing by putting his passionate love into practice. The members of the

Bin Laden terrorist gang did their own thing. The puritan prude may be shocked by such actions, but Nietzsche would be overjoyed to see his joyful wisdom practised with such enthusiasm by the Mafia, Hollywood-types, and university students. Following Nietzsche, what the religious thinker once called ungodly dishonesty is now the noblest display of personal authenticity (Centore, 2000; see also Kreeft, 1999).

Traditional Theism: Both Evil and God

With these considerations we can now do away with the error of those who, because they see evil in the world, claim there is no God. Thus Boethius, in the first book of *The Consolation of Philosophy* (Prose 4), introduces a certain philosopher asking: If God exists, how can evil exist? But it could just as well be argued to the contrary that: If evil is, God is. This is because, since evil is the privation of good, there would be no evil if the order of good were removed. But there would be no order of good if there were no God (Aquinas, 1894a, III, chapter 71).

What does it mean to be real? What does it mean to be good? Are good and evil things, like rocks and trees? If a man hits his wife over the head with a rock, is the rock evil? Is the man evil? Is the mere fact that something, such as a rock, a tree, or a human being, is finite, limited, imperfect, and weak in various ways, evil? Must the good always eliminate the evil whenever the two meet? Must the total amount of good always exceed the total amount of evil? How can we use a negative term such as evil without knowing in a positive way the meaning of the good?

We cannot say that evil is doing evil deeds or thinking evil thoughts because that would use the term to be defined in the definition. The same problem arises if we say that evil means deliberately doing unjustified harm (evil) to another human being. Also, making intention a part of the definition would mean that things such as polio, brain tumours, and the like would fall outside of the meaning of evil. Is your lack of three eyes evil? Do we know what it means to have a healthy pair of lungs? The medical profession does. In the physical realm, we have to know what is healthy in order to know what is unhealthy (dis-ease).

Some forms of evil may be intentional acts by someone who has knowledge and who is responsible, but what kind of acts are we talking about? Are good and evil real as relationships rather than as things? Does good imply having objective standards outside the will of the individual? Can evil be defined as a relationship, as a falling away from an objective standard of good? It is not that the rock or the man are evil in themselves, but rather that some of their relationships are evil. The man should not be angry with his wife and a rock should not be used to viciously attack someone. On this basis, if evil is defined as a real deviation relative to the good, then we would have the universal definition we are seeking. It could then apply to thoughts, actions, and happenings. Where, though, do we find such a standard of good?

Is good just a temporary feeling or is it the fulfilling of our nature, such that we must possess something or someone in an objective way if we are to find true happiness. Just as, in the real world, credit is extended on the basis of something objective, such as real production, real estate, and real collateral, so also our hope for eternal happiness must be based on something real. By the same token, real evil depends upon the existence of real good. If the ideal is only imaginary, then so is any deviation from it. There must be a real standard to measure the evil, so that, by the degree to which something falls away from the good, it can be called more or less evil. This is the traditional theistic approach. There must be a real divine standard in order to speak meaningfully of evil as real. Therefore, parallel to the way that God and science can exist simultaneously, it is not a case of either God or evil, but a case of both God and evil.

Such a standard of good would operate differently in different contexts. For instance, what is evil for a flatworm would not be evil for a horse. God created the world according to certain well-defined patterns. Creatures come with built-in purposes. Fulfilling these purposes constitutes the good of the creature. In general, the good of a thing is defined as that which fulfils its nature. Some criticize this by saying that, for example, what a shovel is good for is not necessarily good for the shovel. Such a statement completely misses the point. It is like asking: If a tin horn is made of tin, what is a fog horn made of? The problem is to define a good shovel, and the answer is a shovel that actually does what it is designed to do. Even though it can be used for other things, in the hands of one person it is supposed to be capable of moving loose material from one place to another place that is close by. A shovel that does its job is a good shovel.

In the moral sphere, real evil requires one set of objective standards for everyone. Human nature has certain set goals and so all human beings have the same needs and rights. Without an unchanging divine standard, we could never know whether or not the dignity of the human person is being violated. What these human needs and rights are is discussed under the heading of the natural moral law as found, for example, in Aquinas. If what constitutes evil differs from one person to another, it would mean that there is no unifying human nature and so no unified human species. This would bring us back to nihilism. Anyone could claim, for instance, that for him torturing cats is very fulfilling and therefore perfectly moral. After all, being self-satisfied is what my life is all about, is it not? This is the socially destructive attitude of the typical moral relativist.

Thus, if evil depends upon a non-arbitrary standard, it follows that good and evil are not symmetrical. We can have light without shadow, but not vice versa; we can have presence without absence, but not vice versa. Just because we say cheese when we have our picture taken does not mean that cheese has to say cheese when its picture is taken. There can be good, such as God, without evil, but there cannot be evil without God. By the same token, there is an asymmetrical relationship between good and evil in terms of substantial things and their relationships. There can be a good thing and a good relationship, but there is no evil thing, only an evil relationship. Considered in itself (for example, the rock, the man, the woman), anything that exists is good.

Compare a situation in which no human beings had cancer. Such a situation would be good, even though there is no disease. Now look at the situation in reverse. The very use of the term human dis-ease indicates a falling away from a common standard of health. Even if everyone had cancer it would still be unhealthy because we know what a healthy human being should be. We need healthiness to understand unhealthiness, but not vice versa. And so also for the relationship of good and evil in general.

When All The World Is Young

When all the world is young, lad,
    And all the trees are green,
And every goose a swan, lad,
    And every lass a queen;
Then hey for boot and horse, lad,
    And round the world away!
Young blood must have its course, lad,
    And every dog his day.

When all the world is old, lad,
    And all the trees are brown,
And all the sport is stale, lad,
    And all the wheels run down;
Creep home and take your place there,
    The spent and maimed among;
God grant you find one face there,
    You loved when you were young.
        Charles Kingsley (1819–75), *The Water-Babies* (1863)

Chapter 3
Naturalistic Theism

Naturalistic Theism in General

There are two very basic ways of looking at the meaning of God, namely, naturalistic theism and supernaturalistic theism. In the naturalistic theism view, God is the same as the world or some fundamental aspect of the world. This view is also known as pantheism. Talking about God is the same thing as talking about the natural world or some energy or force pervading the universe as a whole. This way of thinking seems to come easily to many people. As said by Ronald Arbuthnott Knox (1888–1957), when engaged in writing a book on the Catholic Faith:

> I am the more encouraged to take this course by the fact that in our day many intelligent people who profess themselves Theists hold their beliefs precariously and unreflectively, without troubling to inquire what they involve; nay, that Christians themselves, from a lack of systematic instruction, often misconceive the Nature of the God whom their own theology preaches, and are half-way towards Pantheism without knowing it. (Knox, 1958, p. 44)

As with any view of God, naturalistic theism has practical consequences. What, for instance, becomes of environmental concerns? To Mother Nature, everything is natural. Garbage dumps, micro spheres of plastic in the oceans, atom bombs lost in the Potomac River, and so forth are no more unnatural than the burning sands, the raging waters and winds, volcanoes, and avalanches.

> Ah, love, let us be true
> To one another! for the world, which seems
> To lie before us like a land of dreams,
> So various, so beautiful, so new,
> Hath really neither joy, nor love, nor light,
> Nor servitude, nor peace, nor help for pain;
> And we are here as on a darkling plain
> Swept with confused alarms of struggle and flight,
> Where ignorant armies clash by night.
> Matthew Arnold (1822–88), *Dover Beach* (1867)

Light can be shed on the meaning of naturalistic theism by looking at some long-lived examples. What is interesting about these examples is that, rather than beginning with the facts of experience and then logically working their way up to a conclusion, they begin with mankind's emotional problems and work backward in order to find some theory that will make us feel better. Alleviating anxiety is the main concern. How can we survive under trying circumstances?

One way to get a handle on the situation is by means of the happiness formula, that is, the ratio of your Accomplishments (what you Get) to your Expectations (what you Want). This may be expressed by the formula $H = A/E$ or $H = G/W$. As a subjective psychological state, your degree of happiness is decided by a ratio between what you really want and what you actually get. The formula can be interpreted in a material sense, a spiritual sense, or both.

Naturalistic theism is restricted to the materialistic interpretation. Since everything is already in nature and there is nothing beyond nature, there is no going beyond nature. Ultimately, there is no difference between the 'is' and the 'ought', the natural order and the moral order, the physical and the spiritual, the actual and the ideal. The only gap to be bridged is the difference between one's present illusion of real individual existence and one's final fading back into nature forever.

To illustrate the materialistic approach, if you desire a new sports car and you actually get a new sports car, then your happiness index is one ($H = 1/1$). Theoretically speaking, you are perfectly happy, at least for the moment. On the other hand, if you want a new sports car and you get an old Ford, then you are less happy ($H = 0.25/1$). Although mathematically speaking it may not work out in every case, such a formula seems to be inherent in several of the world's leading religions.

Hinduism

Hinduism began to be formalized about 4000 BC. Its main books are the *Veda*, the ancient writings, including the *Rig Vedas*, the oldest book, going back to about 900 BC. In these works, nature and the parts of nature are personified and divided into good and evil forces. There are many manifestations of the supreme godhead. We also have in the old books stories that seem to prefigure the life and death of Jesus Christ. Then there are the *Brahmanas*, the writings of the Brahmans. Brahmanism goes back to about 600 BC and is noted for its caste system, doctrine of reincarnation, and salvation only for those who have advanced to being members of the Brahman class. For the ancient Hindu, the whole world is said to be the breath of Brahman.

Another important work is the *Upanishads* (Approaches), containing the following points:

- There is the unity of all things, dominated by a universal soul that cannot be sensed.

- The whole universe is Brahman, which is like the air that surrounds us.
- Everything is in Brahman forever.

Brahman, a neuter noun in Sanskrit, is superior to all of the gods and is known only by intuition.

The chief deities (the sacred seven) are Shiva (the destroyer), Kali, Durga, Parvati, Ganesha (wisdom), Vishnu (the preserver), and Lakshmi (or Shri), his wife. Sometimes the deities took the form of combinations of humans and animals. Like animals and humans, the deities could also be reincarnated. So far there have been nine incarnations (avatars) of Vishnu, the seventh called Rama, the eighth called Krishna. More are expected to occur in the future. In all cases it must be emphasized that the many gods and goddesses no more have a truly separate existence relative to Brahman than do humans. In the ancient Hindu tradition, maya is the illusion of separate existence. You have no real separate existence. The ego is reducible to the mind, which reduces to the atman (soul), which is a manifestation of the one absolute.

The important thing is to escape having to return over and over again to a miserable earthly life. Those who finally escape the cycle of rebirth are the enlightened ones. This is salvation. But how, in practice, does one escape? There is no one way. The individual can be liberated by means of knowledge, action, or ritual. Hindus from different sects often attend ceremonies and festivals at each other's temples. While alive, though, it is important to remain absolutely faithful to your caste. In the Hindu tradition, karma is the burden you carry forward because of your failure in the past to live up to the highest ideals of your caste. There is no social mobility while alive. If you deserve to belong to a higher caste, you will be reborn into it. Today, as in the past, the Brahmans, the highest caste, make up about four per cent of the total population of India.

With respect to salvation, we can consult the long story-poem entitled the *Bhagavad-Gita* (Song of the Holy Ruler), which is the most popular and elaborately illustrated Hindu work. It is often called the Hindu bible. Written somewhere between 100 BC and 100 AD, it depicts an ancient war between rival gods and princes for the possession of a large kingdom. In it we learn that, although the way of knowledge is preferred, other ways are also acceptable.

According to the *Bhagavad-Gita As It Is*, wise people lament neither for the living nor for the dead. This is because everyone persists forever in Brahman. True knowledge tells us that killers do not really kill and that the killed are not really dead. Consequently, should Arjuna, the hero of the poem, hesitate to kill, even if the people he is killing are members of his own family? The Lord Krishna says no. A religious war is the best reason for waging a war and Arjuna should never hesitate to do his duty by killing those who oppose him, regardless of who they are.

To be holy, Arjuna must remain indifferent to everything in the world of sense experience, including life and death. This is the Brahman conception. The wise man therefore looks upon everything with the same untroubled attitude. A piece of dirt, a stone, and a lump of gold are all the same to him. He is indifferent to distress and pleasure, friends and enemies, honour and dishonour, praise and blame. He never desires anything nor laments the loss of something. A good action is one which is performed without attachment, without love or hatred, and without the desire for concrete results. Dear to Krishna is the one who is not disturbed by anyone, who is equipoised in happiness and distress, fear and anxiety.

Since the individual atman (soul) and Brahman are really one and the same, the salvation process is not really a transition from one realm of being to another, but only a relative difference in an internal relationship. This means that even those who pursue the most extreme sexual practices imaginable are already in Brahman. Since Brahman is in all things and actions, everything is an act of worship and devotion. 'O Arjuna,' says Krishna, 'I give heat, and rain, and dry spells'. Krishna is both immortality and death personified. Brahman is both spirit and matter. As a result, anyone engaged in devotional service is saintly, regardless of what he does. Ritual prostitution was quite common in many Hindu temples in the past. Prostituting oneself for one or more of the gods or goddesses was considered a form of worship (Bhaktivedanta Swami Prabhupada, 1986).

In addition, India has experienced the most appalling disregard for the poor, combined with the greatest expenditure on the upper classes. This is reflected in the many-layered Hindu social system. At one time, while the members of the two upper classes, the priestly Brahmans and the military ruling class, lived in luxury, the members of the two lower classes, the merchants and the labourers, worked hard and long. But the untouchables, the lowest of the low, had the worst of it. They existed only to serve the other classes. This was not unjust. They belonged to the demonic class, those who were being justly punished for their lack of attention to worship and ritual in their past lives.

Condemned by heredity to do the dirtiest jobs, the untouchables were deprived of all basic human rights. Usually darker-skinned than the others, they were shunned by everyone else. Being reborn as an untouchable was the worse fate imaginable. Merely passing through the shadow cast by an untouchable, of which there are still about 300 million in India today, would render you unclean. Even today, all drinks served in public places from which the untouchables cannot be easily excluded must be served in disposable cups for fear that a cup once in contact with the lips of an untouchable might accidentally come in contact with the lips of someone in a higher caste. As with Black people under slavery in the past, and as with unborn human beings today, being an untouchable means that you can be killed at will, without the killer having to face any form of prosecution.

Overall, in Hinduism there is a mixture of the obscene and the ascetic, with constant emphasis upon sex and sexual symbolism, all justified by a naturalistic theism. Behind everything is the supremely indifferent Brahman, the summation of all contradictions. Ultimately, everything is the same as everything else. (On Hinduism and Christianity see D'Souza, 1959, pp. 13–15; Varghese, 2000a, Introduction.)

Buddhism

Buddhism means enlightenment. Going back to about 500 BC, Buddhism is streamlined Hinduism. Salvation requires quietude. There is no need for divine revelation or doing the will of God. This is because there is no God in any Judao-Christian sense. Since you cannot call upon help from God, you must sort out your own problems. There is no sin in Buddhism; only mistakes in lifestyle.

The programme traces its roots back to Siddhartha Gautama (563–483 BC), a man who left the relatively rich life of his high-caste background in order to bring salvation to all the people. The political founder of Buddhism was Ashoka (or Asoka, ?–236 BC), the third king of the Maurya dynasty in India from 269 BC until his death. The Aryans, a lighter-skinned people than the original inhabitants of India, invaded India about 1500 BC. During the reign of Ashoka, they finally succeeded in conquering the whole of India. Ashoka is largely responsible for the spread of Buddhism. Becoming disgusted with violence and killing, much of which he himself had carried out, he converted from the brutality of Hinduism to the new philosophy and proceeded to make Buddhism the state religion. He even sent out missionaries to preach the doctrine to those outside of India. According to later Christian standards, his reign was very enlightened for the times. He built roads and hospitals and encouraged peace and harmony among his subjects. After his death, however, the dynasty disintegrated and Buddhism greatly declined in India.

In order to succeed within the Buddhistic context, the four noble truths must be accepted as the foundation for this self-help programme.

1. What is the basic problem? Suffering and imperfection. For the vast majority of people life is hard. We are always under the domination of nature and other people. You are lucky to live to be 30 years old. Ravished by disease and oppression, why go on living at all?
2. What is the cause of suffering? Desiring things; attachment to anything at all.
3. What is its solution? Remove all desiring, all craving, all thirsting, and all attachments.
4. How is this to be accomplished? Follow the Aryan (Sanskrit for noble) eight-fold path, which is like a flower unfolding its petals all at the same time. First there must be right understanding (philosophy), that is, the four noble truths. Then there is right thinking (intention, aspiration), which means the willingness to consistently practice the doctrine. Then there is right speech, which means being honest with yourself and others. Next is right action (doing), meaning that you must not kill any living thing or rob

and steal. Then there is right living, which means that you must abstain from all violence, including self-defense. Next comes right effort, meaning pure intentions and a strong will to succeed. Then comes right mindfulness, which means that you must be aware of your bodily and mental states. Finally there is right concentration (rapture), which is the attainment of a higher state of consciousness and the final release from the eternal return.

There are Buddhist monks, but no priests, in the sense of a special class of people who offer sacrifices on behalf of the community. There are sacred places, but no sacred relics, except in a few rare cases. In keeping with Hinduism, though, salvation (nirvana) is still viewed as an escape from the process of reincarnation. We must annihilate ourselves, not just temporarily, but forever. A simple suicide, because it represents a strong desire, will not do. This is a do-it-yourself-salvation, with no mediators or divine grace to help out.

What is nirvana? What happens to a candle flame when it goes out? It undergoes annihilation as a separate individual thing. The key traits of personal imperfection are change and impermanence. This includes physical and mental pain, and being dependent upon other people and things. Where do these traits come from? We must look to the doctrine of the five heaps in sentient beings, namely, mental qualities, feelings (will, desire), perceptions, coefficients of consciousness (ideas), and consciousness itself.

In the Hinayana (Theravada, lower way) Tradition, common to southern Asia, the five heaps are individually and ultimately real. There are no true wholes and unities. There is only a radical pluralism of the parts or aspects of a thing. In the Mahayana (higher way, a term coined by the newer group to indicate its superiority) Tradition, common to Mongolia, China, Korea, and Japan, the five heaps are unreal. Only the whole is real; there is a radical monism.

These two groups have some significant differences with respect to salvation. In the Mahayana Tradition, there is a moving back toward Hinduism by reintroducing various gods and goddesses into its system and even deifying Gautama Buddha himself. The Buddha is said to now reside in the Great Western Paradise or the Pure Land. It also distinguishes between heaven and hell. Moreover, it gives a high place to those monks who, just before achieving enlightenment, choose to remain on earth in order to help others achieve salvation. The Dalai Lama (Ocean of Wisdom), for instance, is regarded by his followers as such a person.

The two main Buddhist sects in Japan are the Shinshu and the Zen. The first allows a high degree of social and political freedom. Its followers are allowed to eat meat, have families, and hold public office. They are encouraged to participate in public rituals, to work for the community, and to go to university. In sharp contrast, the Zen sect rejects all this and concentrates instead entirely upon contemplation, most usually while sitting in the cross-legged (zazen) lotus position.

In general, for the Buddhist, there is only one great reality (Brahman). The ultimate object of life is to reduce the denominator of the happiness formula to zero, to cease all desiring and break all attachments to anything, whether physical or mental, and finally to learning itself. Asking what happens to the human being when the perfect monk finally achieves salvation (nirvana) is like asking what happens to a candle flame when it goes out. The dying flame, like the dying monk, is completely reabsorbed into Brahman, never to return again (Gard, 1963).

Stoicism

What do you do if you happen to live in a cruel and harsh physical and moral environment, one in which you cannot expect very much in the way of food, clothing, shelter, and kindness? In such an environment it would be foolish for you to expect too much. High aspirations are sure to be frustrated. According to the happiness formula, though, you can still be happy by decreasing what you expect, by reducing your wants and desires to a minimum. Expect less, and then, what little you do get, will make you happy. The Stoics were taught to adjust their lives so as to be content with whatever they got. You must write your ego in huge letters across the sky, so to speak, by being so tough, unemotional, and indifferent to the events and happenings in the world around you that nothing could disturb your unfeeling state of mind. It is reason against emotion and passion. Stoicism means virtue without passion. Even if things do not get better, be content with a situation wherein things do not get worse.

Stoicism comes from the Greek word for porch, a covered open platform attached to a building, the sort of place from which the doctrine was originally taught. Stoicism was a Greek version of pantheism. The whole universe is permeated by one great world soul (Zeus, mind, logos, nous, force, law). This makes the world into one reality, one supreme divine thing. We, as human beings, share to a certain extent in the divine nature of the universe. We do this primarily by means of our ability to reason. Consequently, the Stoics were very much interested in the development of logic, especially the logic of the hypothetical syllogism (if P, then Q). Knowing the connection between the cause and the effect will tell us what we must do, thereby allowing us to better adjust to the unavoidable happenings of life.

As beings of reason we are little sparks of the divine fire. It is the world soul or logos, the breath of the world, that is the active principle in the universe. It is responsible for moving things along a predetermined path from age to age. This process goes in cycles, so that, over a long period of time, everything comes back again to the way it was and the cycle starts over again. Logic was important, but only to the extent it trains us to accept the inevitable. The main interest of Stoicism is always fixed on ethics, on how we should behave in order to get along in a world filled with pain and hardship. The answer is to aim low.

The founder of Stoicism was Zeno of Citium (336–264 BC) and its most able promoter was Epictetus (50–120). Epictetius' loyal disciple was Arrian (dates unknown). Stoicism was accepted by the Romans Seneca, Cicero, Horace, and the emperor Marcus Aurelius. Stoicism was thought to be an especially useful philosophy for soldiers. We read, for instance, in Arrian's *Discourses of Epictetus*, that the whole purpose of education is to learn to frame one's expectations in accordance with whatever one gets. Do not expect something and then be disappointed when you do not get it. Learn to accept whatever comes your way without flinching.

> Education is just this, learning to frame one's will in accord with events. How do events happen? They happen as the Disposer of events has ordained them to happen. ... Remembering then that things are thus ordained, we ought to approach education, not that we may change the conditions of life, for that is not given to us, nor is it good for us, but that, our circumstances being as they are and as nature makes them, we may conform our minds to events. (Oates, 1940, p. 248)

We must live this way because everything is controlled by fate, the rule of the logos, the great force that controls all activities in the universe. Only a foolish person would fight against destiny. Consequently, we must not endeavour to change the world or to alter our condition of life. Such actions are not within our power. The best we can do is to accept our circumstances as Zeus has given them to us. We must conform our minds to the events as we find them. Education teaches us what we can and cannot control. As it turns out, the only thing we can really control is the way we react to circumstances. Everything else, from our bodies to our possessions to our society, is outside of our control. You must learn to love what you get, whatever it may be, rather than trying to get what you foolishly want. Theoretically speaking, if you could reduce the denominator of the happiness formula to zero, you would be infinitely happy. If and when things get really bad for the Stoic, suicide is the way out.

Epicureanism

The same formula is also approximated in Epicureanism, named after Epicurus (341–270 BC), a Greek, born on the island of Samos. He studied in Ionia, where he learned the atomistic philosophy of nature, according to which the whole world is broken up (by space) into tiny particles so small that we cannot possibly sense them. Eventually he found his way to Athens where he founded a school in the garden of a house. Before he died of prostate cancer, he freed his slaves. Epicurus taught that the greatest good is bodily pleasure. The primary purpose of his doctrine was to secure peace of mind for people by showing them that they need have no fear of death. Death is simply the coming apart of the atoms that make up the body. After death there is nothing for us. There is no pain and no joy, just nothingness.

This did not mean that he was a complete atheist. In fact the Epicureans claimed not to be atheists. The gods do exist, composed of the finest atoms, residing between the collections of grosser atoms that compose the bodies of the solar system. This is a practical atheism; the gods are effectively removed from day-to-day life; they are irrelevant. Later, David Hume would turn this doctrine to his own advantage.

In the popular press the Epicurean doctrine is often referred to as the 'eat, drink, and be merry, for tomorrow you die' doctrine, as if the only life worth living is one long playboy feasting and sex orgy. As far as ethics is concerned, however, this is not what the Epicureans themselves had to say. The story is that Epicurus himself lived most of his adult life on bread and water. The Epicurean rule was to adjust your lifestyle to what you could reasonably expect to obtain. The rule was to maximize pleasure and minimize pain, adjusted to your particular set of circumstances. If the most you can expect to get is beer and pretzels then do not become accustomed to champagne and caviar.

As one might expect, this made the Epicureans very conservative in social and political matters. The last thing Epicureans want is to be beaten up by the police or deprived by the state of their pleasure-producing possessions, which is exactly what would happen if they were to become involved in social activism. Reasonable people do not stick out their necks for anything. It is recommended that you live unknown, the better to pursue your personal pleasures without interference by other people or the government. The less the tax collector and the police know about you the better.

Concluding Remarks

In conclusion, therefore, we see that naturalistic theism can take several different forms. All of them, though, are variations on pantheism. The one reality is nature, which appears to us in many different ways. Our salvation (ultimate happiness) depends on fitting in to the all-encompassing reality of nature, which is usually personified in one way or another.

Chapter 4
Supernaturalistic Theism

Supernaturalistic Theism in General

In contrast to naturalistic theism, in supernaturalistic theism God is separate from the natural world. This basic fact makes for a world of difference between the two theisms. When God, for instance, is a supreme spiritual being, we are no longer bound by a materialistic interpretation of the happiness formula. What if we interpret the denominator and numerator in spiritual terms? Although this is possible in traditional supernaturalistic monotheism, it cannot work when salvation means fading back into the one reality, never to return again. In naturalistic theism there is no chance of having a personal eternal life more abundantly. Because there is no heaven, there is no storing up treasure for yourself in heaven. We live and die as a part of the one reality of nature. Our ultimate destiny is annihilation. Not a greater sense of spiritual well-being, but a total elimination of the self and self-consciousness, is the goal to be achieved.

In contrast, in supernaturalistic theism there is in fact a real discrepancy between the natural and the spiritual. The goal is to bridge the disparity between the 'is' and the 'ought' while maintaining one's individuality in a more perfect way. In the great monotheistic religions, the denominator is fixed in advance at a high level, namely, the hope for a greatly heightened personal existence in heaven with God forever. The only way to lower the denominator is in physical terms, something which is generally recommended, even when not necessitated by one's material circumstances. For both their physical and spiritual benefit, those well-off must eat less and give away more. Because the spiritual denominator cannot be adjusted, this places upon the believer an obligation to increase the spiritual numerator, which is no easy task. For this reason there is an activism in supernaturalistic theism not found in naturalistic theism.

This activism shows up in evangelization, welfare programmes, hospitals, orphanages, schools at all levels, and in many other forms of individual and group effort. Where possible, and if they can be carried out in peaceful ways, social and political reforms are also on the agenda. Moreover, we see it in untiring scientific research, as people search for a better knowledge of God by investigating his creation. We should also bear in mind that religious activism can be perverted into non-religious programmes and can sometimes make strange bedfellows. Both the capitalists and the anti-capitalists, for instance, preserved the activism aspect of supernaturalistic theism even while removing its religious core. Marx became righteously angry over the conditions of the workers and resolved to do something about it. Those devoted to capitalism become workaholics, never resting until an infinite number of widgits has been produced.

Of course, in order for the capitalist to make money, someone must buy the widgits. As a result, the leaders of industry must see to it that, materialistically speaking, everyone is encouraged to maximize both the denominator and the numerator. Everyone must always want more; everyone must always work harder and harder in order to get more and more. As might be expected, some people rebel against such a system, preferring either a more spiritual supernaturalistic religion or some form of naturalistic theism, such as Buddhism, as a way of escaping the rat-race.

Moreover, the contrast between naturalistic theism and supernaturalistic theism warns us not to confuse one religion with another. Often times it is said that, although, there are many superficial differences among the different religions of the world, underneath it all they are all the same. In fact, just the reverse is true. The Buddhist monk in his monastery and the Christian hermit in the desert, for example, are superficially the same in various ways. Fundamentally, however, there is a world of difference between the religious doctrines of Buddhism and Judao-Christianity.

Supernaturalistic theism comes in several major varieties. There is the view of polytheism. This multiplicity can be as low as two gods, as in Zoroastrianism and Manichaeism, or a much higher number, as in Confucianism and the classical paganism of the Greeks and Romans. Then we can have the view of monotheism, as in Judaism, Christianity, and Islam. Within monotheism we find the traditional position that God is ever-present to us and the non-traditional position of deism, stating that God is absent. Because God is removed from any practical consideration, deism can be called a practical atheism. For the time being, I will supply an outline of the different major subdivisions other than traditional monotheism (Copleston, 1980, 1982).

Polytheism

Zoroastrianism

This is an old Iranian religion founded by Zoroaster (or Zarathustra, 'old camel', 628–551 BC) and written about by Herodotus (485–425 BC), Strabo (63 BC–23), and Plutarch (46–120). Its latest writings are commentaries on the *Avesta* (Law) from the sixth century AD.

Originally, Zoroaster, from the farming region of northern Iran ('the people of righteousness'), wrote against the nomadic horseman of the south ('the people of the lie'). His system was a polytheism of good and evil gods. The leader of the good forces was Ahura Mazda or Ormuzd ('sovereign knowledge') and of the evil forces, Ahriman. Ormuzd is represented by earth, water, air, and fire, which must be kept pure, thus making for an early environmentalism.

Although greater in power, the God of light and goodness is not powerful enough to completely overcome the God of darkness and evil. It is the latter who by and large controls the earth. Individuals can throw the weight of power on one side or the other by their moral decisions.

Zoroastrianism was the state religion from Darius I (550–486 BC) until Alexander's conquest of Persia. It showed up in Europe as Mithraism and emerged again as the Persian state religion after 226. Later it contended with Christianity and Manichaeism and was almost entirely wiped out by Islam in 660. There are still today some followers in Iran and in India (the Parsees, the Persians) around Bombay. The latter are among the most highly educated and economically influential people in India. They are noted for exposing the naked dead on high towers, to be eaten by birds, so as not to contaminate the earth (Boyce, 1975).

Manichaeism

This view was founded by Mani or Manes (216–76), a Persian born near Baghdad. During 240–41, after being expelled by the Zoroastrians, he lived in India. In 242 he returned to Persia and began preaching a combination of Zoroastrianism, Christianity, Buddhism, and Greek philosophy (Plato). He claimed to be the Christian Paraclete, the Holy Spirit of God, come to earth to teach people the truth. In 272 he met with renewed opposition in Persia and was later killed by the Zoroastrians.

Mani saw the world as divided between the realm of light, led by the Master of Light, and the realm of darkness, led by the Master of Darkness. Material beings and the whole earth belong in the latter camp – and so do women, who were created by the evil one. Evil is physical, not moral. There was no original sin. Good people (the elect, the teachers) avoid the material world. Not-so-good people (the auditors, the students), who must care for the elect, are allowed to traffic in the world, but having children is still evil. Children are obtained by kidnapping them from others. All non-Manichaes are doomed to hell. The auditors will keep on being reborn until they become the elect and thus enter into the realm of light forever. In the meantime, the body can do all sorts of dirty things while the spirit tries to remain pure and holy.

Manichaeism died out in the West about 600, but lingered on until about 1000 in Chinese Turkistan. It briefly reappeared in Europe in the Middle Ages from 1200 to 1300, mostly in southern France, its members going under various names, such as Paulicians, Cathari, Albigensians, and Bogomils. From 1209 to 1229 they were attacked by the French and Spanish, whose motives were more territorial than religious. At the time, some members of the cult fled to what is now Bosnia, where they survived for a while.

By rejecting as evil the material basis of human life, Manichaeism makes normal human life impossible. We see this in Islamic cults, such as the Persian Assassins (1090–1256), whose mission in life was to kill any Islamic political leader they deemed unorthodox, and the contemporary fanatical members of

Al-Qaeda, who use western science to destroy western society. We see today something approximating this doctrine in the form of members of a doomsday cult rampaging through the streets destroying everything in sight. Their disrespect for life and property makes them the enemy of anyone concerned about the preservation of civilization. No society can survive such a thing. In fact, the Manichaen sect is so socially destructive that whenever it has shown up it has been crushed out by the leaders of society, whether secular or religious. (See Burkitt, 1925.)

Confucianism

Named after Kung Fu-Tzu (551–479 BC), Confucianism is a Chinese social philosophy. Voltaire said he liked Confucius because he did not claim any divine revelation. Others have said that Confucianism, because of its emphasis on family loyalty and service, was a preparation for Christianity (Sih, 1952). Its main works are the Five Classics: *The Book of Changes, The Book of History, The Book of Poetry, The Book of Rites, The Spring and Autumn Annals*. There are also the Four Classics (collected together about AD 750): *Analects or Sayings of Confucius, The Great Learning, The Doctrine of the Mean or Middle Way, The Sayings of Mencius* (Mencius, 372–289 BC). About 200 BC the state introduced the Shang Ti (Sky God). About 1000 Confucianism became a state religion. An important concept for the state was Li (proper social behaviour), which meant a rigorous adherence to the state-prescribed rituals.

Of central importance were the five relationships, namely, state (emperor–citizen), family (father–child), brothers (older–younger), marriage (husband–wife), and friends (equal–equal). In general, the female must defer to the male and the younger must defer to the older. These relationships cannot be violated. If, for instance, the husband should die, the eldest son would take over as the head of the household. In public affairs, under no circumstances would someone presume to question the emperor, and so on. Each relationship contains mutual responsibilities. For each social action there is a reciprocal social reaction that must be preserved. In Confucianism, reciprocity is the basis for all social relationships. Loyalty and reciprocity constitute the whole doctrine (Confucius, 1955, chap. 4, no. 15, p. 36).

This is sometimes called the Negative Golden Rule, namely, do not do to others what you do not want others to do to you (Confucius, 1955, chap. 5, no. 12; chap. 12, no. 2; chap. 15, no. 24). But is it really a golden rule? Or is it more like a tin rule? Such a rule, for instance, allows you to pass by someone lying injured by the side of the road without stopping to help. What reciprocity really means is that you should stay home, know your place, keep your place, and mind your own business. If and when you do travel, be sure to maintain your proper social relationships. If you do not, then chaos will take over and you can be sure that war horses will breed in the fields instead of rice. The average Chinese person also maintained a belief in many different gods and goddesses. Even today there continues to be a great deal of polytheism in popular Chinese culture and religion.

This is the case even in the naturalistic mystery cult of Taoism, founded by Lao-Tzu, a contemporary of Confucius. According to Taoism (The Way), you must do nothing in order to achieve everything. Fitting in with the flow of nature is the key to success. If you were perfect in this regard, you could go over a great waterfall and not be hurt. Basic to everything is the law of opposites (Yin-Yang). In nature we find being and non-being, presence and absence, light and dark, hot and cold, wet and dry, up and down, male and female, life and death, and so on. Even in the best of times, teaches the Tao, be prepared for the worst of times. Stoicism can be called the western philosophical version of Taoism.

Paganism

> Great God I'd rather be
> A Pagan suckled in a creed outworn;
> So might I, standing on this pleasant lee,
> Have glimpses that would make me less forlorn;
> Have sight of Proteus rising from the sea;
> Or hear old Triton blow his wreathed horn.
> William Wordsworth (1770–1850), *The World Is Too Much With Us* (1807)

A multiplicity of gods, which included many gods taken over from the ancient Egyptians and others in the Near East, was taken for granted in the old Mediterranean Sea civilizations. When the early Christians referred to the Greeks and Romans as pagans, they meant polytheism. Pagans were not atheists, but neither were they people who possessed the Bible.

There is, though, at least one thing that paganism and monotheism hold in common, namely, the fact that the personal religious aspect of human nature is a permanent feature of life and persists through all ages. This is why we should not be too impressed with certain superficial similarities between, say, the old Hercules, Mithras, and Dionysian myths and present-day religions such as Judao-Christianity. Rather than saying that the latter copied from the former, we can just as well say that they all stem from the same common root in human nature.

For the ancient Greeks, the gods represented anything, in a personified form, that had power over their lives. The gods were beings of intellect and will. The Greeks were very fatalistic about their relationship with the gods. They thought of themselves as under the constant control of the gods, who could influence and manipulate events according to their own whims. Hence it was important to appease the gods in many ways. It is not surprising, then, that the popular gods were regarded as 'big people', but with a difference, namely, that the gods, although they shared many good and bad traits with the common human being, lacked mortality. The immortals, as the gods were most often called, had the power of life and death over ordinary human beings because they themselves did not have to fear the ultimate insult of death.

All of the Greek philosophers coming after Thales continued to have reference to the gods, including the materialistic atomists. The world of Plato was as full of gods as was the world of Thales. Even the scientific Aristotle recognized the existence of the gods as the movers of the heavenly spheres. Aristotle, in his *Physics*, rejected both the pantheism of Parmenides (b. 500–515 BC), which held that all reality was one unchanging being, and the pantheism of Heraclitus (535–475 BC), which held that all reality is constant change. The difference between the earlier and later Greeks is that the later ones stripped down the gods to their bare personal essentials of intellect and will.

It should also be added that, for the Greek philosophers, what was divine did not necessarily mean only the gods. Plato's divine world of ideas, for instance, was superior to the gods. This is because, just as the gods are superior to men because the gods never die, so the ideas are superior to the gods because the ideas are completely self-identical and never change in any way. In the case of Plato, as with Aristotle, there is a disunity of ultimate causes. There is no doctrine of absolute creation among the Greeks. The ideas, the gods, the universe, and the parts of the universe are all eternal and uncreated. Each in its own way is an ultimate cause. Many today, brought up with monotheism, find this hard to imagine.

Some lessons can be gleaned from the history of the gods among ancient civilized people, people who had an appreciation of mathematics, logical reasoning, and empirical research. Even though most of their scientific explanations were erroneous, and sometimes humorous, they did know the difference between a naturalistic explanation and a religious one. One indication of this is that, when the difference was violated, as in a play for instance, it was accurately labelled as 'a-god-out-of-a-machine'. When Thales, for instance, said that everything is water he was speaking scientifically and when he said that everything is full of gods he was speaking religiously. As far as Greek philosophy is concerned, there was no transition from myth (religion) to rationality (science).

The same was true of ordinary Romans, who were constantly making sacrifices to the gods and constantly attempting to read the will of the gods in various ways. The popular forms of devotion, objectively speaking, may have been regarded as wrong by the educated classes, but the foundation for the beliefs of the uneducated man remained intact. In this regard, Etienne Gilson (1884–1978) finds classical paganism very instructive. He observes:

> Greek philosophy could not have emerged from Greek mythology by any process of progressive rationalization, because Greek philosophy was a rational attempt to understand the world as a world of things, whereas Greek mythology expressed the firm decision of man not to be left alone, the only person in a world of deaf and dumb things. (Gilson, 1941, p. 23)

According to Gilson, because of our minds and wills, we know ourselves to be superior to the world. For the ancients, if a god is to be at least as elevated as we are, he must be a being of knowledge and will. A god must be a somebody, not a something. This explains anthropomorphism. It provides a minimum personal meaning. Consequently, it is never the river or the mountain that is worshipped, but the god of the thing. This also explains the constant failure of atheism. We know what it means to be superior to cattle and to feel the need to communicate with higher beings.

Viewed from another angle, the ancients could not do without religion because they asked different sorts of questions about the world and our human condition. So today, regardless of how scientific we become, we are still human beings, not just calculating machines. It always comes down to the personal versus the impersonal. The personal includes the arts, the humanities, knowledge, will, love, hierarchy, values, freedom, self-consciousness, world-awareness, meaning, purpose, justice, hope, and talking with angels. As far as talking with angels is concerned, compare the way we today spend millions of dollars searching the heavens for the voices of angels in the form of superior ETs. The impersonal includes the physical and social sciences, technology and engineering, the laws of nature, necessity, and determinism.

The key point is that it is impossible to equate these two concerns. Hence, to eliminate the gods the ancients had to either personalize the impersonal or depersonalize the personal. But they could do neither. This means that the old anthropomorphic mythology was not the first step on the road to science, but an unsophisticated human cry for personal meaning in the midst of impersonal nature. Things are no different today. The human desire for the personal amid the impersonal is as strong as ever, fed, on the modern mythical level, by Hollywood and TV fictions.

By the same token, no human being is ever satisfied with communing with nature. 'Hug a tree' may work for a bear, but not for us. An orphan does not say, leave me out in the woods; he says, take me home. Our greatest suffering is caused by loneliness; we need someone to talk with us and to share our joys and fears with us. We suffer terribly when betrayed by a loved one or when we are cut off from intimacy with another human being on whom we have come to depend for sympathy and support. As Aristotle said long ago, without friends no one would choose to live (Aristotle, 1941, *Nicomachean Ethics* VIII, chapter 1).

> So soon may I follow,
>   When friendships decay,
> And from Love's shining circle
>   The gems drop away!
> When true hearts lie withered
>   And fond ones are flown,
> Oh! who would inhabit
>   This bleak world alone!
>   Thomas Moore (1779–1852), *The Last Rose of Summer*

Continuing, those who claim that the mere diversity of religions discredits all religion are missing the forest because of the trees. Diversity in religion no more eliminates religion than diversity in languages eliminates communication, or diversity in food eliminates eating. We can now understand why the human need for personal relationships means that impersonal science can never act as a substitute for religion. Nevertheless, some thinkers keep insisting that the only reason religion persists is that scientific knowledge has not yet been perfected. This is the god-of-the-gaps theory, which says that religion is only a way of marking time until science explains everything. Human ignorance makes the gods.

With respect to the god-of-the-gaps theory, if it were true, why are there so many questions science is no closer to answering today than it was thousands of years ago? There must be something more involved than our material existence. Sooner or later we always return to our intellect and will. Religion is always related to a someone beyond our material needs. In addition to material things, we must have something to fulfil our spiritual needs. Only personal beings possess religion.

Non-traditional Monotheism: Deism

Deism is a monotheistic way of trying to rationalize religion. Following the revamping of God, man, and nature by Descartes, the doctrine of deism was first popularized by John Toland (1670–1722), an Irishman who left the Catholic Church when he was 16-years-old. His career led him through Glasgow, Edinburgh, Leiden, and Oxford. He published *Christianity Not Mysterious* in 1696 and *Pantheisticon* in 1720. Another famous deist was Matthew Tindal (1655–1733), who wrote *Christianity as Old as the Creation; or, the Gospel a Republication of the Religion of Nature* (1730).

Toland knew from the scientists that the world needed a creator. But then, after creating the world and setting in place all of the natural laws, God abandoned it. God is certainly the great mathematician and engineer in the sky, but not the providential loving Father of traditional monotheism. It was as though a human clockmaker had constructed a complicated clock, wound it up, and then went away, leaving the clock to run on its own. Although exceptional religious leaders may appear from time to time, we certainly cannot accept scripture as literally authentic. An absent God does not inspire Scriptures. By the same token, there cannot be any miracles or divine graces to help people lead better lives.

Deism became widespread in Europe during the 1700s, being adopted by Jean-Jacques Rousseau and Voltaire, and later by Napoleon and the novelist Victor Hugo. Very likely, it was also the view of Edward Gibbon and Darwin. In any event, Darwin's doctrine of natural selection was just what the deists needed in order to complete their programme of rationalizing religion. Science and religion could now go together in a new way. In addition, if we develop some new system of mutual love and respect, we could also put science and humanism together.

Deism also played a large role at the time of the American Revolution, being adopted by Benjamin Franklin, George Washington, Thomas Jefferson, Ethan Allen, and Thomas Paine. Later on, Abraham Lincoln was by and large a deist. Not surprisingly, the American *Declaration of Independence* and *Constitution* are very monotheistic documents, but in a deistic sort of way.

Deism also found favour with the murderous Tzarina of Russia, Catherine II (Catherine the Great, 1729–96), who was praised by the French deists as an enlightened despot. She was so impressed with the thought of the French deist Denis Diderot (1713–84) that she invited him to St Petersburg, where he stayed for six months. She later continued to support him back in France until he died.

As another example, for some years during the French Revolution, in conjunction with the murder of priests and nuns and the confiscation of Church property, the revolutionaries tried to make deism the official state religion. Those who persisted in the old religion were fanatics. The only thing the state could do with them was to chop off their heads (Dougherty, 2000).

Conclusion

Once again, as with naturalistic theism, supernaturalistic theism has taken several different forms. Each of the different forms has some rationale to support it. In both the East and West various forms of polytheism are quite common. Neither is there only one form of monotheism. This means that we must be very careful when we use the word 'God'. We may think we know what it means, but do we really know?

Chapter 5

The As-if Approach to God

The As-if Approach in General

Arguments for the existence of God come in two main subdivisions, the as-if approach and the for-real approach, with several further varieties within each main subdivision. It should be made clear that both as-if and for-real forms of argumentation are rational. All reasonable argumentation presupposes the basic principles of reasoning, such as the principle of non-contradiction. Sound reasoning, in the sense of following the formal rules of rational argumentation (the categorical syllogism, the conditional syllogism, and so on), is required for any approach to be seriously considered. Logic is not something that separates the two approaches, but rather something they hold in common. The difference comes about as a result of the content of the reasoning process.

The first main subdivision within the basic arguments for the existence of God is the as-if approach. There is a certain subtlety here. The as-if approach does not so much prove the existence of God as it proves the need to believe in the existence of God. Some things are really real and some things are as-if real. The as-if approach emphasizes the fact that actions speak louder than words. The emphasis is upon the importance of doing and acting. As people living in the world, we are bound to act. There is no such thing as sitting on the sidelines, forever thinking about what to do. We must act. Words are cheap and, if we let it, mental contemplation (the 'Hamlet syndrome') can go on forever. In real life, though, we must actually move. We are constantly having to make decisions about going that way or this way. In this approach, being a true believer and acting like a true believer are the same thing.

The as-if approach adopts the attitude that the scientific form of argumentation is both unnecessary and unattractive to the vast majority of people. It is unnecessary because we cannot really use science in order to find answers to such lofty problems. Try as we might, we always end up in an agnostic situation. It is unattractive because it would require far too much rigorous thinking for the average person to endure. The as-if aim, therefore, is to find something more closely related to the interests and thinking of the average person, which means an appeal to the practical side of human nature. This is of central importance for the advocates of this approach when the distrust of our intellectual powers is combined with the need to act in matters concerning God. When the intellect fails the will must step in to fill the void.

This does not mean, however, that the as-if people regard their approach as merely an emotional appeal without any objective foundation in the real-life experiences of human beings. It means that, while the speculative aspect of human cognition is played down, the practical aspect is played up. Reason is used, but in such a way as to show its limitations. From the viewpoint of human intellectual knowledge, scepticism is the only really unassailable position to take. However, we can obtain what is true for us by appealing to the creative power of the will. Playing the game of 'let's pretend' can be very rewarding for us as human beings. The most important aspect of human mental life is our ability to direct our attention, to focus on things that are of interest to us, and to create what we need to be happy.

Asking a disciple of the as-if approach whether or not God actually exists will elicit an answer requiring some distinctions. To the ordinary person, saying that the tree is real means that it does not depend upon the perceiver in order to exist. If the big tree falls in the woods and there is no perceiver around to hear it, does the fallen tree make a sound? Well, that depends. If by a sound we mean the objective existence of compression waves in the air, then it does make a sound. But, if we mean by sound what is perceived by the perceiver, then the fallen tree does not make a sound. This can also be applied to God.

Yes, God really does exist, but 'real' is used in the social science sense of the word. Does the idea of God do something positive for you? Is God needed in order to complete your personal lifestyle? If so, then God is real. Is God needed for some very basic social reason? If God did not really exist, would it be necessary to invent him, especially for purposes of peace in society? Must we postulate God's existence in order to make sure that our sincere efforts to act rightly will ultimately be rewarded? If so, then God does exist, at least in the practical way of actually changing behaviour. From the practical viewpoint, therefore, anything that has a real effect on us is real.

Another element of the as-if approach is the willingness to take risks. Living with uncertainty is a normal part of a sane person's life. As we all know from our ordinary experiences in everyday life, it is reasonable to take a chance on various things in various ways. Are you afraid to cross the street, drive a car, fly in an airplane, or take a trip on a boat? If so, then you are not an as-if type of person. To live in this world we must be prepared to face the unknown with an optimistic attitude. We cannot demand certitude before we act. The greatest risk in life in not taking a risk. So why not apply this attitude to God as well as to the many other enterprises we undertake in life? Without any guarantee of success, we leave on a journey, start a business, invest in the stock market, and get married. Let us then also put our faith in God and hope for the best.

Another way of talking about this same process is to talk about the need for taking responsibility and being conscientious in our dealings with other people. Swearing on the Bible, for instance, does not mean that I am affirming the existence of God in an objective way. It means that the great idea of God is operative in my life; that I am willing to step out into the world and take upon myself the role of an actor who sincerely desires the welfare of those around me. My mind is fixed on having a system of peace and harmony in the world, especially as related to human relationships. God, then, becomes the symbol holding together all of the parts that would otherwise fly apart. Practically speaking, therefore, the voice of God issuing commands and my own inner voice of conscience willingly obeying the commands become one and the same.

Pascal's Wager

Pascal the Troubled Genius

Blaise Pascal was born in the Auvergne region of France in 1623. His mother died in 1626 and he was raised by his two sisters and his father, who was a magistrate in the tax court of Clermont-Ferrand. Even though he had no formal schooling and no contact with the classical philosophers, it was obvious from early on that Pascal was a genius. In 1631 the family moved to Paris. In 1639 his father was appointed the tax collector for Rouen. In 1640, at just 16, he wrote his *Essay on Conic Sections*, which became a textbook in mathematics. The family lived in Rouen until 1647, where his father was in favour with Cardinal Richelieu. About 1643 Pascal invented a calculating machine to help his father do his tax work more efficiently.

Pascal's interest was concentrated on science until 1646, at which time he had a semi-conversion under the influence of some Jansenists living in the area. In 1647 he was stricken with a partial paralytic stroke. He went back to living in Paris, where he made several free-thinking friends and led a somewhat wild life, especially with respect to gambling. In 1651 his father died and his sister Jacqueline joined the convent of Port-Royal des Camps near Versailles, which is near Paris. During this time he continued to engage in scientific work. He worked on atmospheric pressure, the existence of the vacuum, the equilibrium of fluids, and invented the hydraulic press based on what is now called Pascal's Principle. In mathematics he developed some thoughts on arithmetic that became the foundation for probability theory.

In 1654 Pascal was almost killed in a carriage accident and underwent his real conversion, which led him, by and large, to give up much of his previous work and move into the community at Port-Royal. During 1656–57, under the pseudonym of Louis de Montalte, he wrote his 19 *Provincial Letters* in defence of Arnauld, a Jansenist professor of theology at the Sorbonne, who was then under review for heresy. A mathematical treatise on the cycloid appeared in 1658. The rest of his short life was spent making converts to Christ, composing the notes for his projected work on a modern apologetic for religious faith (*Thoughts on Religion*), and doing charitable work, such as setting up a bus system for Paris and donating the revenues to the poor. In 1659 his illness returned, making it hard for him to continue on his own. In 1661 Jacqueline died. In the same year he went to live with his married sister, Gilberte Perier. He died during the following Summer (1662) after a painful two-month period of suffering.

Even in his own lifetime Pascal was noted as a great mind. However, he is not highly honoured in the Catholic Church. This is because of his activism on behalf of the Jansenists, founded by the Dutchman Cornelis Jansen (1585–1638), Bishop of Ypres, who wrote *Augustinus* (1642). Jansenism is noted for its doctrines of predestination (very Calvinistic) and its attacks on the Jesuits for making confession too easy. It was often combined with Gallicanism or Frenchism, the view that what the French want should come first and the decisions of the pope should come second.

After Jansen's death, the movement was led by the Frenchman Antoine Arnauld (1612–94), who wrote *On Frequent Communion* (1643), in which he argued that frequent communion is not a good thing. Not far from Paris, the Cistercian convent of Port-Royal became the centre of Jansenist learning and was noted for a series of textbooks, especially on logic and grammar, which were widely used from 1662 into the 1800s. Arnauld's older sister was the abbess. Although some of the reforms advocated by the Jansenists were in fact later adopted by the Church, in 1653–55 the chief doctrines were condemned by Innocent X (1574–1655) and in 1730 any remaining Jansenists were officially excommunicated.

Pascal and the Mediator

Pascal's light was Christ's cross. Nevertheless, he was also concerned with the God who hides himself. The effect appears, but not the cause. We directly observe rocks, trees, buildings, and other people, but why is God's presence not immediately obvious to us? God seems to be continuously present to a few people, such as mystics, but not to the ordinary person. And yet ordinary people do sometimes sense the presence of God. We see too little to be dogmatic and yet we see too much to be sceptics. Why?

Pascal concludes that the world does not exist for the purpose of instructing us about God. For this reason, although he thinks they are possible, he does not place any emphasis on scientific arguments for the existence of God. The real purpose of the universe is for the sake of the Second Person of the Trinity, the Son, as found in Colossians 1. What the world shows us is the absolute need for a personal redeemer. Pascal is sure that any thoughtful person will sooner or later be propelled to go to Jesus Christ for salvation, both intellectually and emotionally. In contrast to the problem of evil, which is very abstract, Pascal claims that we need Jesus Christ in order to solve the problem of personal suffering.

For one thing, everyone is fascinated by the thought of dying. It is like a great adventure into a far away and unknown land. At long last, after many years of thinking about them, the 'big questions' of life will finally be answered. Well, maybe they will and maybe they won't. This is the great source of existential angst. Everyone suffers from a non-specific, nagging, constant anxiety. In contrast to a particular problem to be solved here and now, such as getting a flat tyre fixed or passing a test tomorrow, existential angst has no immediate and well-defined object upon which we can focus our attention. Even if we are in good health, with no broken legs, skin cancer, and so on, we still feel uncomfortable. We fret about whether or not life is worth living. Even if we do not suffer in body, we suffer in mind.

According to Pascal, the world shows us two things simultaneously:

1 Our own wretchedness: If you want to be miserable just sit alone in a quiet room and think about yourself.

> I have discovered that all the unhappiness of men arises from one single fact, that they cannot stay quietly in their own chamber. A man who has enough to live on, if he knew how to stay with pleasure at home, would not leave it to go to sea or to besiege a town. A commission in the army would not be bought so dearly, but that is found insufferable to not to budge from the town; and men only seek conversation and games because they cannot remain with pleasure at home. (Pascal, 1941, section 139, p. 48)

Hence the need for constant entertainment. Most of our activities serve the purpose of preventing us from thinking about ourselves. This is especially true with respect to death. Even if we ignore the death of another, we cannot ignore our own. According to Pascal:

> This man spends his life without weariness in playing every day for a small stake. Give him each morning the money he can win each day, on the condition he does not play; you make him miserable. It will perhaps be said that he seeks the amusement of play and not the winnings. Make him then play for nothing; he will not become excited over it; and will feel bored. It is then not the amusement alone that he seeks; a languid and passionless amusement will weary him. He must get excited over it, and deceive himself by the fancy that he will be happy to win what he would not have as a gift on the condition of not playing; and he must make for himself an object of passion, and excite over it his desire, his anger, his fear, to obtain his imagined end, as children are frightened by the face that they themselves have blackened. (Pascal, 1941, section 139, pp. 51–52)

Just as we can be distressed by a mere trifle, so we can be consoled by a mere trifle. What, after all, do the rich and powerful have that we do not have? More toys and entertainment. They have more means for preventing themselves from thinking about their own personal miserable condition. And so what do ordinary people do? Imitate, as far as possible, the rich and powerful.

2 The possibility of something better: we know ourselves to be deposed monarchs, people who should be rulers but who in fact are slaves to the vicissitudes of nature, to other people, and to our own inner demons. Our thinking shows us superior ways of existing; our worldly experiences show us degradation, oppression, meanness, disease, and death. We both see

and do not see the existence of perfection. If we did not see anything better at all, we would be hopeless and commit suicide. But we do in fact see just enough of the true, good, and beautiful to keep us alive and looking for more.

In modern terms, Pascal would say that this dual vision is what drives the writing and reading of novels and poetry, the making of movies and TV programmes, the participation in sporting events, and so forth. We constantly use fantasizing about other lives and dreaming of something better as a major way of escaping our present low state of existence. This same observation can easily be expanded to include the devoted TV watcher and the bored middle-aged housewife who must shop until she drops.

> We might have been – these are but common words.
> And yet they make the sum of life's bewailing.
> Letitia Elizabeth Landon (1802–39), *Three Extracts from the Diary of a Week*

> For of all sad words of tongue or pen,
> The saddest are these: 'It might have been!'
> John Greenleaf Whittier (1807–92), *Maud Muller* (1856)

Pascal and Original Sin

What is a political conservative? Someone who believes in original sin. For Pascal the fact of original sin is part of natural theology rather than only a revealed doctrine. Our propensity for doing evil is so great that it must be due to a disorder in our nature rather than something accidental or temporary. Why, for instance, is a Hollywood movie only as good as the villain is bad? Why is watching people being tortured and killed on TV the preferred way to kill time in modern society? Why are men so ready to abuse women? Those who deny original sin, such as the followers of Rousseau, Voltaire, and Marx, think that it is possible to bring about human perfection on earth by natural means. In contrast, those who believe in original sin say that man will never reach perfection on earth under his own power. Human beings need divine grace and strong civil laws to counteract the effects of original sin.

Pascal's view of original sin as a part of natural theology was shared by John Henry Newman.

> What can be said of this heart-piercing, reason-bewildering fact? I can only answer, that either there is no Creator, or this living society of men is in a true sense discarded from His presence. Did I see a boy of good make and mind, with the tokens on him of a refined nature, cast upon the world without provision, unable to say whence he came, his birth-place or his family connections, I should conclude that there was some mystery connected with his history, and that he was one, of whom, from

one cause or another, his parents were ashamed. Thus only should I be able to account for the contrast between the promise and the condition of his being. And so I argue about the world; – *if* there be a God, *since* there is a God, the human race is implicated in some terrible aboriginal calamity. It is out of joint with the purposes of its Creator. This is a fact, a fact as true as the fact of its existence; and thus the doctrine of what is theologically called original sin becomes to me almost as certain as that the world exists, and as the existence of God. (Newman, 1927, p. 242)

According to Pascal, because of our original turning away from God, we need someone to once again set us straight with God. For Pascal, the mediator solves both the problem of misery and the problem of pride at the same time. Pascal avoids the two extremes of atheism, which is the self-deception of self-reliance, and deism, which he thinks is based upon a pride in our ability to have a completely naturalistic knowledge of God all on our own without a mediator. In between is Jesus Christ, the perfect mediator. So should we begin by believing in God now, so that we might later progress to other beliefs?

Pascal Places his Bet

The wager argument occurs in Pascal's *Pensées* (Pascal, 1941), a collection of nearly a thousand aphorisms that were collected together from his room and published after his death. Pascal says that Christian love demands that he at least try talking to agnostics and atheists. He has respect for those who are honestly confused and who are sincerely looking for the meaning of life. However, he has no intellectual respect for those who are so self-centred and complacent that they either are not searching at all or have given in to the decadent world of merely physical pleasures. His intended audience seems to be those aristocrats who abuse the poor, who scorn the ordinary believer, and who spend all their time drinking, gambling, whoring, hunting, and making business deals.

Pascal begins by making some stipulations:

1. God's existence cannot be either proved or disproved by science. Let us admit for the sake of argument that uncertainty rules our intellectual life. Reminiscent of Descartes' methodical doubt, it is incomprehensible both that God should exist and that God should not exist.
2. It is possible for us to know that something is without knowing exactly what it is, infinity, for instance, in mathematics.
3. We have all been given a one-way ticket to the grave. We are embarked on life's journey and must act either for or against God's existence, a God who is jealous of our other attachments and who demands our constant love. By the time you are capable of reading Pascal's works you are no longer able to claim any sort of sincere ignorance. The chips in the wager are your actual actions, which always speak louder than words. Call yourself whatever you wish, but we will know the true-you by your actions.

Then comes the wager:

- I bet that God either is or is not. I either win or lose.
- I bet that God is. I win. Heaven.
- I bet that God is. I lose. I have given up a short time (very short compared to eternity!) of some earthly pleasure, but have gained some others. And, after death, I will never know that I lost; the atheist will never have the last laugh on the believer.
- I bet that God is not. I win. I have gained a short period of some pleasures but have lost some others. And, after death, I will never know that I had won the wager.
- I bet that God is not. I lose. Hell. I will have an eternity of suffering, knowing forever that I had stupidly lost my chance for happiness. And those who are in heaven will (in a sense) always have the last laugh on me. This, though, is so only in a sense because those in heaven do not really take any pleasure in the sufferings of the lost ones (Aquinas, 1894b, Supplement, 94, 3).

As far as Pascal can see, because of their eternal natures, the only real issue is heaven or hell. And the only reasonable choice is to bet on God, even though you may be wrong. Given the amount to win over against the possible loss, there is no question about what the really smart person would do. It is like comparing zero and infinity. Doing otherwise would be like betting on a horse lying dead in the starting gate. Atheism is the ultimate bad bet.

Some Objections and Answers

Pascal himself is aware of some possible rebuttals, and attempts to answer them. I will take the liberty of elaborating upon these objections and answers.

1. One objection asks whether or not wagering on a sure loss (of some earthly pleasures) is irrational. Pascal says that it is not. In fact we do it all the time. Using some modern examples, look at lotteries, education, the stock market, and life insurance. In each case we are giving up something relatively small in the hope of getting back something much larger later on. This is called capitalism. How much better is a possible infinite gain. In other words, if it is reasonable to plan ahead for the near future, it is reasonable to plan ahead for the distant (after death) future.
2. Another objection says that I do not know anything about this infinite stuff, whereas I do know about the finite goods at hand. Besides, in the examples given above, we do have cases of people winning and these winners can show us here and now the benefits of the bet (or investment). Has anyone ever come back from the dead to tell us about what happened

to him after he was in the grave? Agreed, answers Pascal, but the whole point of the wager is to act in the face of uncertainty.

3   Another objection says, all right, but still, is not a bird in the hand better than two in the bush? Pascal really has no answer for this. The best he can do is to emphasize the fact that leading a good life is in fact very rewarding, so that the believer benefits even now from believing. In modern terms, why should Hollywood and TV be allowed to define what is enjoyable for us? Acts of charity can be as rewarding as mutilating your enemies and seducing your neighbours.

4   A further objection says, all right, but my psychological make-up is such that I cannot change my ways in order to act like a believer. No problem, answers Pascal. Your view indicates that you are at least trying to really believe. Now what we need is some behaviour modification. Pascal recommends that the intellectual convert go to church, practice praying, take the sacraments, and the like. In time your psychological condition will change to suit your actions. Just as when you act immorally your feelings change to justify your immoral behaviour, so the opposite can happen as well. We can compare what Pascal had to say with modern behaviour modification techniques, often used to stop chain smoking, overeating, and the like. After all, do you really lose out by acting morally? Are those addicted to TV, pornography, drugs, tobacco, alcohol, chocolate, cruelty, body-piercing, or the internet really better off than those who are not?

5   Someone could still object on the grounds of time. Why not wait? That is neither possible nor wise, counsels Pascal. Do you know when you are going to die? How can you avoid action of one kind or another? Even doing nothing is doing something. At every moment in your life you must choose. Life is one long series of forks in the road and you cannot go both ways at once.

6   But what about the nature of God? On which God do I bet? Are there not different definitions for God? Yes, but the only God who would count in such a debate would be one who is jealous of your attachments and who will not stand for idolatry. This is only the God of Judao-Christianity. (Pascal thought that the Muslim God was basically the same as the God of the Jews, which is to say that Muslim theology did not add anything significant to Jewish theology.) This rules out both deism, which removes God from the world, and pantheism, which makes all actions equally good or bad, as possible definitions.

7   Finally, someone might object, but how will God look upon me for treating him as a bet? Is not that alone sufficient to condemn me? Not at all, says Pascal. Remember that the wager is only the first step. There is no hypocrisy in saying: 'Lord I believe; help my unbelief.' With the proper behaviour, you can move all the way up from the first step to sainthood.

Critique of Pascal by Voltaire

Voltaire the Dilettante

Voltaire was one of the bright lights of the European Enlightenment. This was a movement that aimed to maximize reason (science) and minimize religion. It began in the later 1600s when thinkers saw the wonderful results that could be obtained from scientific investigation and the application of mathematical techniques to nature. As a consequence, the movement had no respect for any thinkers coming before the scientific revolution. It was also a reaction to the religious wars that had ravished Europe since the Protestant Reformation. As a part of this reaction, science became the new saviour, and the defenders of the new age never tired of ridiculing old religious works, such as the Bible.

François-Marie Arouet was born in Paris in November 1694. His mother died when he was seven years old. He did not get along well with his father, a middle-class civil servant, whom he rejected and never spoke about. A major influence on his life came from his godfather, a libertine priest. He was educated in Paris at the Jesuit Louis-the-Great College, with the intention of becoming a lawyer, an idea he soon abandoned. The philosophy he learned from the Jesuits was Cartesian in content.

His first job was as the secretary to the French ambassador to Holland. Later, in 1717, he was sent to the Bastille for 11 months for saying nasty things about the Duke of Orleans. His first literary success came in 1718 with the play *Oedipus*. It was after the success of his play that he adopted the name Voltaire, the origin of which is unknown. It may be an anagram on his mother's name. Voltaire never married.

In his first philosophical poem, *For and Against*, Voltaire expressed his deism. In 1726 he was forced to leave Paris because of his heterodox religious views. He travelled to England (1726–29), where he became proficient in English. It was while in England that Voltaire's philosophical mind was formed. He absorbed the science of Newton and the theory of knowledge promoted by John Locke (1632–1704). For Locke, experience is the foundation of knowledge. This sounds very concrete, but those who read Locke carefully see that what we experience is our own idea of the thing, not the thing itself. Ironically, Voltaire never understood that Locke himself was very much a Cartesian. While in England, Voltaire composed his work *The Henriad*, a plea for religious toleration on all sides.

About 1732 Voltaire became a complete convert to Newton's view, which then became the centre of his unitarian deistic theology. From 1734 to 1737 he composed a set of notes for himself called a *Treatise on Metaphysics*. This work, which was not written for publication, was heavily inspired by the scepticism of Pierre Bayle (1647–1706). At this point in his life Voltaire surrendered any hope for finding answers to the 'big questions', such as the exact nature of God, the mystery of human freedom, and the immortality of the soul. Aside from the mere certainty that God exists as the maker of the world, we cannot know anything with respect to our ultimate destiny or the rules of proper human behaviour.

With the publication of his *Philosophical Letters* (1734, also known as the *English Letters*) he once again had to leave Paris. He went to Cirey in Lorraine where he lived with the du Chatelet family. Later, he became a court favourite at Versailles, where he was made a gentleman of the king's bedchamber. After this royal approval, his reputation was firmly established and he no longer had to fear government reprisals. For a while, in 1743, he was sent to Prussia as an unofficial diplomat.

In 1746 Voltaire was elected to the French Academy. The following year he published a work entitled *The Metaphysics of Sir Isaac Newton, A Comparison Between the Opinions of Sir Isaac Newton and Mr. Leibniz*. In this work he sided with Newton in his view that the world is not a perfect place and that maybe God has to intervene once in a while in order to keep the mechanism working properly. Newton, for instance, held the view that God used comets to create and destroy parts of the universe. This could also be a reference to entropy, meaning the running down of the available energy in the universe as a whole. The term entropy was first used in 1865 by the German physicist Rudolf Clausius (1822–88), who formalized the three laws of thermodynamics. From 1750–53 Voltaire was at the court of Frederick II of Prussia (Frederick the Great, 1712–86). In 1756 he published his longest work, *An Essay on the General History, Customs, and Characteristics of the Nations*, arguing that deism is the only rational form of religion.

In 1758 he settled in Ferney, France, near the border with Switzerland, for the rest of his life. There he wrote *The Lisbon Disaster*, an account of a great earthquake that destroyed Lisbon in November 1755. This work also served as an attack on the idea that this world is the best of all possible worlds, a view popularized by the famous mathematician Gottfried Wilhelm von Leibniz (1646–1716). While in Ferney he also wrote *Candide* (1759), concerning education, and *The Philosophical Dictionary* (1764). *Candide* is probably his most famous and widely read work. In it, a naive young man is taught how everything is for the best, how noses are designed for eyeglasses, legs for trousers, and so on. Later on, after going through a series of unpleasant adventures, the young man discovers that this is not the best of all possible worlds.

A short time before he died in May 1778, Voltaire received his greatest honour when he was elected president of the French Academy. During his later years, when he saw that his new message was not being accepted by society, Voltaire became a very bitter old man. He turned fanatically anti-papal, popularizing the phrase, 'let us crush the infamous thing', referring to the Roman Catholic Church. In rejecting the abuses of religion, however, he also rejected its useful parts. Throughout his life he showed very little interest in helping the poor, used women freely, and was known for being greedy, selfish, and avaricious. And, unlike Jean-Jacques Rousseau (1712–78), Voltaire was not opposed to monarchies.

Although Voltaire had respect for God, he claimed to really love humanity. However, this did not rule out a strong strain of anti-Semitism on Voltaire's part (Mosse, 1978). Voltaire also loved his position in society. In fact, he was always jealous of the power, wealth, and prestige of the nobility. He distinguished between intellectuals and others. For the ordinary 'Jacques', in order to keep him moral, we must resort to fables, such as stories about heaven and hell, while the educated classes can be told the scientific truth about nature, man, and God. If heaven and hell do not exist, it is necessary for intellectuals to invent them. With respect to morality, the absolute truth is that we are on our own. When commenting on Voltaire's *Treatise on Metaphysics*, Rosemary Z. Lauer states that:

> God has not handed down from heaven, Voltaire says, any set of moral laws for the individual or society; in fact, those who have pretended to impose God-given laws on man have not given even a ten-thousandth part of the rules necessary for the conduct of life. Although Voltaire does not say so, it would seem from the context that God has no more concern about one man's injustice to another than he has for the sheep eaten by the wolf. (Lauer, 1961, pp. 126-7)

Overall, Voltaire was a dilettante, dabbling a little bit here and a little bit there. Consistency was not something he worried about. He would say one thing in one place and then say just the opposite in another place. He was very adept at throwing out things he did not like, but not at all adept at replacing them with workable substitutes. He was, though, consistently repulsed by the idea that we are sinners who must beg God for mercy and forgiveness. His constant attacks on traditional religion helped prepare the ground for the French Revolution and its Reign of Terror.

The leaders of the revolution engaged in the mass murder of all those they thought were the enemies of the new France. Its chief achievement was the guillotine, a device for fast, efficient, and entertaining killing, invented by the French doctor, Joseph Guillotin (1738–1814). Ironically, the state also killed Antoine Lavoisier (1743–94), one of the founders of modern chemistry; unfortunately for Lavoisier, he was also a tax collector. Voltaire's legacy to France was death. The king soon returned in an even worse form in the figure of the megalomaniac dictator Napoleon Bonaparte (1769–1821), who then proceeded to reinstate slavery in the French colonies, and to bring even more death down on the French, especially as a part of his arrogant military campaign against Russia. Altogether, Napoleon was directly responsible for the unnecessary deaths of about three million people. He ended his days in prison, dictating a fictionalized account of his military exploits to a bored secretary.

Voltaire the Deist

Voltaire is one of Pascal's biggest fans as well as one of his severest critics. As we learn from his essay on Pascal in his *Philosophical Letters*, Voltaire praises

Pascal for his great literary talents, ranking him with Moliere (1622–73), as well as for his mathematical and scientific genius (Voltaire, 1961). However, Voltaire also lambasts Pascal for his pessimism. Although this world is certainly not the best of all possible worlds, it is also not the worst. What is a major problem for Pascal, namely, your being a nobody and royalty at the same time, is merely the ordinary course of nature for Voltaire.

Pascal also condemned self-love. However, in Voltaire's outlook, self-love is a divinely established good, as necessary to our welfare as are our five senses. Self-love is given to us for the preservation of our being and, when properly regulated by religion, can be just as useful to us as our senses. Man is really not such an enigma, but is just where he belongs in nature, situated between the animals and the angels. Man is a mixture of pleasure and pain, of good and evil. He is provided with passions so that he may act and with reason and thus regulate his actions. Man's passions and reason complement each other.

On occasion, though, Voltaire is more like Pascal than he realizes. Voltaire is a very as-if fellow. For instance, is the human soul immortal? Voltaire says that we have no way of rationally knowing such a thing. Nevertheless, in order to prevent all sorts of evil actions by ordinary people, we must assume that it is. Since reason cannot prove the immortality of the soul, religion must reveal it to us. Voltaire asserts that the good of mankind requires that we believe the soul to be immortal and so the question is settled.

And what is the nature of the human soul? Here Voltaire takes his cue from John Locke and brings up the possibility of thinking matter. Could God have bestowed upon matter the power of thought? According to Descartes, there cannot be any such thing as thinking matter. Thought and matter (extension) are mutually exclusive. Such a view has a serious consequence for Cartesians. Not only does it return us to the Platonic dualism, it also means that anything without a soul-substance is a mere machine. Now, since anything of a feeling, cognitive nature belongs to the soul, sub-humans do not really sense or feel anything. Neither do they have any emotions. Locke observes that the understanding of man so surpasses that of brutes that some are of the opinion that brutes are mere machines, without any manner of perception at all (Locke, 1876, vol. 2, p. 495). This view, though is ill-grounded.

For both Locke and Voltaire, ordinary experience shows us that animals feel pain. When you cut an animal and it screams, it is not comparable to the squealing of tyres on pavement or the sound made when you scratch your fingernails over a chalkboard. In his essay on Locke in his *Philosophical Letters*, Voltaire goes out of his way to prove that animals cannot be mere machines. If animals are simply mechanical devices, why has God given them the same sense organs as human beings? Does God work in vain, giving his creatures useless organs? In this way, religion comes to the aid of commonsense and science.

Thus does Voltaire find himself in bed with Pascal. As with the vast majority of the other scientific thinkers of the time, Voltaire took it for granted that

Descartes had completely destroyed Aristotle's matter and form philosophy of nature. In his essay on Descartes and Newton in his *Philosophical Letters*, Voltaire says that Descartes had eliminated the absurd chimeras that had held us captive for thousands of years. No longer would students learn about the hierarchy of natural types based on the combination of matter and form. In the new philosophy of nature there is only one matter, with its parts arranged in many different ways. Descartes is wrong about its continuous nature, but right about its basic definition. And most wrong of all was Aristotle, who made nature into something basically qualitative rather than quantitative.

On the basis of such a view, we can see why Locke and Voltaire must have a material world that is capable of producing ideas and thought. They are caught in a dilemma. Either animals are mere machines, which goes against commonsense, or animals have human-type souls, which goes against religion. The proper rational way to escape such a dilemma is, first of all, to return to Aristotle's psychosomatic view of the natural world. However, given their prejudices, this is impossible for them to do. The next step is to see, with Aquinas, that the human soul possesses its own act of existing, which it communicates to the body in order to form a unity while alive on earth, but which allows for the immortality of the soul after death. However, going along with Aquinas is even more out of the question than following Aristotle. Consequently, Voltaire must settle for an as-if immortality.

Voltaire, however, cannot abide an as-if God. As a practical person he knows the importance of a firm belief in God. Although a deist, and therefore an enemy of the traditional monotheistic view of God, Voltaire feels that he has at least one very great advantage over Pascal, namely, that his own (Voltaire's) deistic God is at least a really existing God in comparison to the subjective deity of his fellow Frenchman. In his essay on Pascal in the *Philosophical Letters*, Voltaire, after mentioning in passing a few of the possible rebuttals against Pascal's wager argument, gets down to his main point. He says (quite rightly) that even though someone might sincerely want to believe in something, such a desire in no way shows the real existence of the thing in question. Voltaire uses the example of someone who is told that he can rule the world if he really believes that he is the ruler of the world. Obviously, this will not work.

But how, then, do we know that we are creatures of God, that religion is important, and that we must take moral laws seriously? Voltaire insists that we must not talk about games of head or tail and wearing a crown of thorns. Talk instead about the way all of nature forces upon us a belief in the existence of a wise creator of the world. In other words, Voltaire's approach is the same as that of Newton and Paley.

Voltaire, it seems, holds a relatively optimistic view of nature: nature is pretty good. It is not until the next century, under the guidance of Darwin, that nature begins to look very ragged around the edges. And it is not until our own day, under the influence of atomic bombs and pollution, that we begin having serious worries about the disappearance of man. As far as Voltaire is concerned, though, God did a pretty good job, and his existence must be taken seriously by both the common man and the political leaders. As Voltaire's famous saying goes, if God did not exist, it would be necessary for mankind to invent him.

Kant's Internal Moral Sanction

Kant the Resolute

Immanuel Kant's grandfather had moved from Scotland, where his name was Cant, to Königsberg in eastern Prussia. His father was a saddle-maker and his mother was greatly under the influence of the Pietism movement within Lutheranism, which taught the importance of inner devotion and ethical perfection and which played down external denominational practices. Social activism was not the way to help people. Instead, each individual must undergo an inner conversion of will. The basic appeal must be to the indwelling presence of God in each individual.

This was the atmosphere into which Kant was born in 1724. He attended the local schools and later studied theology, physics, and mathematics at the University of Königsberg. At the time, philosophy in Germany was ruled by the Spanish Jesuit, Francis Suárez (1548–1617), and the German philosopher, Wolff, both of whom thought of philosophy as the supreme science of essences, from which the thinker could deduce a knowledge of reality. Kant's philosophy professor at the University of Königsberg was Franz Albert Schultz, one of Wolff's pupils.

Freiherr (Baron) Christian von Wolff (1679–1754), a pupil of Leibniz, was a professor's professor. He wrote works in theology, psychology, botany, mathematics, physics, and philosophy. In 1707 he was appointed a professor of mathematics in the University of Halle. In 1723, however, he was banished from the area by the Pietists because of his anti-religious rationalism. From 1723 to 1740 he taught at the University of Marburg, which became the first Protestant university in 1527 and where Luther and Zwingli debated in 1529. In 1741, under orders from the King of Prussia (Frederick II, 1712–86, king from 1740), Wolff returned to the University of Halle as chancellor, where he remained until his death. For a while (1716–25), Wolff acted as the science advisor to Tsar Peter I (Peter the Great, 1682–1725) of Russia.

Wolff is important because of his influence on the method used for the teaching of philosophy as well as for the content of his philosophy. It was Wolff who began the practice of breaking up philosophy into subdivisions covered in textbooks, some of which he wrote himself. He was also a part of the Enlightenment, an intellectual movement that aimed at rationalizing religion. Along with the earlier John Locke, Wolff wanted to move religion away from the superstitious beliefs of the older churches, especially the Roman Catholic Church, and into the modern age of science.

When Kant's father died in 1746, Kant had to work as a private tutor in order to earn a living. In 1755 he was hired as a tutor in the Count Kayserling family, which helped his finances. In 1756 he read Hume's *Enquiry Concerning Human Understanding*, a work that broke his dogmatic slumbering in the philosophy of essences. This led to *The Only Possible Foundation for a Demonstration of God's Existence* (1763) in which he insists that, if you cannot go from the intra-mental idea of something to its extra-mental reality, then the existence of God cannot be proven by reason alone. In 1766 he became an assistant librarian at the University of Koenigsberg. In 1770 he finally obtained a full-time teaching position in the University, holding the chair of logic and metaphysics. In his inaugural address he agreed with Leibniz on the need for a pre-established (by God) harmony between mental and physical events. Up until then his main interest was in science and mathematics. Soon after, though, his thinking underwent a radical change.

In 1771 Kant entered into his long period of silence, contemplating how both Hume and Newton could be right at the same time. How can science be saved in the face of Hume's scepticism? What role can reason have in a world made up of disconnected sensations? The result was his chief work, *The Critique of Pure Reason* (1781, second edition 1787). A critique means an evaluation of the subject, an attempt to put something in its place relative to other things. This lengthy and complex work was not well-received at first. Consequently, taking his cue from Hume, Kant produced a much shorter and simpler work, covering the same main points of the longer work, under the title of *A Prolegomena to Any Future Metaphysics* (1783). There quickly followed a series of other works, including *The Foundations of the Metaphysics of Morals* (1785), *The Critique of Practical Reason* (1788), *The Critique of Judgment* (1790), *On the Real Advances in Metaphysics Since Leibniz and Wolff* (1791), and *Religion Within the Bounds of Reason Alone* (1793).

Politically speaking, he supported the revolutionary (American and French) causes of the day and was anxious to keep up with the latest news reports of current events. At home, from 1792 to his death, he was in trouble with the Lutherans. To keep the peace, Frederick Wilhelm II (king from 1740–97) made him promise not to lecture on religious matters, a promise that he kept. In 1794 he began withdrawing from society, giving only one lecture a year, until he stopped completely in 1797. The same year saw the publication of *The Metaphysics of Ethics*, and in 1798 he published *The Contest of the Faculties*, an attack on censorship, and *Anthropology from a Pragmatic Viewpoint*, a precursor to the thought of Renouvier and James.

He died in February 1804, after being nearly blind and in poor health for some years, never having travelled more than 40 miles from his home town. On his tombstone was written, 'the starry heavens above and the moral law within', indicating the two great irreconcilable sides of man, science and morality. He left behind many half-finished works, some of which were published in 1920. These later musings show Kant's true colours as an atheist.

He says, for instance, that God is not a being outside of himself, but only a thought in himself (Kant, 1920, section 341, p. 819).

Kant's Practical Necessity

Kant tackles the question of God's existence in his *The Critique of Practical Reason* (1956 [1788], Book II, chapter 2, section 5). He had already shown to his own satisfaction in *The Critique of Pure Reason* that the human intellect is incapable of reaching God on its own. In summary, it is not possible to know about the existence of God through scientific reasoning, which would require that our knowledge of God have a foundation in sense experience. We cannot get God into a test tube. So we must turn from the intellect to the will. This means that we must postulate the existence of human freedom and immortality in order to explain how it is possible for human beings to behave morally in a material (scientific) world. Likewise, we must postulate the existence of God in order to guarantee the ultimate happiness of those who freely act in accordance with the categorical imperative (the will to duty), which is sure to cause them pain and suffering in this life. In this way our own reason tells us that we can postulate God's existence.

We know from everyday experience that there is no necessary connection between doing what you are supposed to do (duty) and personal happiness. In fact it is often just the reverse. In this life, all too often good people suffer while evil people prosper. So it must be the case that the achievement of happiness lies outside of this world, provided by a being who has the knowledge and power to do so. This being is God, who must be personal in order to know and will the coincidence of action and happiness for those who do what is right. God did not create the world for our happiness, but as a testing ground for our worthiness of happiness. We must make ourselves worthy of happiness by following the categorical imperative. In other words, without God there would be no lasting justice for anyone. It would mean that, if someone could get away with some evil act until he died a natural death, he would have gotten away with it forever. So we need God in order to fulfil the moral will to duty. Hence the proper names of God are all related to moral (action) attributes. These attributes are what make God into an object of personal religious devotion.

Kant sees three such attributes that God must possess in order to be useful to us:

- God must be holy, meaning that God is a creator and lawgiver.
- God must be a ruler, meaning that God is an executive, someone who sustains things.
- God must be wise, meaning that God is a judge, someone who rewards and punishes.

Furthermore, if you act rightly you are a believer. This is the case regardless of what you call yourself. All those who follow the will to duty, and who therefore act rightly without any thought of reward in this world, are in fact true believers.

Kant and Atheism

The obvious rebuttal to this line of reasoning is to ask: If God is only a postulate, that is, something I must will into existence, could I not also will God out of existence, especially if I am willing to take the consequences, as in the case of Nietzsche and his disciples?

In his *Critique of Practical Reason* Kant insists that being moral requires a pure will, the will to duty. The moral law is absolute and unyielding. This is what it means to be holy. Being holy requires that each man be resolute in his adherence to the law. As it turns out, though, since there can be no speculative (theoretical) knowledge of morality based upon the world as it really is, the only way to be moral is to come up with a practical rule to guide the will in an absolute fashion. This rule is nothing other than the categorical imperative. It is both unyielding (categorical) and absolutely necessary (imperative). It tells us (or rather, we tell ourselves) that we must never act in any way that we could not will into being a proper way of acting for anyone else. For example, if I allow myself to take something that I do not own, then I must also be willing to allow everyone else to do likewise. This, according to Kant, would undermine the whole concept of private property, which would make robbery and theft meaningless, which in turn would produce chaos. In everything we do we must take into account the needs of society. Practically speaking, it is essential to human life that everyone possess a well-developed social conscience.

At the end of the day, though, our will to duty is just that, our own will. No moral action is to be based on either the fear of punishment or the hope of reward. To do so would destroy the entire moral character of the act. Morality can never, if it is really pure, be considered as a means to an end, even if that end is ultimate happiness itself. Acting in accordance with duty is the necessary rational condition for happiness, but it is not an instruction on how to achieve happiness. Kant insists that a pure and true morality must always be a completely disinterested and selfless mode of behaviour. Being moral means following the categorical imperative for its own sake, which means that virtue is an end in itself. Looking for rewards is a sure sign that someone is not really virtuous.

In his old age Kant finally made explicit what was implicit all along, namely, that he was an atheist. As described by the Kantian scholar Hans Vaihinger in his 1935 classic study, God is only a thought in Kant's mind. When God acts as a sanction for human actions, it is really the human agent who is acting as his own sanction. It is as-if there were a real God who really speaks to people. It is as-if there were divinely instituted purposes built into human beings that had to be respected. What rules we have we have given to ourselves and so what rewards we have we must also give to ourselves. Virtue must be its own reward. Undoubtedly, this sort of self-imposed morality can be very rigorous; and maybe too rigorous (Vaihinger, 1952).

Kant makes law an end in itself, with the result that virtue becomes inhuman. For example, Kant was very fond of eating dried fruit and on one occasion became extremely angry with the crew of a ship that was transporting an order of fruit to him from France. He had invited some friends over for dinner and was looking forward to the special treat. However, due to a storm at sea, the ship was delayed long enough to run out of food and so the crew ate the fruit. This infuriated Kant, who asserted that, if the members of the crew had been truly moral men, they would have starved to death rather than violate their duty to deliver the fruit as promised. What would human society come to if each individual did not feel an obligation to honour his contracts? When a friend asked him if he was really serious, Kant said yes.

For Kant there was nothing good except a good will. Duty was the great sublime name of morality. He even thought that duty played the same role in human moral life as the biblical Golden Rule and the Sermon on the Mount. As far as Kant was concerned, acting morally was the same thing as religion. Morality was a realm entirely within the person. Kant expected people to be moral for the sake of being moral. The idea of duty, and the particular maxims that could be derived from it, was Kant's substitute for divine Revelation. As a result, one's personal conscience is everything.

However, despite its claim to being absolute, the will to duty is just as variable as any other form of moral relativism. It is all a matter of my own will. Whatever I do I am doing to myself. So when an adherent of Kantian philosophy talks about duties that must be performed and rights that cannot be taken away he is like a man who locks himself in a room, puts the key in his pocket, and who then bemoans the fact that he cannot escape. However, such a self-binding is in no way necessary.

James Wills to Believe

James the Psychologist

William James was born in 1842 in New York City, where he attended the local schools. His younger brother was Henry James (1843–1916), the famous novelist who switched his citizenship to England a year before he died. James's grandfather was a wealthy Presbyterian who had immigrated from Ireland. His father was a wealthy lay theologian who followed the new religion of Emanuel Swedenborg (1688–1772), a Swedish mining engineer who had a private revelation that allowed him to move freely in the spirit world. In 1788 some of his disciples founded the Church of the New Jerusalem.

According to this religion, the Second Coming of Christ has already occurred in the form of some 30 volumes of writings in which Swedenborg explained everything about the Bible. His basic approach turned out to be very pantheistic.

God is the great power within all things. The Trinity is essentially related to the world, while a human being is a microcosm of the world. The Father is the great soul of the world, the Son is the material embodiment of the soul, and the Holy Spirit is the activity of the Son in the world. In this way, Jesus can rightly be called the divine human. Swedenborg's aim was to be completely rational and eliminate the mysteries of faith.

James's father was well-connected and hobnobbed with the famous philosophical and literary figures of America and Europe. From 1855 to 1860, money being no obstacle, James studied in Europe. For a while in 1860 he studied painting with the American artist William Morris Hunt (1824–79) in Newport, RI.

During the Civil War, from 1861–63, James attended the Lawrence Scientific School at Harvard. In 1864, the same year in which his family moved to Cambridge, MA, he entered the Harvard medical school. After a year, though, James took a break in order to travel through Brazil for a year with the famous Swiss naturalist Louis Agassiz (1807–73), who had come to settle in the United States in 1846. Agassiz was critical of Darwin's theory, wondering, for instance, how there can be change in species if there are no species in the first place. From 1867 to 1868 James studied in Berlin. He was well aware of Darwin's theory and, in 1868, even wrote reviews of some of Darwin's works. In 1869 he finally received his medical degree from Harvard, but never practised.

By this time he was truly troubled by the relationship of faith and reason. James's graduation was followed by a period of severe mental stress (1869–71), as he contemplated the fact that, if it is true that human beings are nothing but matter in motion, then there is no freedom for us. Where science starts, freedom ends. We would all be machines and so there would be no point to ethics. Furthermore, if human life is meaningless, why not commit suicide?

Significantly, from the viewpoint of his intellectual development, James began to conquer his depression in February 1870 by reading the French philosopher Charles Renouvier (1815–1903), a somewhat loyal disciple of Kant. According to Renouvier, there is no world existing independently of the human thinker. The world is as we make it to be. This would include the world of religion and human freedom as well as everything else. James learned that the secret to happiness is to emphasize one's creativity as a human being. What James needed was a series of useful fictions. He thought that there must be some really existing force in nature that allowed humans to be pragmatic, but he did not know what it was. It took James several years to overcome his angst, during which time he remained at home, virtually an invalid, his problem compounded by the publication in 1871 of Darwin's *The Descent of Man*.

After his recovery in 1872 he taught anatomy and physiology at Harvard until 1880, at which time he switched his public persona entirely to philosophy and the new science of psychology, which he taught at Harvard until 1907. In

1874 he began to show an interest in mysticism and mystical experiences and later founded the Society for Psychical Research. In 1876, the same year in which the German engineer Nikolaus Otto (1832–91) built the first workable internal combustion engine, he established an experimental laboratory at Harvard for doing studies in psychology. In 1878 he married Alice Gibbens (1849–1922), a religious woman in a non-denominational Christian sort of way, chosen for him by his father. They proceeded to have five children. After travelling in Europe for a year (1882–83), he began to write in earnest.

1890 saw his *Principles of Psychology* in two volumes. Two years later, a one volume *Psychology: Briefer Course* was published. In the *Principles* he developed the notion of a stream of consciousness as an alternative to the notion of a substantial soul in each human person. He later abandoned the view that each successive state of consciousness is a unity unto itself; it should instead be defined as a relationship. He also advocated the notion, in agreement with Darwin's conceptualism, that species were only intra-mental creations of the human mind, useful for making things more convenient for those studying nature. In 1896 he travelled to Yale University to deliver a talk on the will to believe. About that same time he also praised Freud for beginning the process of doing scientific work in abnormal psychology. In 1909 James actually met Freud on a visit to Clark University in Worcester, MA.

After a talk given by James in California in 1898, his pragmatic turn solidified and the term 'pragmatism' became a part of the popular American vocabulary. Following the same force that motivated James, modern pragmatists think that they have managed to salvage some semblance of human honour in an otherwise completely impersonal scientific universe. In the new order, nothing is eternal and even the best science is only probabilities and approximations. With respect to ethics, mankind cannot appeal to anything God-given, but must instead look to the total human experience for guidance.

During 1906 James lectured at Stanford University in California. He lectured at Oxford University from 1908 to 1909. Toward the end of his life James was defending vivisection as a necessary means for scientific research and advocating, as a moral substitute for war, the conscription of young men for manual labour instead of for the army. In the summer of the same year in which Mark Twain died (1910), James died at his extensive farm complex on Silver Lake near the little town of Chocorua in central New Hampshire.

His works include *Human Immortality* (1898), *The Varieties of Religious Experience: A Study in Human Nature* (1902, the Gifford Lectures, given at Edinburgh, in which he concluded that God is only a higher force in the human psyche), *Pragmatism: A New Name for Some Old Ways of Thinking* (1907), *A Pluralistic Universe*, and *The Meaning of Truth*, both in 1909. After he died there appeared *Some Problems of Philosophy* (1911) and *Essays in Radical Empiricism* (1912). For a while after James's death, several people claimed to receive messages from him. (On James and Darwin see Myers, 1986, pp. 589–91.)

James the Pragmatist

> The abdication of belief
> Makes the behaviour small –
> Better an *ignis fatuus*
> Than no illume at all.
>
> Emily Dickinson (1830–86)

There is no doubt that James places the will above the intellect in human affairs. At the end of his *Psychology: Briefer Course*, James emphasizes the fact that our acts of will are the most important thing about us. What we will is the most revealing thing about us. James, like Kant, is convinced that actions speak louder than words. Our greatest contributions to the betterment of the world come from our deepest wellspring of emotional commitment, which is revealed in our actions. What we do shows what we will, and what we will shows our true inner life-force (James, 1963, pp. 400–401).

This is as true of religion as it is of anything else. If everyone thinks that old Mr Kris Kringle, as in the movie *Miracle On 34th Street* (1947), is Santa Claus, then he really is Santa Claus. James's pragmatic argument for believing in God is found in his brief *The Will to Believe*, which he regarded as a sort of sermon on your right to be righteous. The talk was originally delivered to the philosophical clubs of Yale and Brown Universities, places where, unlike his own Harvard University, religion was still taken seriously. He said that he was arguing against the growing trend at the time of rejecting anything that did not meet the rigorous standards of inductive scientific experimentation. His own counter-view is that, in the spirit of Kant, reinforced by Darwin, whatever is useful for earthly survival is right and true (James, 1968, pp. 717–35).

As a psychologist, James thought his position much better than the cold, calculating position of Pascal. Such an unemotional approach would never work for 'us Protestants', said James. Nevertheless, Pascal was right when he said that we must choose. There is no doubt that the God-choice is a genuine choice, which means that it is alive (you can actually act on it), forced (unavoidable, with definite options to choose from), and momentous (irreversible, there is much at stake, you must act now). The important point is that we have to be pragmatic in such matters.

The key question for James is whether or not it is reasonable for us to follow our emotional nature (the will) when something cannot be decided on scientific grounds. The answer is yes. In fact we act on incomplete scientific evidence all the time. We believe in molecules, the conservation of energy, progressive evolution, democracy, and in the possibility of attaining the truth, even though we do not see such things (with our eyes) for ourselves. Playing the agnostic is itself a definite decision that puts us in danger of losing the truth and that is, in practice, the same thing as a negative decision. Why deny the obvious fact of secular faith? And then why not extend faith or trust into religious matters?

This is especially true in moral matters, where we cannot await the gathering in of all the evidence and where not acting is itself a moral decision. Also, in many cases, how we act becomes a part of the evidence; our actions create the data. Do not forget the self-fulfilling promise. We can create a positive cycle, for example, by assuming that someone likes us, or a negative cycle, for instance, by assuming that we are not liked. This is so in the vast majority of human interactions. How could society possibly survive if we did not have faith in the cooperation of others with us, in the law-abiding wills of others, and so on? A modern example would be driving a car.

As a general rule, it is perfectly reasonable in social settings, thinks James, to have our faith (our emotional life) run ahead of the current scientific data. This, after all, is what we find in business, the stock market, insurance policies, and marriage. Who, for instance, would ever get married if he or she had to wait for the perfect mate? Who would ever stay married if he or she insisted upon living a life without squabbles, arguments, disagreements, and moments of regret? It would be most unreasonable to expect that everything will always go along in a smooth and unperturbed fashion. The consequence is that, if you are thinking about getting married, you must be prepared to take a chance and hope for the best.

In cases of human interaction, those who preach eternal scepticism are the unreasonable ones. They follow the foolish idea that it is better to risk the loss of truth than the chance of error. Remember what America was like back in 1890. It was time of vast economic growth; the thing to do was to take a chance, invest, get rich, and be a self-made man. Anyway, agnosticism and scepticism are impossible in practice. And, before we miss the forest because of the trees, they are also cases of taking up an option, which requires a definite act of the will. Therefore the will to believe is perfectly reasonable.

James's own view, in light of our social needs, is that it is better (more useful) to be religious than not to be religious. In general, religion teaches us that eternal things are better than non-eternal things and that we are better off believing than not believing. Religion, therefore, serves a very useful function. A belief in God actually changes our behaviour for the better. Although he agrees with Darwin's scientific view of nature as promiscuous and open to endless variation, James has no use for the ruthless self-made tycoon and the competitive approach of social Darwinism. Individualism is fine, but people must also take into account the needs of other people. Family relations are very important to the welfare of the individual. In addition, man remains, after all, a social animal. Pragmatically speaking, this social aspect of human life proves to James that God is real (Myers, 1986, pp. 422–45).

However, unlike Pascal, who insisted that the reasonable person must believe in God, James wants to leave it an open question. As we know from James's work *The Varieties of Religious Experience* (1902), polytheism is the most common kind of religion among ordinary people. For the critical mind, though, God does not really exist. God is only the higher self. God is really only me knowing myself. When conversing with God I am really talking to myself. This is very much in line with the as-if view of Kant.

But Does it Work?

'Yes, Virginia, there is a Santa Claus; he really lives in your own mind and heart.' The game of 'let's pretend' may be suitable to children, but not for adults. Although the ventriloquist view of God can be entertaining, it is not convincing. How can you be a sincere believer if you know that your belief is the creation of your own will? A self-deception is still a deception. Is my religious experience an experience of God or only of myself? Saying that God is real for me says something about me, but not about God. In everyday English, real means that the thing is there independently of my willing it or thinking it. Speaking ordinary English, therefore, both Kant and James are atheists. As understated by Alfred Jules Ayer:

> This is in line with the view of some contemporary theists that the doctrine associated with the religious practices in which they engage is acceptable as a useful myth. This view is so modest that it is hard to take issue with it, unless one wants to argue that the myth is harmful, but it does appear open to the practical objection that the satisfaction which most believers derive from their acceptance of religious doctrine depends upon their not judging it as mythical. A myth which is generally seen to be a myth must be in some danger of losing its utility. (Ayer, 1978, pp. 234–5)

Chapter 6

The For-real Approach to God: The A Priori Method

The For-real Approach in General

In contrast to the as-if method, the other main approach to the existence of God adopts the attitude that, in order for someone to be truly reasonable, the human intellect must be accorded primacy over the will. A rational approach demands that the thinker adhere closely to the methodology of gathering evidence from things as they really are. We must investigate the issue until the evidence firmly tilts the scales toward God. In such a realistic procedure, God's existence is discovered, not invented. The for-real method aims to say something objective about the world. In contrast to the as-if approach, the for-real approach cannot accept any procedure that regards God as a mental construct, whether on an individual basis or on a social basis. It insists upon maintaining the ordinary usage of the words 'real' and 'true'.

When I say that something is really there I mean that it does not depend upon me and those around me for its existence. The tree in the yard is real; the tree will go on existing even if I should drop dead in the next second. Even if the whole society were to disappear, the tree would still go on existing. If we are realists, that is also the way we should speak about God. We do not create God; God creates us. God is there eternally, whether or not there are any human beings and whether or not there is any world at all.

We must also demand certitude in our proofs for God's existence. Risk-taking is fine in many ways and it may even be necessary in some cases. However, it is not the ideal situation. We must always aim for certitude and trust that we will be able to achieve true and certain knowledge in the important matters of life. This attitude must also apply to the existence of God.

Within the for-real approach there are two main subdivisions. One main method for rationally reaching the existence of God is the strictly a priori or deductive method. An a priori approach means one that comes before something else, usually referring to the senses. There is no immediate connection to facts about ourselves or the world. According to this method, there is no need to employ any sort of human experience of the world, either of our internal world of mental experiences or of our external world of sense experiences. All we need do is concentrate on the idea of God and the solution of the problem becomes self-evident. We can know with certainty that God exists simply by knowing the definition of God. It is a very direct and easy method for proving God's existence. Indeed, it may be too easy.

And this is exactly how it is viewed by those who favour the other main subdivision within the for-real approach. Advocates of this second main subdivision need some sort of actual experience of ourselves in the world in order to rationally reach God. An a posteriori approach means one that comes after something else, with the something else usually referring to knowledge derived from the senses. The a posteriori method does not deny the need for logical reasoning. All rational argumentation presupposes the use of correct logical formations. What the a posteriori method does insist upon, though, is that the formations be filled with some content derived from human experience. In this sense it is an inductive procedure as opposed to a strictly deductive procedure. According to the inductive way of doing things, a mere definition or set of concepts is not enough to justify a move from the idea of something to the real existence of something. Ideas must have some worldly content, either internal or external.

In the internal experience branch of a posteriori argumentation, one's own experiences of one's own feelings, thoughts, hopes, fears, psychological condition, and state of mind rise to the top in importance. The predominant theme is that in knowing ourselves we also know God. By examining the way I am made in terms of my mental and psychological life as a human being, I am empowered to move to the one who is responsible for making me the way I am. In one way or another, it can be argued that we are made to be happy with God and that we cannot be happy in any other way. Just as we know that thirst implies water, in order to be happy we must know with certainty that there is a being who guarantees that our quest for happiness will be satisfied. This approach has the advantage of always being with us. To find God, all we need do is to look within ourselves, something we can do at any time or place.

On the other hand, according to the external experience branch of a posteriori argumentation, while admitting that the realization of our own psychological needs is important to us, appealing to our internal ideas and psychological condition is not the best way to proceed. We live in a real world of real physical things. Surely we should be able to acquire a knowledge of God's real existence as the real creator of such a real world from our experiences of the real world. This approach is in fact the one closest to the ordinary person, who knows first and foremost the things of the world that exist outside of his mind. The advantage of the external experience approach is that it is public. There is no need to call upon one's own private experiences that may or may not be shared with others. This branch of argumentation has two main subdivisions, to wit, the scientific design argument, which depends upon grasping the essences of real things, and the existential way, which emphasizes our grasp of the existence of things.

The classical case of the a priori approach is Anselm. However, others, such as Baruch (Benedict) Spinoza (1632–77) and Leibniz, would also fit in here.

Anselm of Canterbury

Anselm versus The State

In 1033 Anselm of Canterbury was born into a well-off family in northwestern Italy. At 15 he tried to join a monastery in his hometown area, but was turned down. After that he lived a carefree life, with much time devoted to travelling. Nevertheless, he was known for his brilliant mind even from his youngest days. In 1057 he underwent a conversion and left for Burgundy in Normandy in order to study with the famous Lanfranc (1005–89). At 27 he was allowed to join the Benedictine monastery at Bec in Normandy, where Lanfranc was also a member. Anselm entered Bec in 1060, became prior three years later, and abbot in 1078. He was on friendly terms with William the Conqueror (1027–87), who had invaded England in 1066. Anselm's two main works, the *Monologium* (A Monologue) and the *Proslogium, sive Fides Quaerens Intellectum* (An Address, or Faith Seeking Understanding) were both written about 1070.

Trouble began, however, in 1093 when Anselm was appointed by William I's second son, William II (1056–1100, called Rufus), as the archbishop of the cathedral priory of Canterbury, succeeding Lanfranc. In the four years between Lanfranc's death and Anselm's appointment, the new king had robbed the cathedral of its land and anything else he could get away with. William II also wanted the power to select bishops in England, thereby making sure that he was in absolute control of everything, especially the money. Anselm refused to even consider such a takeover of the Church by the state. He said that he would accept the post if the king gave back the stolen property and if his appointment was confirmed by Urban II (a Benedictine, 1042–1099, pope from 1088), thus emphasizing the need for ecclesiastical approval for the English bishops.

The king refused and in 1095 the other English bishops sided with William Rufus. Anselm was exiled from England. Always active, in 1098 he was a leading figure at the Council of Bari in Italy, which ruled against the king. Anselm, though, convinced the pope not to excommunicate William II. Urban II was succeeded by Paschal II (?–1118) in 1099.

In 1099 Anselm was living in Rome, where he wrote his *Cur Deus Homo* (Why God Became Man), explaining the need for a sacrifice of equal rank (Jesus) with the one offended (God) by original sin. In 1100, after Rufus was 'accidentally' killed by an arrow during a hunting expedition, Anselm was recalled by Henry I (1068–1135), who wanted religious peace so that he could consolidate his kingdom in both England and France. Nevertheless, Anselm was again banished (1103–1106) for not being compromising enough. One reason for the falling out, in addition to the investiture fight, was that at a Westminster synod in 1102 Anselm had come out very strongly against the practice of slavery. According to the *Doomsday Book* of 1086, about 10 per cent of Englishmen were still slaves. For Anselm, in the sight of God all human beings are equal and any law saying otherwise is wrong. Some time later, Pope Alexander III (?–1181, pope from 1159) issued a letter condemning slavery, but, comparable to the condemnation of things such as contraception and abortion today, with little effect.

Finally, in 1107, at a synod in Westminster, a compromise was reached, in which the king could recommend people for Church posts, but the pope had the final say on who was actually chosen. In return for the king's cooperation, the pope would allow the bishops to become the vassals of the king, thus allowing the king to take money from them. This allowed both sides to claim victory. Anselm was then able to return to England, where in 1108 he was even appointed the king's regent, acting for the king when the king was away. Anselm died in 1109. He was canonized by Pope Alexander VI (1431–1503, pope from 1492) in 1494 and in 1720 he was declared a Doctor of the Church by Clement XI (1649–1721, pope from 1700). Because of his emphasis upon the combination of faith and reason, Anselm is known as the father of scholasticism, a form of education that was to last until the time of Descartes.

From the political viewpoint, Anselm's life was of great importance. He knew very well that, if God did not exist, then either the individual would become God or the state would become God. In either case human life would be just as miserable in the future as it had been in the past. If the individual is the highest being, he would have the right to oppress anyone he wishes. This spells chaos and eventually the rule of the strongest and meanest. If the state is the highest being, then the state can become as oppressive as it wishes. Hence the importance of the real existence of God, thereby providing an objective foundation for peace and justice for everyone living in society.

Anselm Defines God into Existence

Anselm's famous definitional approach to the existence of God is found at the beginning of his *Proslogium* (Anselm, 1958). Although Anselm himself knew nothing of the name, after being named by Kant, his argument has become known as the ontological argument. In his Preface, Anselm asks if there is one simple proof for the existence of God that anyone who thinks at all can understand. This was something of importance at the time. Although the clergy were expected to be more or less literate, everyone else, including the political leaders, generally were not able to read and write. Consequently, long involved treatises on profound matters were of little use when dealing with the average person in society. What was needed instead was something short and neat.

In chapter 1 Anselm insists that faith must precede knowledge. You must first believe in order to understand. This was something he got right out of the Bible. However, there is no reason why you cannot understand for yourself what you first accepted on faith. Several paths can lead to the same destination and faith lets you know what that destination is. Far from retarding the work of reason, faith greatly stimulates reason to work harder and achieve more.

In chapter 2 he begins his simple argument by setting out some preliminary facts on which, he is sure, everyone would agree. Let's stipulate:

1. God is defined by everyone who thinks as 'That Than Which Nothing Greater Can Be Conceived'. This is an awkward expression in both Latin and English.
2. Even for the fool to say in his heart that God does not exist means that he must at least understand the meaning of the word God. It would be irrational to be against something when you do not know what it is you are against. Is it rational to declare unequivocally that 'paufkiffinughs' do not exist when you do not even know what they are?
3. Everyone will admit, for example, that having the completed artistic work outside the mind is a far greater thing than having only the idea of the work in the artist's imagination. By the same token, when you are hungry, having a real hamburger in your stomach is greater than having only the idea of a hamburger in your mind. In general, assuming there is some good to be achieved, such as a poverty-free world, the real thing is better than only the dream or vision. And, even assuming for the sake of argument that the idea is perverted, such as taking revenge on an enemy, the thinker still thinks that the completed deed is better than only the thought of the deed. At this point, the moral nature of the idea is irrelevant. The main point is that everyone admits that the real thing is greater (more perfect) than only the idea of the thing. Anselm then proceeds with the proof.

- Whatever is understood exists at least in the mind.
- That Than Which Nothing Greater Can Be Conceived is understood.
- Ergo, it exists at least in the mind.

- To truly be the greatest being conceivable is to have extra- as well as intra-mental existence.
- That Than Which Nothing Greater Can Be Conceived is truly the greatest being conceivable.
- Ergo, it has both intra- and extra-mental existence.

In chapter 3, only after completing his proof, does Anselm call 'That Than Which Nothing Greater Can Be Conceived' by the name of God. The main point is that denying God's real existence would be contradictory. The problem for Anselm is to see how he can understand that God, in whom he already believes, cannot not exist. His answer is – by God's very definition. To say that the greatest being conceivable lacks extra-mental existence contradicts the meaning of the greatest conceivable being. This is the case because, if the being did not possess extra-mental existence, we could conceive of a greater being, namely, one that did. To deny its existence, then, in this one unique case, would be most absurd. In other words, the most perfect being must also be the most real being.

A rebuttal to Anselm's argument was written by a monk named Gaunilon from Marmoutier and called the *Book in Behalf of the Fool*. Gaunilon said that what begins in the mind must end in the mind. So it is certainly true that God is the greatest, but only as a concept in the mind.

Anselm's response was to point out that talking about God is not like talking about some perfect little island somewhere in the ocean beyond the Pillars of Hercules (the Strait of Gibraltar). God is a special case. Only in God's case does the argument hold. The existence of God is not like the existence of any imagined finite thing; nothing finite can be a greatest conceivable being. There is only one Supreme Being and his existence is assured by the very thinking of human thought, something from which we cannot possibly escape. So the fool destroys his own mind in the very act of saying that God does not exist (Matthews, 2001).

However, as later critiqued by Aquinas, Anselm's argument is faulty for at least two reasons. First, essences are existentially neutral and so cannot yield anything real. Second, the reasoning is circular, assuming the reality of the thing the reasoning is supposed to prove. He observes:

> Even granting that everyone understands by God something than which nothing greater can be conceived, nevertheless it does not follow that the one who understands what the word signifies understands it to exist actually, but only that it exists mentally. Nor can it be argued that it exists actually unless it is admitted that there actually exists something than which nothing greater can be thought. But this is precisely what is not admitted by those denying the existence of God. (Aquinas, 1894b, I, 2, 1, ad 2)

Later in history, Kant again raises the first objection. The existence of something cannot be deduced from its concept. For financially poor Kant, it would certainly be nice if he could think a large amount of money into his pocket. Such a thing, though, is impossible.

In conclusion, Anselm had every good intention in the world. The notion, though, that we can go from the idea of something to the reality of something does not in any way correspond to ordinary human experience. In order to end up in the real world outside the mind we must begin in the real world outside the mind. Later on, Aquinas will fully exploit this fact of human experience.

Chapter 7

The For-real Approach: A Posteriori Internal Experience Method

Augustine and Self-fulfilment

> O Thou who dry'st the mourner's tear!
> How dark this world would be,
> If, when deceived and wounded here,
> We could not fly to Thee ...
> Then sorrow, touch'd by Thee, grows bright
> With more than rapture's ray;
> As darkness shows us worlds of light
> We never saw by day!
>
> Thomas Moore (1779–1852), *Sacred Songs*

Augustine Bares his Soul

Before Boethius and Saint Anselm there was Saint Augustine (354–430). At the very beginning of *The Confessions*, largely an autobiographical work (the first ten of 13 books) and his most influential work, Augustine says directly to God that: 'You move us to take delight in praising you, because you have made us for yourself, and we are restless until we rest in you.' Augustine's main philosophical interest was in truth, because, if there is any truth at all, it can only be explained by the existence of God.

Aurelius Augustine was born in the Roman province of Numidia, in what is now Tunisia in North Africa, where Latin was the official language of government and education. His father was a pagan and his mother a devoted Christian, Saint Monica (332–87), who constantly (for 15 years) prayed for her eldest son. His formal education took place in his home town of Tagaste (Hippo Regius), nearby in Madaura, and in the great city of Carthage (now Tunis), where he specialized in the study of rhetoric, and where he also taught rhetoric from 370 to 383. He then moved to Rome for a year, and then to Milan, to do the same. At the time Milan was the centre of the Western Empire and the place where the emperor resided.

All along the way, his life was one long party in which he tried every sexual permutation available. He was also constantly lying and stealing whatever he could get his hands on. This included stealing from his own father. In addition, he tried out various religious options, including Manichaeism, and finally ended up as a sceptic. Augustine had at least one illegitimate son, in 372, that we know of. This son, Adeodatus, died in 389.

Augustine's move to Milan, though, was fateful. There he read Plotinus, who he thought was Plato (*Confessions* VII, 9, 13 in Augustine, 1948), met Saint Ambrose (340–97), the bishop of Milan, and began reading the letters of Saint Paul. In May 386, while sitting in a Milan garden, he heard a child singing, 'take, read', (*Confessions* VIII, 12 in Augustine, 1948), and so he opened at random a copy of Paul's letters. The place he landed on was Romans 13:13, telling him to give up all vice and follow Christ, which is what he did thereafter. He immediately went on retreat for a year and wrote his first philosophical work, *Against the Academics*, in which he attacks the scepticism of Plato's Academy during its middle and newer periods (300–100 BC).

On Easter eve, 25 April 387, Augustine was baptized by Ambrose in Milan. Augustine then began to make plans to return to Africa. Before he could return, however, his mother, who, along with other members of his family, was in Italy with him, died. Her last word to him was to remember her whenever he said mass. Upon his return he set up a monastery in his home town. In 391 he was ordained a priest and in 395 he became the bishop of Hippo Regius. In the same neighbourhood he established a convent for women, headed by his sister, and for which he wrote a constitution, the Rule. Afterward, the Rule was widely used by other religious orders.

The year 410 saw the sack of Rome by Alaric the Visigoth (370–410), a terrible event, which many Christians thought was the end of the world. Augustine, though, lived on to debate with the Donatists and the Montanists, who, during Augustine's lifetime, greatly outnumbered the Catholics in North Africa. They held that only sinless people can be in the Church, that the sacraments are not valid if the priest is bad, and that people must be rebaptized in order to enter the true church of the Donatists and Montanists. Augustine also debated with the Pelagians (Pelagius, a British monk, 360–420) who denied original sin and who held that divine grace and Christ are not needed for salvation. In addition, he spent time challenging the Arians, named after Arius (250–336, a priest from Alexandria), who was heavily influenced by the doctrines of Plotinus. The Arians denied that Jesus Christ is one in being with the Father. Augustine was prepared to defend all parts of the Nicaean Creed (Council of Nicaea, 325), including the Trinity.

Augustine died in August 430 (a good union man always quits at 4:30) during a siege of his city by Vandals from Spain. He left behind a large number of works, including the *Soliloquies* (387), *On the Immortality of the Soul* (387), *The Teacher* (389), *The True Religion* (391), *Free Choice* (395), *Against Faustus the Manichae* (400), *Confessions* (400), *The Good of Marriage* (401), *The Nature of the Good Against the Manichaes* (405), *Literal Commentary on Genesis* (415), *Nature and Grace* (415), *On the Trinity* (416), *Against a Sermon of the Arians* (419), *Handbook of Faith, Hope, and Charity* (421), *The City of God* (426), *On Christian Doctrine* (427), and *Retractions* (427, not meaning to take back, but from *retractare*, meaning to review or repeat something). He also wrote many letters and sermons, many of which have been preserved for us today. To this day, Augustine himself is the subject of many books and articles.

Augustine's Assent to God

When reading Augustine, it soon becomes clear that he held a very Platonic view of being and, consequently, of God. 'To be' for Augustine means to be immutable. We can see this in his works on *The Nature of the Good* (19), *On the Trinity* (V, 2, 3), and *The City of God* (XIX, 15) (Augustine, 1948). How, then, are we to attain a knowledge of God? It can only be by means of working up from what is relatively permanent, unchanging, and immutable to what is absolutely permanent, unchanging, and immutable. And where is such stability to be found? In Book VII, chapter 17 of the *Confessions*, Augustine describes, in a fashion reminiscent of Plato's *Symposium* and Plotinus' *Enneads*, his personal assent to God by means of the hierarchy of perfections found in the world of human experience (see Augustine, 1948). He is looking for the real thing, not some phantom or mirage that will vanish in a moment. So the senses are out. This real thing can be grasped only by means of the mind. However, to fully utilize the powers of the mind requires leaving the body.

In matters pertaining to both the mind and the body we are constantly passing judgment on what is fair and unfair, just and unjust, and on the degree to which something is good. We know from our own experiences that we are able to pass judgment on what is beautiful in the mutable world of material things. For example, human beings spontaneously respond in a positive way to certain arrangements of parts in architecture, such as the symmetrical placement of windows in a wall. On the mental level, seven plus three equals ten. We are absolutely sure of this.

To find God, then, all we need do is continue the process of what comes naturally. Augustine sees the process of finding God as one of consciousness-raising, whereby we move in steps from a lower plateau to a higher plateau as we come to realize more and more the difference between the ugly and the beautiful, the false and the true, the evil and the good. So by degrees we move from the body to the soul, from what is changing within the soul to what is unchanging, and finally to the source of all that is beautiful, true, and good. This must be God, the one being who is absolutely immutable, beautiful, true, and good.

Augustine, however, cannot sustain this vision of God and soon falls back into the ordinary habits of a human being on earth. He is, after all, both body and soul. The body is good. The material world is good. It was created by God. God became man, which is the Incarnation, the embodying of the Second Person of the Trinity. Jesus Christ rose from the dead in a bodily way. Human beings are destined for the resurrection of their bodies. Therefore, the Platonic tradition of material things as evil must be rejected. Like it or not, we are in the good world of material things.

This causes him to realize the importance of the Church (the community, the Body of Christ), the sacraments, and the central role of Jesus Christ as the intermediary between man and God, in order to maintain a constant relationship with God. All of this activity requires both the intellect and the will, both the head and the heart. The will must have an intelligible object toward which it can move and the intellect must have a motive force to kept it going in a positive way.

Boethius and Self-fulfilment

Boethius Seeks Consolation

Anicius Manlius Severinus Boethius was born 50 years after Augustine's death. He was given the best education by his stepfather Symmachus, who later became his father-in-law. He quickly achieved high office in Rome: in 510 he was a consul and by 523 he was the master of the government offices, the bureaucracy of the king. He is noted for his emphasis on the liberal arts (logic, grammar, rhetoric, arithmetic, music, geometry, astronomy) in education, and especially for his realization of the importance of music in the educational process. In his lectures on the importance of music he explains how some music is conducive to peace and harmony and some is not. Without a doubt, much of modern popular music, such as that produced by the punk groups of the 1980s, would be rejected as harmful.

Boethius divided his time between scholastic and political matters, with the latter proving to be his undoing. Because of his Roman background, he desired to see more republican political freedom in Rome. He wanted, for instance, to see the restoration of the Roman senate, with real powers. This brought him into conflict with the dictatorial Ostrogoth king, Theodoric the Great (454–526), who was part of the wave of invaders that had finally conquered the Western Empire. In 523 Boethius was arrested on charges of treason and tortured to death in prison a year later.

Philosophically speaking, Boethius was most influenced by Plato by way of Plotinus, his disciple Porphyry, and Augustine. He was the last Roman scholar to seriously study Greek. Scholastically speaking, his aim was to reconcile all of the great Greek and Roman thinkers with Christianity, a task cut short by his untimely and cruel death. Despite this, however, he did manage to produce an impressive array of commentaries, as well as philosophical and theological works of his own. He wrote four commentaries on Aristotle's *Categories* (the logic of terms), two on Aristotle's *Perihermeneias* (the logic of propositions), while also translating Aristotle's *Prior Analytics* (syllogistic logic), *Posterior Analytics* (philosophy of science), *Refutations of the Sophists*, and *Topics* (on probable arguments). In his commentaries he brought to bear the work done in logic by the post-Aristotelean Stoics. In addition, he wrote books on arithmetic, geometry, and music. In theology, he wrote works *On the Holy Trinity*, *On the Person and Dual Nature of Christ*, and *On the Six Days of Creation*.

Boethius' major work is *The Consolation of Philosophy* (Boethius, 1962), written while he was in prison. In this work he imagines a conversation between himself and Lady Philosophy, who acts as his guide through some especially troubling philosophical problems. His work quickly became one the most widely read works of all time in Europe. In this work he does not quote from the Scriptures or from the saints, but appeals instead to reason and to the familiar sources of Greek and Roman culture. His key point is that the only winners in the game of life are those who find God.

All of his works had a tremendous influence on later Christian thinkers. Largely due to his influence, for instance, logic was usually used as an introduction to philosophy. One extraneous reason for Boethius' important status in the development of European intellectual history is the fact that in 529 the emperor of the Eastern Empire, Justinian I (483–565), to whom the emperor of the Western Empire officially owed allegiance, closed all of the pagan schools of philosophy in the empire. Since they could not go west, the scholars went east. This deprived European scholars of direct access to the teachers and works of these schools for a period of time that turned out to last a long 600 years. During this time, Boethius' commentaries on Aristotelian and Stoic logic were among the few philosophical texts available during the early Middle Ages in the West. The major works of Aristotle, which survived in places such as Damascus and Bagdad, did not become available again in central Europe until 1140 and thereafter.

On the basis of his reading of Plato and Aristotle, one of the main problems Boethius transmitted to later thinkers was the problem of how something can be the same and different at the same time. Peter is a human being, but then so are John, Mary, Andrew, and Jane. This led him to distinguish between the existence of the individual (for example, Peter) within the species (human being) and the essence of something (for example, humanity) in which the individual participates. The singular thing is certainly real, but how real is the essence? Does humanity exist? Boethius seems to have finally gone along with Plato's view that two things (for example, Peter and John) equal to the same thing (the idea of man in the heaven of ideas) are equal to each other. It was not until Aquinas that a more satisfactory solution was found (Aquinas, 1949).

Boethius Finds Fulfilment

Book I of *The Consolation of Philosophy* discusses the problem of good and evil and the true cause of anxiety in humans, which is worry about achieving personal happiness and fulfilment (Boethius, 1962). At the beginning of the work Boethius asks how, if God exists, evil can exist? But, if God does not exist, how can good exist? Lady Philosophy comes to his aid by assuring him that evil cannot be used as an argument against the existence of God. Being aware of evil may remain a source of mental anxiety for people, but, rationally speaking, the fact of evil cannot be used to disprove God's existence. If anything, evil proves God's existence.

Book II discusses how everyone wants a complete personal satisfaction, an ultimate good that cannot be lost. Where can I find such a thing? Boethius argues as follows: it certainly cannot be found in anything mutable; you cannot achieve personal fulfilment if you must constantly worry about losing what you need to be happy; without a sense of security, no one can be at peace. This is certainly true as a fact of life. Judging by the number of contemporary self-help gurus, money managers, and politicians promising more health insurance, we are as concerned about security today as were people of old.

- Nothing perishable is the ultimate good.
- All results of chance are perishable.
- Ergo, no results of chance are the ultimate good.

- No ultimate good for rational beings depends upon uncertainties.
- But happiness is the ultimate good for rational beings.
- Ergo, no happiness depends upon uncertainties.

Book III discusses the existence of God as the solution to the basic human problem of the meaning of life and death. Boethius reminds his readers not to miss the forest because of the trees. Certainly, change and mutability are everywhere. Yet, amid all the variation there is also stability. Whether it is a mathematical formula, a law of nature, or a probability function (the laws of probability are not probable), we experience the same pattern of understanding. All rational judgments must have an unchanging standard against which they can be evaluated in terms of their truth. The amazing thing is that we, who are part and parcel of the ever-changing world, can recognize and hold on to such standards.

- Only if there is an eternal standard of perfection are we capable of judging good, better, and best.
- We (even atheists) are capable of judging good, better, and best.
- Ergo, there is an eternal standard of perfection.

Yes, but why not a multiplicity of eternal standards, maybe something after the fashion of Plato's realm of ideas? Boethius says that this is not possible. If the supreme good were broken up into parts, we could never be sure that we have everything we need all at once. Instead of solving the problem of self-fulfilment, we would only be moving it from a lower level to a higher level. There would have to be a unity above the ideas. In Book III, Prose 11, Lady Philosophy concludes that all lesser goods can only satisfy us when they are gathered together into a single form and operation, so that sufficiency becomes one with power, honour, fame, and pleasure. Without such unity the ultimate good would not be viewed as desirable by us.

- Only if there is one real supreme being can our desire for ultimate happiness be fulfilled.
- But there is (namely, the eternal standard of perfection).
- Ergo, we can fulfil our desire for ultimate happiness.

Boethius is careful to note that the existence of God is a necessary condition for happiness, not a sufficient condition. It is like saying, only if I have oxygen can I survive. Oxygen is one of the things we must have; it is not the only thing required. Likewise, in order to achieve happiness other factors are also required, for example, obeying the will of God rather than our own will.

- To strive for perfect happiness is to strive for God.
- We all strive for perfect happiness.
- Ergo, we all strive for God (whether or not we know it).

Book IV goes on to discuss fatalism, free will, and divine providence. Boethius says that we are not predestined to either heaven or hell. It is up to us to use our free will so as to cooperate with God's wish that all should be saved (1 Timothy 2:4). Salvation means being with God forever.

- All those who honestly seek God are those who will be satisfied.
- All good people are those who honestly seek God.
- Ergo, all good people are those who will be satisfied.

- All those who get what they want are powerful people.
- All those who achieve happiness are those who get what they want.
- Ergo, all those who achieve happiness are powerful people.

Boethius' point is that, although the wicked people of the world may appear to be the powerful ones, in fact they are not. In the end the good people will triumph and the evil ones will be put down. In this sense, evil people do not exist, even though they appear to be so numerous. Holy people are the only ones who really get what they want. Thus, if being able to get what you want is the sign of a powerful person, then it must be the case that the really powerful people are those who do the will of God instead of following their own inordinate desires. Holy people are the only ones who ultimately succeed in life.

René Descartes the Mathematician

Descartes' Mission in Life

While Claudio Monteverdi (1567–1643) was inventing opera, Descartes was being born in 1596 in La Haye, a little town near Tours, in west-central France. Tours was famous for the Battle of Tours, in which the Frankish king Charles

Martel (688–741, Charles the Hammer), the grandfather of Charlemagne (742–814), defeated the Muslim invaders in 732. René was the son of a wealthy nobleman with a large estate. When his mother died a year later, his father remarried and moved to the big city, leaving his young son in the care of his maternal grandmother (Vrooman, 1970).

From 1606 to 1615 he attended the Jesuit college of La Flèche in Anjou, where he was impressed by the power of Euclidian geometry. The college had only recently (1553) been established by Henry IV (assassinated in 1610) for the purpose of training men in military engineering. Very likely he also picked up the notion that will is the basic creative force in the world from his teachers there. According to Descartes' later views, not only are the laws of nature arbitrarily imposed by God, but also the basic laws of logic and mathematics. Although he knew that laws are not things (like rocks), he believed that the way in which things relate to each other is willed by God. Instead of basing reality on being (what is), thus giving, for example, the mutual exclusiveness of being and non-being (the principle of non-contradiction), Descartes based the reality of everything on God's will.

In contrast to Descartes' view, according to Aquinas, God cannot go against his own nature. Thus, without denying God's infinite power, it is not possible for God to change the past or make a square circle. God can do anything, not any no-thing. Descartes' emphasis on the will, though, did fit in much better with his philosophy of nature, which viewed the physical universe as merely one matter undergoing many motions. In such a world there cannot be many essences, each following its own internal set of laws, but only a set of rules imposed from outside by a wilful power.

From his earliest days, Descartes was in the habit of sleeping in late, a habit he blamed on the fact that he had a weak constitution, one requiring 12 hours of sleep a day. W.W. Rouse Ball reports that when Descartes visited Pascal in 1647 he told him that the only way to do good work in mathematics and preserve his health was never to get up in the morning before he felt inclined to do so. Ball notes that this is an opinion that could benefit many schoolboys (Ball, 1912, p. 269).

The 1600s was a time of growing technology, with an emphasis on the practical. In philosophy, this was an age of scepticism, a time when trust in the power of the human intellect to find truth was at a low ebb. In politics, it was a time of the rise of the nation state. In religion, the Reformation was in full swing, throwing Europe into turmoil. In business, world trade was on the rise, with whole new areas of the world being recently discovered and available to explorers and adventurers. In many ways it was a time of great confusion. There was a great need for some solid foundation for the new world in the making and especially for the prospects of a renewed natural philosophy (science) that had been growing since the Middle Ages, 'science' being a term coined by those in the Renaissance who were looking ahead to a new future. While in school Descartes began to suspect that the new foundation would be mathematics.

In 1616, the same year in which the Roman Catholic playwright William Shakespeare died, Descartes received his law degree from the University of Poitiers. However, he never practised. In 1618, at the beginning of the Thirty Years' War that so devastated Germany, he volunteered, at his own expense, as a gentleman soldier in the Dutch army under the Protestant leader Maurice of Nassau, the Prince of Orange. While in the Netherlands he met Isaac Beeckman (1588–1637) for whom he wrote in 1618 a *Compendium of Music*, a work for which Beeckman himself later claimed credit. In 1619 he volunteered for the Upper Palatinate Bavarian army and moved into Winter quarters at Neuberg on the Danube River. Descartes never did see any actual fighting.

Years later he claimed to have used his many hours of quiet solitude discovering his method of methodical doubt and using it as a basis for beginning afresh in order to establish some great truths about man, God, and nature. He said he used his methodology to establish the new science of analytic geometry, a feat accomplished on 10 November 1619, after being inspired in a dream by what he called the Spirit of Truth, which he took to be the Holy Spirit. He thought that he had found the one universal method for all science, and it all started from within his own mind. Now his main problem was changing the minds of people who thought in qualitative terms and who were sure to resist his quantitative approach to nature. He thought about it for 18 years.

In the meantime, during 1621, a year after the first Pilgrim Fathers went ashore on Cape Cod, Descartes travelled in Austria and Poland. In 1622 he sold his part of the estate in France, invested the money, and received an annual income of 6500 Francs. He then travelled through Switzerland and Italy. For some time he was back in Paris, often meeting with the intellectual elite of the day and carrying on research in optics. In 1628 he turned over his business affairs to the reform-minded priest Pierre de Berulle (1575–1629, made a cardinal in 1627 by Urban VIII) and moved to Holland, which at the time was the leader in world trade. In the same year he wrote *Rules for the Direction of the Mind*, but the work was not published until 1701. A fragment of another work, called *The Search After Truth*, was also published in 1701. Before then, though, a disciple of Descartes, the French priest Nicolas Malebranche, used *The Search After Truth* (1674) as the title of his own major work.

In 1630 Descartes moved to Amsterdam, crossed the water to visit Charles I in England, and spent some time studying at the University of Leiden. He moved to Deventer, the home of the Brethren in 1632. During this time he was working on a book (*The World*) in natural philosophy concerning the operations of the universe, a work that was basically Copernican in content. However, in 1633, hearing of Galileo's troubles, he decided not to publish the work in the form he originally intended. It was published in 1664, after he died. In 1634 he visited Denmark and later had an illegitimate daughter, Francine, by a Dutch housemaid. In 1635 he moved to Utrecht and then to Leiden in 1636.

In June 1637 he finally published his *Discourse on Method: Of Rightly Conducting the Reason and of Seeking for Truth in the Sciences*, which acted as an introduction to three scientific works, one on optics (*The Dioptics*), one on the explanation of various atmospheric phenomena (*The Meteors*), and one on geometry (*Geometry*). The whole work was published anonymously in Leiden in the French language. The *Discourse* part was written in a personal style imitating the essay style of the French sceptic Michel de Montaigne (1533–92). Montaigne, who introduced the essay style of writing in 1571, took the easy-going approach of simply relating to people what he was thinking, without saying that others had to think the same way. Descartes then moved to Santport.

The part of Descartes' work on optics was mainly concerned with the law of refraction, something he got from the Dutchman Willebrord Snellius (1591–1626), a professor of mathematics at the University of Leiden. Descartes was also concerned with the best shape for lenses in a telescope. With respect to light, he thought that the speed of light was infinite, a sort of pressure in a medium, and he could not decide whether, in the seeing process, light emanates from the eye to the object or moves from the object to the eye. In the part of his work on the atmosphere, Descartes was especially interested in explaining rainbows.

Of primary interest, though, was the part on geometry, which was subdivided into three parts. The first two subdivisions outlined his famous discovery of analytic geometry. The third subdivision showed how his new discovery fitted in with the old geometry and introduced a way of writing formulas ($x = y$, the use of exponents, and so on) that is still in use today. Descartes also started the digital revolution, the idea that something continuous can be broken up into little parts, stored, and reconstituted elsewhere.

In the *Discourse* Descartes advocated a methodical scepticism that doubted everything. This doubt was then counteracted by starting within one's own mind in order to establish the unshakable truth that I am a thinking substance and then moving out to the extra-mental world. By using this method he was able to redesign the whole world. Descartes, who was a genius, wanted to remake the whole world so as to render everything material open to an exclusively mathematical treatment. Surprisingly, he actually got away with it, at least for a while. Descartes quickly became world-famous as a mathematician. In time, his methodology came to be regarded as the standard antidote to scepticism. In one mighty stroke, he thought that he had conquered scepticism and had made the world forever safe for science. Many others agreed. Little did his immediate disciples realize how illusory this really was. Later on Hume would say sarcastically that he learned his renewed scepticism from the Jesuits at La Flèche, Descartes' old school.

In 1640 Descartes developed the *Discourse* into his *Meditations on First Philosophy*, which he sent to his old schooldays friend, now a theologian, Marin Mersenne (1588–1648) in Paris so that Mersenne might send it out for comments before publication. He moved to Leiden and then to Endegeest.

That same year his father and young daughter died. The latter he interpreted as God's punishment for his sin of fornication with a young Dutch housemaid. In 1641 the *Meditations on First Philosophy* was published in Latin in Paris and dedicated to Catholic professors of theology. Along with it went six critiques, including critiques by the English materialist Thomas Hobbes (1588–1679), the Jansenist Arnauld, and the atomist Pierre Gassendi (1592–1655). Descartes provided responses to each set of critiques. The second edition of 1642 added a seventh critique by the Jesuit Pierre Bourdin, who Descartes regarded as a fool for defending Aristotle's view of nature as a hierarchy of natures and for ridiculing the idea that the earth could be moving either daily or yearly. At that time he also began using the Latin name Renatus Cartesius, which gave rise to the habit of calling his followers Cartesians.

During 1643–49, he moved to Egmond-op-den-Hoef, visited Princess Elizabeth Stuart (1596–1662) of Bohemia, who was living in The Hague, moved to Egmond-Binnen, often visited Paris, where he met Pascal in 1647, and corresponded with Christiaan Huygens (1629–95), the Dutch physicist who formulated Huygen's Law and the wave theory of light. It was in a letter to Princess Elizabeth that he explained how the body and the soul meet at the pineal gland in the middle of the brain. In August 1648, during a revolt of the nobility against the king, Descartes left Paris.

During this same period he published *The Principles of Philosophy* (July 1644), which he said superseded all his other works. In this work he enunciated ten laws of nature with respect to physics, only two of which turned out to be right, namely, the conservation of motion (the principle of inertia) and the law of momentum (force is proportional to weight times acceleration). He did, though, correct Galileo, who erroneously thought that if you let go of a body circulating around a centre it would continue to move in a circle. Descartes showed that it would fly off on a tangent. Descartes' work was later used by Newton as the basis for his synthesis of terrestrial and celestial mechanics. Newton changed weight to mass and explained the orbits of the bodies in the solar system as a result of a balance of forces.

Descartes stayed in Holland for 22 years, living in 18 different places. Why so much moving around? One reason was to avoid having all his time taken up by admiring followers and budding mathematicians seeking his advice. Another reason was to avoid his enemies, especially among the Protestants. At one point, the rector of the University of Utrecht, Gisbertus Voetius (1589–1676), a staunch Calvinist, who had become the leader of the Calvinist congregation in Utrecht in 1637, banned his books at the University and encouraged the people of Utrecht to burn them in public. Although delayed, there was also a Catholic reaction. In 1671 the teaching of Cartesian philosophy was banned at the University of Paris. Much earlier, Pascal expressed the opinion that Descartes had no other use for God than to give matter its initial quantity of motion. After realizing that, Pascal had no further use for Descartes.

Employing his own method, Descartes planned on spending the rest of his life solving all of the major problems in human health, an extremely ambitious programme indicating just how great was the ignorance concerning such things at the time. In 1649 he published *The Passions of the Soul*, describing how the body operates, physically speaking, when we experience things through the senses. It was overwhelmingly wrong. He thought, for instance, that the bodily nerves were little hollow tubes through which the animal spirits travel around the body. In that same year he also made a fatal medical error with respect to himself.

In that year he was invited by Queen Christina of Sweden (1626–89, queen 1632–54) to tutor her in philosophy and science. She may also have been interested in secretly learning about the Catholic faith, not an easy task in a country where Lutheranism was the official state religion. The lessons started each morning at sunrise. Why he allowed himself to be treated in such a fashion is not clear. Although she promised him safety, money, and all the time he needed to do his own work, his reward for changing the habits of a lifetime was to contract a lingering respiratory disease, most likely pneumonia. This caused his death in February 1650, only four months after he had gone there. His last piece of writing was a letter to his brother asking him to take over the payment of a small pension to their old nurse.

Before he died he made Queen Christina promise to give him a Catholic funeral, no easy task in Lutheran Sweden. He was buried in Stockholm. Sixteen years later his body was moved to Paris and buried in the churchyard of Saint Genevieve-du-Mont. In 1819 it was transferred to Saint Germain-des-Pres. A few years after Descartes' death, Christina became a convert, went to Rome, and was buried there when she died. Also, after his death, in 1664, there appeared an unfinished work entitled *On Man and the Formation of the Fetus*. Generally speaking, it must be said that Descartes was certainly not a very good Catholic. Like Montaigne, he might be called an inertial Catholic.

Overall, although he did his greatest work in mathematics, and although he publicized the important work of others, such as Galileo and William Harvey (1578–1657), the English physician who proved that the blood is circulated in the body by the pumping action of the heart, his own contributions in physics were limited to supplying a foundation, such as the principle of inertia, that others could build on. He never did do anything noteworthy in medicine. And in philosophy, where he thought he had made his greatest contribution, the results were absolutely disastrous (see Maritain, 1944).

Descartes' Reversal

Opinions are easy to come by; proofs are hard to find. The best place to find proofs is in mathematics. Descartes therefore endeavoured to reduce all rational knowledge to the one science of mathematics. He began this process by out-doubting the doubters and showing that there is something beyond all doubting, namely, his own consciousness. Thus, 'I think and therefore I am' (*cogito ergo sum*), reminiscent of Augustine's 'I doubt and therefore I am' (*dubito ergo sum*). For the king of the one-liners, nothing could be closer to him and more certain than his own thoughts. The more one tries doubting them, the more certain they become. The more pressure is applied, the more resistance is offered.

As a result of this thought experiment, Descartes had a clear and distinct idea of himself as an immaterial substance without a body, and so that was what he really was. Thinking must be the essence of his mind. Now, in order to find the truth about anything else, he had to repeat the process of analyzing his own ideas. One idea is the idea of God. The certitude of God's existence, taught Descartes, could be established purely through his own ideas. Descartes claimed to know God better than he knew the material world through his senses. In fact, we are all born with the idea of God within us. There are no atheists among those who live by their minds.

Moreover, since his idea of God is that of the perfect being, God must exist, for existence is one of the perfections proper to the perfect being. Another trait would be honesty. God cannot deceive. After this point, then, if his future clear and distinct idea was not truly representative of reality, then God would be a deceiver, which is impossible. So he proceeded with his next idea.

His clear and distinct idea of the material world outside the mind is pure extension. Despite what his senses tell him, that is what physical nature really is. Since extension is the only trait that cannot be removed from the idea of matter, the essence of matter must be nothing but extension. What, though, of motion? Motion must come from outside of matter. Descartes concludes that it was given by God. Thus, all we have to deal with is matter in motion, both of which are fixed in terms of the total quantity originally bestowed upon them by God. This in turn gives rise to conservation laws, including the law of inertia, which Descartes states for the first time. It is not the result of an induction, but of a deduction.

Separating mind from matter is of central importance for Descartes. Mind and matter follow different laws. The conservation laws apply only to the physical world, including the body. They do not apply to the mind and to human reason. Reason discovers the laws of nature, but is not subject to the laws of nature. It stands outside of nature. While the mind is free and independent, the physical world is strictly governed by iron-clad laws. The object of the physicist's study cannot change itself in any way. In the unfree realm of physics there is no problem with spontaneous motions and unpredictable events. Descartes thinks of himself as having granted an everlasting licence for the doing of mathematical physics. Since the total amount of matter and motion is forever fixed, we can be sure that every correct formula will always balance, not just now, but for all time. In this way the world is made safe for science.

As far as Descartes is concerned, the existence of himself as a thinking essence, of God as the one perfect being, and of the material world as mindless, formless, textureless, colourless, soundless, odourless, tasteless extension, are all equally certain. All three are on the level of absolute truth. There is no hierarchy of forms in nature; there are no essential differences among natural things. Matter in itself is one inert mass. Body = matter = 3D = space = extension = parts outside of parts = pure quantity = the real physical world. Such a world is a disaster for the poet, but fine for the mathematician. In the real world outside the mind, everything except the human species is a mindless machine. Such things have no subjective life.

Indeed, subhuman life is really only a mechanical turning of gears. On this basis one could justify vivisection. The screeching of the creature is only the sound of mechanical parts scraping against each other. As far as human sensations are concerned, they are all in the mind. Since extra-mental reality is nothing but extension, all sense qualities (textures, colours, odours, sounds, tastes) are purely subjective. This means that when you are smelling a rose it is not the rose that has the nice aroma; you smell sweet. Likewise, the terrible stench of polluted water is really only in you.

Descartes' Idea of Perfection

If God did not really exist, how could we even think of God? Consider, for instance, Ivan's confession of faith to his brother Alyosha in Fyodor Dostoyevsky's (1821–81) *The Brothers Karamazov* (1880).

> And what's strange, what would be marvellous, is not that God should really exist; the marvel is that such an idea, the idea of the necessity of God, should enter the head of such a strange, vicious beast as man. So holy is it, so touching, so wise and so great a credit it does to man. As for me, I've long resolved not to think whether man created God or God man ... And I advise you never to think about it either, my dear Alyosha, especially about God, whether He exists or not. (Dostoyevsky, 1912, p. 257)

Following his confession to Alyosha, Ivan goes on to say that, although he does not reject God, he does reject the evil world. The real problem is not the existence of God, but how the world can be reconciled with God. After all, the idea of God was there in my mind all the time.

In chapter 3, 'Of God, That He Exists', of his *Meditations* Descartes begins by telling the reader that he plans on appealing only to the internal experiences of his own mind.

> Now I shall close up my eyes, stop up my ears, still all my senses, and even the images of physical things I shall either delete from my mind, or, since that can scarcely be done, count them not worth a straw, as being vain and misleading fancies; and so, holding converse only with myself, delving ever deeper within me, I shall endeavour to become little by little better acquainted and more familiar with myself. (Descartes, 1960, p. 117)

We learn that the Perfect Being is sovereign, eternal, infinite, all-knowing, all-powerful, immutable, independent, and absolutely trustworthy, the traditional characteristics of God in supernaturalistic theism. This was very important for scientific reasons. In order to do science, nature must be absolutely law-like. At no time could anything be added to or subtracted from nature. If, on account of some miracle on God's part, anything were added or subtracted, all previous science would become outdated. We would have to start all over again. Only a deity who never changes his mind can guarantee a scientifically dependable world. He then goes on with the argument, which can be summarized as follows.

- Everything has a cause.
- My idea of a Perfect Being is something.
- Ergo, my idea of a Perfect Being has a cause.

- The cause of anything is at least as real as the thing caused.
- The cause of my idea of a Perfect Being is the cause of something.
- So, the cause of my idea of a Perfect Being is at least as real as the thing caused.

- No imperfect being can be the cause of an idea of a Perfect Being.
- I am an imperfect being.
- Ergo, I cannot be the cause of my idea of a Perfect Being.

- Either the idea of a Perfect Being is from inside me or outside me.
- It cannot be from inside me (see above).
- Ergo, it must be from outside me.

- Either the external cause is imperfect or perfect.
- It cannot be imperfect (see above).
- Ergo, it is perfect.

In fact, then, God exists. Such an idea could not have come from a collection of bodily sensations, from my own imagination, or by way of a negation of the finite. It must have been implanted in me at conception and is anterior to my experiences of imperfection. I know God before I know the world. Thus I can know the differences among good, better, and best, and between perfection and imperfection, and that I am an imperfect being. He states at the end of chapter 3 in the *Meditations*:

> The whole force of the argument I have used in proving the existence of God resides in this, that I understand that my nature could not be what it is, that I could not have in me, that is to say, the idea of God, if God did not truly exist, that same God whose idea inhabits me, who possesses all of those perfections of which I have some idea without, indeed, being able to comprehend them altogether, and who is subject to no defects. It follows that God does not deceive us, for deceit is the sign of a defect. (Descartes, 1960, p. 133)

Descartes does not seem to have been especially confident in his proof. Hence the need to return to the question in chapter 5 of the *Meditations*, 'Of the Essence of Material Things, and, again, of God, That He Exists'. Here Descartes repeats Anselm's ontological argument. Just as you cannot think of a valley without also thinking of a mountain, so you cannot think of God without also thinking of existence. Yes, but how much real existence is in the idea of existence? Can any abstraction, even existence, exist?

Moreover, Descartes says that his God of science is the same as the God of the Judao-Christian religion. But is this really the case? Is the proper name of God the author of nature or He Who Is? Judging by the later development of the Cartesian doctrine into deism, it seems that the opposition between the God of science and the God of religion was indeed something firmly established by the Cartesian doctrine. This fact led Pascal to dismiss the Cartesian God as useless for religious purposes. It seems that when the subjectivist sets out to discover the world, the most he can discover is himself, and not even his whole self.

Georg Hegel's Idea of Being

Hegel the System-builder

Born in Stuttgart, Prussia, in 1770, Georg Hegel was the son of a minor government official. In 1788 he entered the University of Tübingen as a theology student, obtaining degrees in theology and the classics. In 1799 his father died and in 1801 he took up a teaching position at the University of Jena, where the pantheist Friedrich W.J. von Schelling (1775–1854) was the intellectual leader. At the time, Hegel agreed with Schelling, who, in addition to the great absolute of the whole, insisted on the existence of the natural world as something absolute in itself. This view served to pit both Hegel and Schelling against Johann G. Fichte (1762–1814), who insisted on the existence of only one pantheistic absolute, the great ego. Later in life, though, Hegel moved much closer to the more unified position of Fichte.

While at Jena, Hegel wrote a dissertation on the planetary orbits, showing that there could not possibly be a planet situated between Mars and Jupiter. This was unfortunate, because an Italian astronomer had just discovered its remains in the form of what is now called the asteroid belt. Working out of an observatory in Palermo, Sicily, Giuseppe Piazzi (1746–1826) first discovered an asteroid in January 1801. Piazzi also began the policy of naming them after Greek and Roman gods and goddesses. Later, when Napoleon entered Jena in 1806, unlike Ludwig van Beethoven (1770–1827), who was greatly distressed by Napoleon's invasion of the German-speaking world, Hegel carried on his teaching as usual.

Hegel's reputation escalated when, in 1807, he published his *Phenomenology of the Spirit*. He then left his university teaching career, became an editor of a newspaper, and later the principal of a high school in Nuremberg (1808–16). In 1811 (at 41) he married a 19-year-old girl and had a large family. Socially speaking, despite the fact that he had a bad stutter in his voice, Hegel got along pretty well. He loved to attend dances and play cards. He also had one illegitimate son, whom he cared for fairly well.

1812 saw him move to the University of Heidelberg. In 1816 he published his *Science of Logic* in three volumes. *The Encyclopedia of the Philosophical Sciences*, his most comprehensive work, appeared in 1817. In 1818 he made his final move, to the University of Berlin, replacing Fichte as the guiding intellectual light of the day. His *Philosophy of Right*, a work on ethics, came into print in 1821. Throughout his life Hegel always claimed to be a good Lutheran, while also claiming that he could accommodate many different religious trends. As he got older, he became less anti-Jewish and more anti-Catholic.

In 1830 Hegel was made rector of the whole university, which at the time had a total enrolment of about 2000 students. As rector of the largest university in Germany, located in the capital city, Hegel had achieved the most prestigious position possible for a German academic. Not surprisingly, he also became a staunch supporter of a strong centralized Prussian government and predicted that Prussia was due for its day in the sun. A year later he left Berlin to avoid the cholera epidemic that had started in northern India a few years before. Unfortunately, he returned to Berlin too soon and died in November 1831 of the dreaded disease. (See Pinkard, 2000.)

Hegel and the Absolute

Spinoza has his one eternal unchanging substance; Hegel has his one eternal ever-changing subject. Spinoza offers us a rationalized version of Cartesian religion. Hegel offers us a rationalized version of Hinduism. Hegel himself seems to have been aware of this. The older he became the more interested he became in Hinduism. His philosophy, though, was superior to any religion. Hegel believed that his philosophy was so complete and comprehensive that it could adequately translate Hinduism into a European scientific language. His one absolute subject, he thought, transcended all times and cultures. (See Hegel, 1984, pp. 515–16. For a comparison of Descartes, Spinoza, and Hegel see Descartes, 1901, Introduction.)

Early in his life Hegel was greatly influenced by Kant, who ruled over Prussian philosophy in the later 1700s. After Kant, attempts were made to either restore existence as an a priori deduction (Hegel) or deny that it had any part at all in pure thought, as with Søren Kierkegaard (1813–55). Kierkegaard, for instance, could not understand how the impure thinker (Hegel) could think the pure thought. For the Dane, the more you think the less you exist. For Hegel, though, the philosophy of being (metaphysics) is the same thing as the science of logic in its most generalized form. To discover what is real we must study the idea of being. Hegel wants to get to God by means of pure internal thought. Even the sense-data 'given' of Hume and Kant is too much non-thought for Hegel. Pure thought must be complete and uncompromising. The rational is the entire content of reality. 'To be' means pure, infinite consciousness, the absolute subject.

This can be proven by examining the way the mind deals with things in a logical way (Hegel, 1975). Consider, for instance, a particular flag, say an American or Canadian flag. Such a thing belongs to several classes or mental categories simultaneously. There is the genus of flags in general. Then we have various subdivisions, including national flags. Then, within national flags, we have all the different national flags of the world at a particular time in history. This process of dividing and subdividing is true of anything that we might care to consider. Everything concrete is in a class, which is in a class, which is in a class, and so on until we arrive at the ultimate class of all classes, which is being.

What, though, is the situation outside the mind? Extra-mentally, every real Canadian flag is a real national flag, just as every real dime is a real coin and every real man is a real rational animal. Concepts distinguish within the mind what is undivided outside the mind. As a result, pushed to the limit, no matter where we start the process, everything will end up being identified with everything else. All subordinate classes merge into the supreme class of all classes. This is the one ultimate genus, the set of all sets, which Hegel chooses to call God, the Idea, or the Absolute. Hegel is thus the supreme pantheist, even while claiming that he is not a pantheist. He manages this denial by identifying pantheism with the doctrine of Spinoza, from whom he claims to differ in a radical way. Spinoza's one substance was completely unchanging. In contrast, Hegel's God is incessant becoming, with no element of unchanging Greek Being.

Hegel and Non-being

Hegel had an early attraction to Spinoza's doctrine, but not for long. Hegel soon came to see Spinoza's one substance as too materialistic and static to be suitable to a truly speculative system of pure consciousness. Hegel wants constant change to be the one and only reality. He sees reality as a continuous historical process, a constant dialectic in which contradictories constantly clash and overcome each other, always moving ahead into a more developed and unending future.

But how, then, can change be explained within this one being, the most broad and empty of all categories? Are we not back with the one immutable ultimate reality of Parmenides? How can being be becoming? Enter non-being: not only must being be something, it must also be nothing. Non-being (nothingness) must be as real as being (something). The Absolute can be defined as the ultimate something, or it can be defined as the ultimate nothing. Hegel reasons that only if there is non-being can there be change. Now obviously there is change. Therefore, there must be non-being. The clash of being and non-being gives becoming. Contradiction is thus at the heart of reality.

Hegel is thus doubly strange. He claims that the abstract is more real than the concrete (that the law of falling bodies is more real than the falling bodies) and that it is possible to have your cake and eat it too, which he holds up as the height of rationality. There is an inverse relationship between the concrete and the abstract. The more concrete something is, the less real it is. The less concrete it is, the more real it is. We see this attitude in Hegel's proof for the existence of God. Ordinary syllogistic reasoning must be abandoned. Instead of going from true and certain premises to an unavoidable conclusion, Hegel insists upon the need to negate the finite (that which is sensible, the concrete, the premises) so that he can reach the infinite, the conclusion, which is God, the Great Spirit, the Something-Nothing.

His thinking leads him to the one being that is both everything and nothing at the same time. Anyone who thinks must arrive at the same conclusion. Hegel therefore rejected Kant's rejection of Anselm's ontological argument for the existence of God. In God's unique case there is something that can only be thought of as existing; that must be thought of as real. Being is obviously an aspect of everything and so God is everything. This should not vex philosophers. After all, being is the poorest, emptiest, and most abstract of all ideas. It is the very least you can say about anything. It is simply the broadest category, the highest genus, the widest possible logical class. To think at all is to think being, which is the same as thought itself, that is, the supreme subject, when thought takes itself as its own object.

Hegel and the God-State

This endorsement of contradiction as the norm has produced the madness of modern politics. The uncompromising application of an abstraction to actual human life has wreaked havoc in the world for generations. It has produced communism, fascism, Nazism, and pseudo-democracy, all of which regard the society, state, race, or people as more real than the individual. And if bloody conflict should arise resulting in the torture and murder of millions, as between the Marxist Party and the oppressive capitalists, this is to be welcomed, because contradiction is at the heart of reality. In the socialistic stage of the dialectical process, as the workers move ahead into the new final stage of the communist paradise on earth, the workers must negate (kill) the capitalists.

In Hegel, every essence is only a partial reality, always waiting to be overcome by some greater essence. There is a constant dialectic, that is, a contradictory passing back and forth of one thing into and out of other things. The appearance of something, as actually there in its own right, is what the uninitiated (non-Hegelians) take to be a really existing thing. But, for Hegel, such things are illusions. For Hegel, existence is only the superficial appearance of an essence.

In this way the Supreme Essence, the Concrete Universal, the Absolute Spirit, the coincidence of all contraries, is absolutely free, and is the only thing that is really free. The supreme task of the supreme spirit is to know itself. The more it advances in self-knowledge, the more free it becomes. Freedom means that something is for-itself, that it has an awareness of itself. It means grasping everything together, comprehending all in all, uniting the one reality with all of the little partial realities. In effect, man, as the Absolute Idea knowing itself, is divine and the leaders of men are gods. Thus does the state become divine for Hegel. The work of the state is the work of God. Within human experience, the state is the closest thing we have to a God that we can see and feel. The Prussian authorities were very happy to hear this and, for a while in the mid-1800s, Hegel's philosophy (religion) was the official state doctrine (Hegel, 1967).

And so, contrary to Kant, we do know the thing in itself, what is really out there. Or rather, God knows us and we know ourselves and the world through God. It is not so much that we think God as it is that God thinks us, thereby making us to be. This is Hegel's notion of creation. Moreover, God wants to be with us and save us from our ignorance, with God's chief prophet being Hegel himself. This is Hegel's notion of Judao-Christianity and, in particular, Lutheranism. We know God because being and thought are the same thing. We can deduce reality in general. This one reality is the Absolute Spirit. The whole world of human life can be explained in general as the Idea marching through history. Its marching is history and its most comprehensive earthly manifestation is the nation state. The forward march of the Idea is a never-ending conquering and overcoming of all of its own necessary and intrinsic internal determinations. The Idea is the only really real thing. All things (plural) are only 'real'.

To say the least, Hegel's great system is very strange. Gilbert Keith Chesterton (1874–1936) has the following to say on this point.

> Since the modern world began in the sixteenth century, nobody's system of philosophy has really corresponded to everybody's sense of reality; to what, if left to themselves, common men would call common sense. Each started with a paradox; a peculiar point of view demanding the sacrifice of what they would call a sane point of view ... A man had to believe something that no normal man would believe, if it were suddenly propounded to his simplicity; as that law is above right, or right is outside reason, or things are only as we think them, or everything is relative to a reality that is not there. The modern philosopher claims, like a sort of confidence man, that if once we will grant him this, the rest will be easy; he will straighten out the world, if once he is allowed to give this one twist to the mind. (Chesterton, 1956, pp. 146–7)

Hegel and Pseudo-liberalism

Blessed are the flexible, for they shall tie themselves in knots. True liberty means the ability to do what you are supposed to do. Pseudo-liberty means doing whatever you feel like, usually justified by maintaining contradictories as true at the same time. Since Hegel's day, the compatibility of contradictories has become the chief trait of pseudo-liberalism. As described in the novel *1984* (1948) by George Orwell (Eric Blair, 1903–50), Big Brother controls people by getting them to accept contradictories as true at the same time. This kind of education is called double-think and double-speak. Thus, war is peace, sickness is health, poverty is wealth, hunger is being well-fed, vice is virtue, suffering is pleasure, and being religious is being irreligious. This technique effectively prevents someone from engaging in critical thinking.

At present, it is politically permissible to say that your moral position is right, but you are not allowed to say that contradictory positions are wrong. For example, you are allowed to maintain that sex has the God-given purpose of reproduction within a loving family context, but you are not allowed to say that actions that contradict your position are immoral. If you, being a rational being, publicly rebel against such nonsense, those in the public media condemn you as an intolerant bigot.

We see pseudo-liberalism, for instance, in the desire of the average citizen to have both a high standard of material living and environmental conservation at the same time. Economically speaking, vast numbers of people claim to desire an uncorrupted natural environment, and yet two or three of them live alone in a huge house. They consume everything in sight at a fast pace, even while decrying the depletion of unrenewable natural resources.

In sexual matters, some women sell themselves into sexual slavery by deliberately degrading themselves into being mere bodies that are temporarily useful to men, while at the same time demanding that they be treated as full human beings by their customers and employers. It is like the goalkeeper in a soccer team complaining about being hit by soccer balls.

In natural theology, process philosophers claim that God both is and is not the world. Ecological feminists, for instance, claim that they are concerned about equality and justice in the world, even while advocating nature-worship. Body and spirit are rolled up into one, being only two aspects of the same underlying stuff of the universe. For them, as with Hegel, everything is ultimately the same as everything else. Consequently, it becomes impossible to distinguish right from wrong and justice from injustice. Nevertheless, the feminists, often using traditional language, insist upon having their cake and eating it too.

In the realm of education, we see school administrators, for instance, claiming an allegiance to X, even while supporting all sorts of anti-X doctrines and activities. In the area of politics, politicians claim to respect human life and dignity, even while promoting various kinds of legalized hate literature (for example, all forms of pornography) and legalized murder (for example, abortion). Many today think that the latest fad is the final truth about everything. For example, in the past, many 'Catholic' thinkers embraced Marxism, fascism, or Nazism, thinking that it was the culturally avant-garde thing to do. Adjusting to the times (being 'relevant') was all-important. Nowadays, many 'Catholics' embrace feminism for the same reason. These 'Catholics' demand priestesses and regard an authoritative statement by the pope as just one more opinion among many.

How long can such pseudo-liberalism continue? Regardless of the context, the practical consequence of trying to live a contradiction is always the same, to wit, destruction. Many people, thinking that living a contradiction is the very meaning of toleration, open-mindedness, and inclusiveness, follow the road to destruction in blissful ignorance. This seems so obvious today with respect to communism, fascism, and Nazism. It is just as true with respect to democratic states.

Critique of Hegel by Schopenhauer

Schopenhauer the Pessimist

Depression ran in Arthur Schopenhauer's family. Schopenhauer is known for being a brooding, philandering, woman-hating pessimist. Monogamy, he thought, was a terrible burden on the human male. His only solace was the combination of philosophy and music. Schopenhauer was born in 1788 in Danzig, Poland, into a German family in the banking business. His parents named him Arthur because it is the same name in German, French, and English. The family later (1793–1805) moved to Hamburg, Germany. As was common at the time, in 1803 Arthur took the standard Grand Tour of Europe, which was largely an excuse for the sons of the rich to go drinking and whoring. In 1805, the same year in which the German playwright Johann von Schiller (1759–1805, who wrote the poem *Ode to Joy*) died, Schopenhauer's father committed suicide.

Schopenhauer, though, had no intention of taking over the family business. His interests were much more aesthetic. In 1806 he began his studies at Göttingen University, founded, strangely enough, by George II of England in 1734. He also studied in Berlin and Jena. In 1809, instead of going into business as his family wanted, he took an annual pension of 150 pounds, which allowed him to pursue his academic interests.

In 1814 Schopenhauer had a further falling out with his mother and he left home forever. He did not even attend his mother's funeral in 1838. Over the years he tried to get a full-time teaching position, but was constantly turned down. He attributed much of his problem to the Hegelians, whom he came to despise with a passion. In 1833 he moved to Frankfurt-am-Main, where he spent the rest of his life, constantly in fear of being robbed and/or assassinated by the many evil forces that were out to get him. Finally, one day in 1860 while sitting at the breakfast table, he dropped dead, alone and abandoned by everyone.

During his life he produced some influential works. In 1819 he published his major work, *The World as Will and Idea*, in 1833 *The Four-Fold Root of*

Sufficient Reason appeared, in 1836 he produced *On Will in Nature*, while 1844 saw a greatly enlarged edition of his *Will and Idea*. And in 1851 a series of short essays entitled *Parerga and Paralipomena* appeared.

Schopenhauer the Selective Orientalist

Like Hegel, Schopenhauer was a pantheist. And also like Hegel, he did not want to be known as a pantheist. When it comes to the moral consequences of pantheism, however, Schopenhauer was much more alert than Hegel. Hegel believed in the importance of historical development, necessary progress, and the manifest destiny of Prussian domination in Europe. Schopenhauer, like Nietzsche later, rejected all such ideas with a moral revulsion and acidity of language that could hardly be published today.

As far as pantheism is concerned, claims Schopenhauer, any view that attempts to equate God with the world is worse than useless. As he tells us in his *Parerga and Paralipomena*, his chief objection to pantheism is that it is vacuous. Trying to view the world as a living thing simply exchanges one unknown for another unknown. All we get from 'the world is God' is 'the world is the world'. No sane person would ever imagine the world to be divine. And certainly God would never transform himself into the world. If God really existed, why would he make himself miserable? This gives rise to one of Schopenhauer's most famous remarks, namely, that pantheism is simply the polite form of atheism (Schopenhauer, 1970, pp. 217–18).

With respect to the moral consequences of pantheism, Schopenhauer knows that, if the world were God, it would support all ethical choices equally well, that is, it would be an absolute relativism. Schopenhauer draws his metaphysical and moral inspiration from Hinduism and Buddhism. However, he is very selective about what he uses from them. He strips these religions down to their bare core, keeping only what he thinks to be their rational essence. For Schopenhauer, nature knows only the physical and has nothing to do with the moral. Physical nature and ethics are incommensurable. The world cares nothing for the individual, but only for the species.

In contrast, the individual cares only for himself and nothing for the species and his fellow man. Individuals are mean, miserable, narcissistic egotists, intent only upon following their own desires and having their own wills obeyed down to the last detail. The rule of human behaviour is short-term selfishness. Also, since there is no distinction between good and evil, truth and error, there is nothing to argue about. In such a world, life does not get better and better; it only gets more boring. Hence, explains Schopenhauer, the pantheist can draw no comfort from his own doctrine. All the world shows us is poverty, suffering, misery, dissension, wickedness, infamy, and absurdity.

Schopenhauer's own position is that, even though life is miserable, he will nevertheless not commit suicide, but instead spend his time reflecting upon life. We learn from his *The World as Will and Idea* (or *The World as Will and Presentation*), indicating the dichotomy between the really real (will) and its fleeting manifestations (the material, structured, scientific, mathematical, world of ordinary experience), that the only reality is the eternal universal will surging through the apparently real world of our sense experiences. We know of this one true reality by means of our own internal awareness of our self as a centre of willpower. The intellect is of secondary importance. The intellect is only the tool of the individual will, which is itself only a passing manifestation of the great will. The great will, however, Schopenhauer insists, is not to be called God. It is simply an impersonal force in the universe.

This, however, will not do. If there is only one reality and if everything must be explained by it, then whatever has developed, in whatever manner, must have come out of this one source. This one source of creativity, whether personal or impersonal, whether progressing or not, can only be the one necessary being. Schopenhauer's paradigm, as with Hegel's, is a pantheism whether he likes it or not. His method for trying to get himself off the hook in this regard, as found toward the very end of the later editions of his major work, is to simply refuse to talk about it. He admits that there is only one reality and that only he has revealed its true nature (will), but, since will does not produce any of the doctrines that have normally been associated with the pantheistic view, especially as found in Hegel, it would be wrong to label his view as pantheistic. A neat subterfuge.

Schopenhauer, Boredom, and Justice

What is the meaning of life? Would you rather be worked to death or bored to death? For Schopenhauer, the main feature of life is boredom, and atheism is the same thing as terminal boredom. The world as going nowhere in particular. It is precisely because of his rejection of progress that Nietzsche will later refer to Schopenhauer as the first true atheist (Nietzsche, 1974, section 357).

According to Robert Martin Adams, a main theme of all the outstanding literary figures of the nineteenth century is boredom, defined as the lack of any directed intention. Boredom is the one unbearable suffering in the life of the healthy person. Yet, if reality is meaningless, then one must think meaninglessness. And if this necessarily means ennui, monotony, dullness, and dreariness, then so be it (Adams, 1966, pp. 217–24).

According to Adams, boredom is not natural to human beings and when we find ourselves in a bored condition there is no telling what we will do to escape. This can be seen, for example, in *Hedda Gabler*, a play by the Norwegian playwright Henrik Ibsen (1828–1906). Hedda is attractive, rich, a community leader, and healthy. Yet she commits suicide. No identity crisis here. Hedda knows very well what she is, namely, a bored middle-aged (for her time) housewife and she cannot take it any more. Many other examples could be used to fill in Adams' meaning. Bored youths often go on rampages of vandalism, bored millionaires take up politics, and bored housewives become feminists. Small families, in order to overcome boredom, consume more natural resources than large families do.

What is the cause of boredom? Schopenhauer's answer is to call upon ancient Buddhism, which he dresses up in modern philosophical terminology. Reality is the will-to-life, of which we are a small part. He insists that the force working and operating in nature is identical with the will that is in ourselves (Schopenhauer, 1958, vol. I, p. 591). As in Buddhism, wanting things is the cause of all our problems. To be happy we must eliminate desiring. Nothing can be said about our existence except that it would be better for us not to exist. This is the most important of all truths and must be boldly stated, however much it stands in contrast to Judao-Christianity (Schopenhauer, 1958, vol. I, p. 605).

Schopenhauer also explains, in sections 63 and 64 of his *The World as Will and Presentation*, that, unlike the justice administered by the state, in which there is a sequence of events such that crimes must first be recorded, then adjudicated, and then punished, in nature the offence and the punishment occur simultaneously (Schopenhauer, 1958). Virtue must be both its own end and its own reward. By the same token, vice is its own punishment. Everything in nature gets exactly what it deserves all the time. Justice is the eternal equilibrium of guilt and punishment.

This then proves to him the true status of human life. Since the human condition is full of poverty, wretchedness, misery, lamentation, and death, it must be that human beings are of no importance in the universe. Since everything in the world gets exactly what it deserves, it must be that justice is being done to us as well. We are getting what we deserve for the crime of being born. We are all guilty of existing. As with modern feminists, pregnancy is a disease. This same theme was later taken up by Franz Kafka (1883–1924) in his novel *The Trial*. So, says Schopenhauer, when Hegel says that we and the state are God incarnated, he could not be more wrong.

However, Schopenhauer's pantheism also has serious problems. In order to argue for justice here and now he must deny the reality of what is obvious to the ordinary person. He insists that we must raise our consciousness up to the level of realizing the unity of all things, such that the criminal and the victim are truly one and the same reality. All individuality is fake and so are all temporal sequences of cause and effect, that is, those situations in which something appears to be the sufficient reason for something else. The difference between the sufferer and the one who inflicts the suffering is only a superficial appearance. The tormentor and the tormented are one. They are both only passing manifestations of will.

Does this make any sense? To Schopenhauer's way of thinking, if you do something evil you are immediately punished. Virtue is its own reward and vice is its own punishment. Yet one wonders: What practical difference could such a doctrine possibly make? How would I ever know that I had been rewarded or punished? If I kill someone and get cancer, is that my punishment? If I give money to someone and win a lottery, is that my reward? Anything could be interpreted in any way. If so, why not do whatever I feel like doing and rest assured that sooner or later everything will fade back into the one reality and be forever forgotten? In effect, every day would be a moral holiday.

For Schopenhauer, when you hurt someone you simultaneously hurt yourself. The greatest good anyone can do is to do nothing. It is better to suffer in silence than to be active in the world. This is why suicide is not recommended: it would be a strong act of personal will. All such acts must cease. Stay out of trouble, stay away from political controversies and physical confrontations. Remain unperturbed, quietly accepting the order imposed upon you by the government. Nothingness is our final reward for being virtuous. For pessimists such as Schopenhauer and Shakespeare's Macbeth, life really is a lie told by an idiot, signifying nothing. There is really no point in fighting for anything, because, in the end, everything comes to nothing (Copleston, 1947).

In rebuttal to Schopenhauer, one must wonder (using one's intellect) why the will should throw up obstacles to itself. Why would the will deliberately frustrate itself in such a fundamental way so as to rule out in advance any relief? Anyone who starts down this road will be forced to regard the world as the ultimate irrationality. It is no wonder that he should then start talking about thinking logically and thinking illogically as being on a par. In the end, I am my own worst enemy.

The Personalism of John Henry Newman

Newman the Man of Controversy

Newman was born in London in 1801, into a financially well-off banking family. He attended private schools. But then, in 1816, his father's bank failed, throwing the family into turmoil. Nevertheless, Newman was able to attend Trinity College, Oxford (1816–20) and was later (1822) made a fellow of Oriel College, Oxford, where he came under the influence of the logician Richard Whately (1787–1863). In 1825 Newman became an Anglican priest and, starting in 1828, served as vicar of St Mary's, the university church in Oxford. He was also a tutor in Oriel, an examiner in classics, and a university preacher.

His study on *The Arians of the Fourth Century* appeared in 1833 and brought him immediate respect as a scholar. During 1831–33, he travelled in Italy for a while with a fellow Oxford tutor, Richard Hurrell Froude (1803–36). While in Italy, Newman became seriously ill and nearly died. In the Summer of 1833, on his trip back to England via France, he wrote the hymn 'Lead, Kindly Light' ('The Pillar of the Cloud'). As it turned out, his friend Froude died young of tuberculosis, while Newman lived a long life.

Between 1833 and 1841 he participated in the Oxford Movement, started by another Oriel fellow John Keble (1792–1866), who thought that England was undergoing a 'national apostasy'. Newman wrote 26 of the 90 tracts that examined the relationship between the Anglican Church and the Roman Catholic Church, finally coming to the conclusion that Henry VIII was wrong in what he had done. The proof of the king's mistake was that the whole Anglican enterprise had become little more than another department of the government. Instead of being society's conscience, it was going along with every neo-pagan, pseudo-liberal practice that the secular state could imagine. The branch cut from the vine was withering. At the same time, the other organization had remained true to its origins and purpose in the world, often bringing down upon itself the wrath of the world for having done so.

In 1845, the same year in which his *An Essay on the Development of Christian Doctrine* (second edition 1878) appeared, Newman converted to the Catholic Church and was ordained a priest in Rome in 1847. In 1848, the same year in which *The Communist Manifesto* of Marx and Engels was published, Pope Pius IX encouraged Newman to establish an Oratorian Foundation of Saint Philip Neri (1515–95) in Birmingham. In 1850 the British government allowed Catholics to openly have their own bishops and dioceses in England. To help ease the process along, Newman wrote a series of lectures *On The Present Position of Catholics in England*, in which he mentioned the sins of an Italian ex-Catholic priest. In 1851, due largely to widespread anti-Catholic prejudice in the England of that time, he was sued over his revelations. The court ruled against him and in 1853 he was ordered to pay a large fine of £100. Altogether he had to pay out many thousands of pounds for all of the legal costs associated with his defence. By then he had been asked to become the rector of the first Irish Catholic university, to be located in Dublin.

The new university, with only 20 students, began operations in November 1854, the same year in which the religious test for tutors in Oxford was abolished. Newman served as rector until he resigned in 1858, due largely to policy disagreements with the local bishop and other educators who thought that he was too 'liberal'. Newman wanted a broad-based education, not a glorified seminary for laymen. During his time as rector he established colleges of arts, science, medicine, and Celtic studies. He even founded a scientific journal called *Atlantis*, after the title of Francis Bacon's (1561–1626) story concerning a *New Atlantis*, outlining a scientific society of the future.

Within a short time, though, because of continuing policy disagreements with the local Church leaders, and unable to maintain its financial base, the university closed. However, Newman's work there did produce a series of nine lectures entitled *Discourses on University Education*, published in 1853, and a later series entitled *Lectures and Essays on University Subjects*, published in 1858. The two series of lectures were then combined into his world-famous *The Idea of a University* (1859), which he dedicated to all those who had made contributions to his legal fund so that he could pay off the huge legal costs.

In 1864, after the talented poet, novelist, and Anglican clergyman Charles Kingsley called him an opportunist, Newman wrote his *Apologia Pro Vita Sua, Being a History of His Religious Opinions*, published in weekly instalments, with a second edition in 1865. Over the years this became his best-known work and served to make him somewhat popular even among Protestants. *An Essay in Aid of a Grammar of Assent* appeared in 1870. The government ban on Catholics studying in Oxford and Cambridge was lifted in 1871. Although, because of their Protestant atmosphere, some Church leaders opposed sending Catholics to such places, Newman thought that Catholics should be allowed to attend the schools as long as they had Catholic tutors.

In the later 1860s a controversy erupted over whether or not it was wise for the bishops about to gather together for Vatican Council I to declare the infallibility of the pope. Given that the Church cannot fail, it necessarily follows that Simon-Peter must be protected against failure in those areas essential to the preservation of the Church. Newman did not doubt infallibility, but wondered, given the prejudice against Catholics, whether it was a good idea to declare the doctrine at that time, especially if the case was overstated and every word of the pope was accorded a definitive status. As it turned out, the Council did exactly the right thing in restricting infallibility to matters of faith and morals. From then on, Newman vigorously defended the doctrine in public.

Later in life (1878) Newman was made a fellow of Trinity College, Oxford, and a cardinal in 1879 by Leo XIII (1810-1903, pope from 1878). Always Augustinian in outlook, he did not participate in the pope's initiative to establish Aquinas as the model of Catholic education, something confirmed by Vatican Council II. Newman died quietly of pneumonia in August 1890. On his tombstone he asked for the words: 'Out of shadows and illusions into truth'. At present, he is being considered for sainthood. (See Ker, 1990.)

Newman's Conscience Argument

When it came to convincing people that they should believe in God and act accordingly, Cardinal Newman did not put much stock in syllogisms and scientific arguments. You cannot expect to have much influence over people unless you can arouse them emotionally as well as intellectually. Nobody was ever converted to Christ by a syllogism. As Newman says in his *Idea of a University*, you may as well try quarrying granite with razors or mooring ships with silk threads as trying to overcome the passion and pride of mankind with fine-tuned reason (Newman, 1959, p. 145).

Newman did not, however, reject reasoned argumentation; far from it. Human beings, when freed from the grosser effects of ignorance and prejudice, are quite capable of rational thinking. He exercised his own intellect on the existence of God in a book with the ungainly title of *An Essay in Aid of a Grammar of Assent* (Newman, 1985). The main argument for the existence of God is contained in Part I, chapter 5, section 1, 'Belief in One God'. The main points concerning the existence of God are repeated in Part II, chapter 10, section 1, 'Natural Religion'. In this latter place he once again discusses conscience. He also brings up the prevalence among all human societies of atonement rites and sacrificial practices, as well as the wonder felt by people when viewing the beauty and orderliness of the physical universe.

Even though, thinks Newman, there may not be a hard and fast experiment or syllogism proving the existence of God, when all of the convergent evidence is taken into account the probability of God's existence becomes so overwhelming that only a very unreasonable person could reject it as a fact. The right kind of circumstantial evidence is quite capable of proving something. After all, working on the basis of probability is normal for us. We are ruled by faith, not science.

The section in Part I on the existence of God is followed with a section on 'Belief in the Holy Trinity'. Although it cannot be proven by reason alone, Newman thinks that the doctrine of the Trinity is nevertheless also congenial to human beings. It is only fitting that God should have an inner life. It is also proper for the family to have a spiritual foundation with an eternal significance. Moreover, how often have fathers longed to have a truly intimate relationship with their sons? And how often have sons wished that they could truly be one with their fathers? That the things of the world, and especially human beings, should reflect their creator seems perfectly reasonable.

Newman wants to restrict the name of theist to those who believe in a personal God, one who is separate from the material universe. He is well aware, though, of the dangers inherent in producing a proof for the existence of God that renders God little more than a distant great engineer or mathematician in the sky. In fact, Newman is so concerned about such a regressive possibility that he does not even want to call his proof a proof, as if God could be encased within a set of propositions. He is much less interested in having an inference than he is in having a description of how God satisfies our inner human need for a feeling of fulfilment. What he is after is more the feeling of a loving father with his hand resting on the shoulder of his child than the picture of a remote genius piecing together a wonderfully complicated mechanical device. As a good psychologist, Newman is interested in real assent, that is, in real motivational power.

Moreover, Newman wants to treat his subject-matter as a natural truth, one that is open to any human being. No appeal to scripture, revelation, or the teachings of the Church is necessary. In this regard, conscience is independent of books and dogmas. In this way, even in the poor lighting of natural theology, we will be able to see God in a religious context, that is, one in which God is real, sensual, physically and emotionally active, rather than in a strictly theological context, that is, one in which God is only notionally, theoretically, and intellectually active. Believing in a distant God is no better than being an atheist.

Newman knows that we cannot separate the heart and the head. In any real human person, the mental enunciation of propositions and the emotional swelling of the heart always go together when there is a true awakening of the spirit. There cannot be any antagonism between the statements of dogmatic truth and the vital feelings of real religion. The emotions follow the intellect and the intellect is buoyed up in its contemplations by the emotions. We cannot in fact become excited by something about which we have no knowledge. Hence, we need to know God, just as we need to know our parents.

Even religious devotions, says Newman, must have their objects, something to which we can direct our attention. You can, for instance, in a non-religious context, be devoted to a baseball or football team. What happens, though, when there is no concrete material thing capable of being sensed, as happens in the case of real things that are supernatural? In that case what is set before our mind is a proposition to be considered. Newman has no use for those who use feelings as an excuse for rejecting reason and logic. One thing Newman is certainly not advocating is a touchy-feely approach to religion. A pure sentimentality, without the support of reason, is as much a perversion of true religion as is a pure intellectualism. We cannot pretend that human beings lack intellect any more than we can pretend that human beings lack will and emotions. A real, active, relevant religion needs theology to survive.

This being said, it is still the case that, if the existence of God is to be shown to ordinary people in a meaningful way, the emphasis must be kept on those aspects of God's nature that immediately touch upon the feelings of ordinary people. Does God save individual people through love or through dialectic? The answer is through love. And where do we find this aspect of God displayed most poignantly if not in our personal relations with loved ones? Where there is real human love, there is an opening to divine love.

The main part of the argument begins by pointing out that we all make moral judgments of one kind or another. If we do not make moral judgments about racism then we make moral judgments about child abuse, environmental pollution, the plight of the poor, or the proliferation of weapons. Such judgments cannot be based solely upon the facts as we might observe them in a cool and objective fashion. As simply data, they are neither good nor evil. All of our moral judgments must necessarily transcend the facts. Moral judgments are evaluations of the facts. Such evaluations may then themselves become facts to be reported upon, but they would still be a different sort of fact. Observing that someone is burning a child with a hot iron, for example, is quite different from proclaiming that such an action is reprehensible. Yet such differences are just ordinary human knowledge, common to all normal human beings.

On this basis, claims Newman, we can come to an understanding of God that is just as immediate and intense as if we were to see God directly, as someone might see his loving mother or father face-to-face. We know by a natural instinct that the objects of sensation really exist. Following the usual path of inductive science, we come to know the nature of a naturally existing thing by an examination of its properties. Force it to interact with other things and see what happens. In parallel fashion, our naturally occurring sense of moral obligation (our conscience) leads us to accept as real the existence of a moral governor.

This moral sense, or the feeling of conscience, is both a judgment and a sense of duty. We know that there is a difference between right and wrong and that we must do what is right. It must be emphasized that this sort of moral judgment is not a rule of what is right. It is rather a sanction of right conduct. Newman is well aware of the fact that different cultures have different rules of right conduct. Nevertheless, all people have the sense of a sanction for their actions. This awareness of a sanction must not be confused with merely a sense of good taste. Acting with good taste contemplates its object only in an impersonal sense. It is quite possible that acting with bad taste will be very remote from us in an emotional way. Conscience, however, is always something of a very personal concern.

We can understand what Newman is talking about by way of an example. Imagine a situation in which someone attends a fancy dress party dressed in an old T-shirt. Now imagine a situation in which a child is being tortured with a hot iron. In the first case, the person in the old T-shirt might be embarrassed for a while, but then that would be the end of it. Bystanders might get a momentary laugh out of the situation; Hollywood could even make money out of the situation. Not so in the second case, in which there would be real moral outrage and some real motivation to do something about stopping the evil. Once the guilty party realizes that they have done something terribly wrong, they would not be able to forget about it. Bystanders would insist that they be stopped and arrested. It is important not to confuse manners and morals. Newman is talking about morals.

The key question for Newman concerns the source of this indisputable sense of conscience. He insists that there is no way it can come from the natural world. The world of nature is only a world of facts. Darwin's world, the world of the chemist and the physicist, the world of the medical doctor, is a world of natural laws. It has neither manners nor morals. This leaves only one alternative for the reasonable person, namely, the supernatural world. Conscience can only come from a world that transcends the world of our fleeting senses and ideas. The voice of conscience must be the voice of God speaking to each person in a personal way. Conscience is the connecting link between the normal individual and God.

Newman asks us to consider the case of a child who has done something wrong and who must now seek forgiveness for her bad deed. In order to find relief from their guilt feelings, the child will spontaneously seek out the loving attention of someone who is familiar, powerful, present, able to read their heart, forgiving, and whose goodwill can be counted upon. Newman is not saying that what constitutes good and bad will be defined by everyone in the same way all the time. He is saying that all normal human beings have a moral sense and that this moral sense (conscience) must be accounted for in a supernatural way.

Newman is even willing to admit that this moral sense or conscience can be lost later in life. It is a fact of experience that many people are callous and hard-hearted. He is well aware of the many cruel and detestable actions of which people are capable. Often, people are their own worst enemies. Atheists, for example, suffocated by their own physical senses and worldly concerns, do as much damage to themselves as they do to others. That, though, is not the way we start out in life. Snuffing out your conscience so that you can be callous about torturing, maiming, and killing takes time and practice.

Such cruel actions might even be rationalized in some way. Some people might even claim that there is no difference between right and wrong, or that wrong has as much right to exist as does right, or that right and wrong are on a par. Some people might even assert that evil has a greater claim on us because it is so widespread in the world. Such assertions, however, do not represent normal human thinking. The normal thing is to grow in our moral development so as to have a more refined conscience as we mature.

Thus does Newman think that he has shown not only the existence of God but the nature of God as well. Conscience is the living connection between two personal beings, one finite and one infinite. He rejects the notion of God as merely the soul of the world, the idea that God created the world and then abandoned it to run on its own, and the theory that God is really the same thing as humanity taken collectively. Newman, it seems, must have been reading people such as Ralph Waldo Emerson, Darwin, Ludwig Feuerbach, and the Marxist philosophers. According to Newman, such views of God are completely useless to human beings. Newman wants instead to speak as a theist, something that can be accomplished only on the basis of God as a supreme personal being, who is not identified with the world he created and who is continuously in contact with the world, including each and every individual human being.

Critique of Newman by Freud

Freud the Viennese Neurologist

Sigmund Freud was born in 1856 in Freiberg. In order to avoid anti-Semitism, Freud's family, which was non-practising, left for Leipzig in 1859 and later moved to Vienna while he was still a child. His family was poor and lived in the Jewish ghetto. At first he could not decide what to do, but he finally decided to study medicine, concentrating on the nervous system, which he did from 1873–81 at the University of Vienna. The atmosphere in the medical school was generally materialistic and atheistic. In 1878 and 1879 Freud was supported in his studies by various Jewish charities. Even at this early period in his life Freud held a very low opinion of the human race and especially of the poorer people living in Vienna. At one point in 1877 he commented that ordinary people are a low rabble and he wished that a thunderbolt from heaven would strike them all dead. (See Ferris, 1998, pp. 20, 42, 49–50, 63.)

Following graduation, Freud worked in Vienna's general hospital for three years. In 1884 he developed an interest in hypnosis and in 1885 went to Paris to study with Jean Martin Charcot (1825–93). Freud taught at the University of Vienna for a year and then, in 1886, began a private practice. In 1893 Freud co-authored (with Josef Breuer) *Studies in Hysteria*.

In 1896 Freud began in earnest to push his psychoanalysis project. His basic premise was that all mental problems encountered in adult life can be traced back to troubling situations (traumas) experienced during childhood. The adult is not consciously aware of the source of the problem because it has been repressed into the unconscious level of mind. The purpose of psychoanalysis is to uncover these psychic cuts. There must be an analysis of the childhood psyche in order to find the source of the adult problem.

At this point in Freud's career (later 1890s) we begin hearing about the free association of ideas, the unconscious, repression, infantile sexuality, the Oedipus Complex, and intra-mental conflict, such as the id-child versus the superego-parent versus the ego-self. The role of unconscious forces controlling our lives and the Oedipus Complex were the chief themes in Freud's philosophy of human nature. According to his Oedipus theory, boys are (unconsciously) in competition with their fathers for sex with their mothers, a wish their fathers will not let them fulfil. As a result, sons do not get along well with their fathers. This frustration then becomes the nucleus for all male neuroses later in life. Outright warfare between fathers and sons is prevented by various forms of sublimation, such as more mild forms of rebellion against authority and various dream states, sometimes revealed by 'Freudian slips' in speech. The existence of such slips, as well as the therapy technique of 'free word association', shows the iron-clad causal relationship between what appears on the surface and what is locked up in the unconscious mind.

Some commentators wonder if Freud is consistent here. New York University psychologist Paul C. Vitz, for instance, asks if the Oedipus Complex could also apply to those who reject God, the ultimate authority figure. According to Freud's own position, thinks Vitz, atheism should be an unhealthy, neurotic condition, something that must be cured if we are to lead a normal human life (Vitz, 2000, pp. 293–306).

In 1900 Freud published *The Interpretation of Dreams*, in 1902 be became a professor, in 1906 he began to make converts, and in 1908 the International Congress of Psychoanalysis was established. Freud's major work, *A General Introduction to Psychoanalysis*, consisting of 28 lectures, was delivered in the Psychiatric Clinic at the University of Vienna during the 1915–17 academic years. The lectures were well attended by members from all the faculties. In the sixth lecture we are told that human freedom of choice is an illusion. Freud tells us that the deeply rooted belief in psychic freedom and choice that we have is quite unscientific, and that it must give ground before the claims of a determinism that governs even mental life. Freud here is consistent with his basic philosophy of atheistic materialist. In such a world there is no room for freedom of choice for any kind of being, including a human being (Freud, 1963, p. 112).

Some modern thinkers, though, such as Edward Osborne Wilson, try to get around this fact by defining human freedom as a lack of predictability. In his gambling casino view of decision making, mere randomness is enough to give us the impression of having free choice. Since all overt actions are determined by the motions of subatomic particles and since such motions are so complicated that we will never be able to map them out in any great detail, we will never be able to completely predict human behaviour. As a result, human freedom is forever safe from scientific prying. Does this mean that human beings have freedom? Hardly; all it means is that we are ignorant of the causes of our behaviour (Wilson, 1998).

At the end of Freud's eighteenth lecture we learn that, after Copernicus and Darwin, Freud's own doctrine represents a third revolution, one that deprives human beings of their rational core. We can no longer claim to be masters of ourselves. In the same place, we also learn that he has been compelled to disturb the peace of the world in yet another way, as he will explain later. The new shock occurs in the twentieth lecture, wherein Freud describes infantile and childhood sexuality, and even perversion. In the twenty-first lecture, true to Darwin, we learn that perverted sex is sex that does not lead to reproduction. Here he develops the notion of a child desiring sex with his or her mother or father.

For most of his life Freud was a chain smoker, loving his cigarettes and cigars. But then, in 1923, he developed cancer of the jaw. His illness required several major operations, the result of which finally made it almost impossible for him to speak. Things became so bad that he would always eat alone, because the process of eating was so disgusting.

The 1920s also saw Freud turn his attention more toward religion. For years he had been an avid collector of masks and statues, all of which showed him the anthropomorphic nature of religion. His written works in the area of religion were aimed mainly at explaining away anything of a supernatural nature about religion. From this period of time we get *Totem and Taboo* (1913), *The Ego and the Id* (1923), *The Future of an Illusion* (1927), *Civilization and Its Discontents* (1930), and *Moses and Monotheism* (1939). Although each is interesting, none of these works can be considered scientific. In fact, Freud's whole psychoanalytical approach has been attacked on scientific grounds. He has been criticized for working with extremely small samples, falsifying his data, and prescribing addictive drugs to his patients. (See Fisher and Greenberg, 1996; see also Gilman, 1993.)

In the 1930s, during the depression, at the request of his financially troubled publisher, Freud wrote a series of *New Introductory Lectures on Psychoanalysis* (lectures 29 to 35), in which we hear about penis envy and other such things that so alienate him from modern feminists. Why do women continue to have babies, even though child-bearing is so painful? Because having a baby is the female way of growing a penis. For Freud, your biology is your destiny. After all, Darwin was right when he said that women are really nothing but baby-producing machines.

The 1930s saw the rise of Nazism in Germany and Austria. In 1938 Freud hurriedly fled to London, leaving behind his worldly goods. Ironically, Freud's own philosophy relieved Hitler and his minions of any guilt in their persecution of the Jews. According to Freudian doctrine, Hitler, like everyone else, was forced to do what he did by virtue of his troubled childhood and bad experiences. Freud died in 1939. Coincidentally, Freud died on Yom Kippur (the Day of Atonement, the Sabbath of Sabbaths), the most holy of the Jewish religious days. On this day the Jews, as a whole people, beg God to forgive their sins (Ferris, 1998, pp. 396–7, 446).

Freud's Attack on Religion

After the Copernican revolution of 1543, which displaced man from the centre of the universe, and the Darwinian revolution of 1859, which displaced man from the centre of the biosphere, the time was right for a revolution that would displace man from the centre of reason. Instead of relying on reason, man is driven by instincts and powers buried deep in his unconsciousness. However, in order to carry out this third revolution, it is not enough to be materialistic. Other recent thinkers, such as Karl Marx (1818–83), have been materialistic but without being scientific. In the last lecture of his *New Introductory Lectures on Psychoanalysis*, which provides the best summary of his views on religion, Freud goes out of his way to point out the anti-scientific character of Marxism.

Freud asks: What is religion supposed to do for people? First, it gives us information about the origin of the universe and our place in it. He claims that this aspect of religion is of greatest significance because it comes into direct conflict with science. As a rival to science, religion expresses itself in such a way that the ordinary person can understand what is being said, thereby placing religion in competition with science for the minds and hearts of ordinary people. For this reason, religion must be taken seriously by anyone wanting to substitute science for superstition. Religion also provides comfort and consolation in life, as well as assuring its followers of ultimate happiness. In addition, it involves placing obligations and prohibitions on its members. In this last respect it is most removed from science. In summary, religion:

1 teaches an overall explanation of how and why we are here;
2 performs a consolation function; and
3 provides specific rules and regulations regarding behaviour.

According to Freud, Marxism fits on all counts, and so it cannot help but generate illusions comparable to those of the old religions. Two of these illusions are:

1 the view that the New Order will produce a New Man; and
2 the view that there will be a future paradise on earth for the true believers.

Before rejecting the Marxist claim to being scientific, however, Freud had already set out his main objections to religion. In 1932, in his lecture 'The Question of a Weltanschauung', Freud defines a world-view as an intellectual construction that solves all the problems of our existence uniformly on the basis of one overriding hypothesis, and so leaves no question unanswered, and in which everything that interests us finds a fixed place (Freud, 1965, p. 158).

In contrast to religion, Freud defends the view that all dependable knowledge must come from the working over of carefully scrutinized observations. He wants research, not revelation. He insists that truth cannot be tolerant, that it admits of no compromises or limitations, that research regards every sphere of human activity as belonging to it, and that it must be ruthless in rejecting any other power that might try to take over any part of it (Freud, 1965, p. 160).

How, though, can there be intellectual knowledge in a materialistic world? Is not Freud's view paltry and inhuman? Freud says no. Psychoanalysis has already answered this objection by including mind among the sciences. With respect to his own new field of study, its contribution to science lies precisely in having extended scientific research to the mental field (Freud, 1965, p. 159). Psychology, he goes on, must adhere to the same methodology as the natural sciences. In a universe of iron-clad natural laws, anything smacking of an unexpected breakthrough from on high must be rejected. The doctrine of creation is also wishful thinking. As far as science is concerned, the world is eternal and that is that.

Unfortunately for religion-phobic Freud, the Abbe Georges Henri Le Maître (1894–1966), a Belgian priest, who was also a professor of astrophysics at the University of Louvain, had only recently (1927) proposed the idea of an expanding universe that had begun from a primordial quantum of matter (the Big Bang) about ten billion years ago, with the earth being about three billion years old. His theory was praised by Einstein in 1933 for being both beautiful and satisfactory (Vecchierello, 1934).

Le Maître lived long enough to see his theory verified in 1964–65 from observations made by two radio astronomers, Arno A. Penzias and Robert W. Wilson. They discovered a background microwave radiation level, coming from all parts of the universe, that matched up very well with what would be expected from the remains of a primeval fireball. The present temperature of the heat radiation, only a few degrees above absolute zero, is just what we would expect if the Big Bang had taken place some ten to 20 billion years ago. Among scientists, the Big Bang view is now generally accepted as the one best fitting the data.

Also, for Freud, any notion of divine providence is without merit. Religion has been replaced by modern technology and medicine. According to Freud's fatalistic doctrine, hidden, unfeeling, and unloving powers determine our fate. The system of rewards and punishments that religion ascribes to the government of the universe does not exist. We are not under the loving care of God and we are not the captains of our own ships, but only the playthings of uncaring natural forces (Freud, 1965, p. 167).

In the end, thinks Freud, there are only two real sciences, namely, psychology and physics. The latter deals with the world outside the mind, while the former deals with the inner world. Later on, B.F. Skinner will attack Freud for his inconsistency. According to Skinner (a stimulus-response behaviourist who denied that there is any mental world), Freud should have ended up with just one science, namely, physics. In Skinner's book, Freud's appeal to the psyche as something real and different marks him as being unscientific (Skinner, 1974).

Freud and the Origin of Religion

Be this as it may, if Freud's world-view is correct, how could religion have ever begun in the first place? As far as the origin of religion is concerned, Darwin believed that animals showed signs of religion. Modern human religion began among primitive people when they projected their dream images into the world and came to regard such images as spiritual beings. They also projected personal human traits on to natural forces, such as the wind. Thus polytheism emerged first, to be followed later by monotheism. Modern man, thought Darwin, possesses the most advanced form of religious morality, namely, Christianity.

With respect to the origin of religion, compared to Darwin, Freud's approach was more psychological than biological. The father of psychoanalysis did not care to speculate about the mental life of animals. Yet he could not avoid asking why, in a strictly materialistic world, there is any religion at all? Freud was in basic agreement with Darwin's gradual development view, namely, that people went from no religion to animism to magic totemism to modern forms of religion. However, he gave it a psychological twist. The process was greatly helped by language, which allowed the notion of spiritual beings to become entrenched in human thinking. Along with totemism (the worship of animals) went the rise of taboos and finally the personification of evil in the form of evil spirits, which also became entrenched in human culture.

In his world-view lecture, while discussing the great absolute truth that reality is nothing but matter in motion, Freud found himself in the position of having to also discuss the rivals to science, to wit, art, philosophy, and religion. Art is quickly dismissed. It works with illusions and does not pretend to say anything significant about reality. Anything it knows it borrows and it can serve any master with equal skill. Philosophy can also be dismissed as a rival to science. For Freud, philosophy was Kant and Hegel. The writings of such men might be interesting to a small number of people who are as obscure as their masters, but they can never become a force in the world to rival science.

Not so with religion. At every point it pits itself against science. It claims to explain the origin of things, particularly human beings. It uses an appeal to revelation running directly counter to the scientific method. It attempts to guide the lives of people in all sorts of unrealistic ways. It is not so much that religion is dogmatic, says Freud; after all, science is also dogmatic. What troubles Freud is that religion is both dogmatic and wrong at the same time.

To Freud's mind, there is only one way to finally get rid of religion and that is to completely discredit it by explaining it away and then replacing it with science.

By his method of psychoanalysis, which he defines as an analysis of the origins of human thought and behaviour, Freud says that the origin of religion is found in human fear and primitive ignorance. Deep down in the human psyche is a desire for security. This is the same sense of security we feel while in our mother's womb. Outside the womb, we fear the thousand dangers that await us at every turn. Thus, claims Freud, thinking especially of Judao-Christianity, religion is an obsessive-compulsive neurosis. It is an unrealistic concentration upon obtaining an impossible goal. It is both a personal and a communal disease. It began as a psychological crutch in times of trouble. The gods are nothing more than the projections of the parent image into the heavens by our earliest ancestors, hoping thereby to be saved from their adversities. Sometimes, as in the Old Testament, the image is that of an unbending father, the stern disciplinarian. At other times, as in the New Testament, the image is more that of a sweet mother. In any case, though, it is an illusion, the one most responsible for retarding scientific progress.

What response can religion make to his analysis? None, says Freud. Some might claim that, because of its divine origin, religion is not subject to scientific analysis. Freud says that this begs the question. Prove to me its divine origin. What about the claim that religion is so important to life that it must evade scientific analysis? Freud thinks that this is a very dangerous position. Instead of a dictatorship of science, such an attitude would allow emotions to rule us, with deadly consequences. Science alone gives us the truth. What about the truth of religion in a higher sense? Religion gives us beautiful personal inspirations rather than truth. Nonsense, says Freud. Such a view would be the end of science. There is only one truth. In effect, an appeal to personal insights and private aesthetics would be a prohibition against science (Freud, 1965, p. 171).

So what about the claim that religion is needed in order to answer the 'big questions', questions not addressed by science, even though the religious answers may be only provisional? Freud says that this is the religion-of-gaps view. It has some merit, but only temporarily. Science is still young; we must give science time to provide the absolutely true answers to our questions. Although he does not give any specific examples, he says that we already have some truths from the older and more mature sciences. Overall, though, we are still better off with a little bit of science than with a whole lot of nonsense based upon wishful impulses (Freud, 1965, p. 174).

Freud also takes a minute to dismiss another possible rival to science, which is nihilistic scepticism. This anarchist doctrine teaches that either we cannot know anything at all at any time or that all knowledge is totally relative to the time and place of its enunciation. Since you can know nothing with certitude, you may as well believe anything you wish. Such a view is rejected by Freud as anti-scientific. Freud says that it is perhaps acceptable as a game in theory, but that it could not possibly be acceptable in the practical affairs of life. Imagine, for instance, trying to build a real bridge out of cardboard rather than using stone or steel. If scientific truth is indistinguishable from mere opinion, what difference would it make if we gave a patient a large dose of morphine rather than a small dose or gave him tear-gas rather than ether? Science gives us the true and certain knowledge we all depend upon to survive.

Freud's Philosophy Today

In his *Totem and Taboo*, Freud asserted that, at the beginning of human history, the young men ganged up to kill the dominant male father. In his *Moses and Monotheism*, Freud asserted that the crime was repeated among the early Jews when Moses was murdered by the young bucks. They later felt guilty about their act and decided to adopt monotheism in order to please the memory of Moses. In Freud's theories, women play little if any role. Today everyone agrees that Freud's history of the Jews and the origin of guilt feelings are pure fantasy. Moreover, why would some primitive sons feel guilty about killing their father? And why, even if they did, should the guilt be carried on over so many generations? In addition, his answers to the rebuttals offered by religion are self-contradictory. Freud's system, according to his own words, attributes all human actions to hidden instinctual drives. How can science be the final truth if his own 'scientific' theory is founded upon something irrational? Has rational science discovered that there is no such thing as rational science?

The key question, though, concerns the direction of flow of the influence. Is the master taking the dog for a walk or is the dog taking the master for a walk? Is the heavenly father modelled after the earthly father, as Freud asserted, or is it the other way around? Is it that the child is to the father as the adult is to God or is it that God is to the adult as the father is to the child? Is it a top-down model or a bottom-up model? This problem has already been pointed out by numerous commentators on the Freudian theory.

One of the most comprehensive critiques is provided by the psychiatrist Karl Stern (Stern, 1961). Stern observes that Freud is perfectly consistent in his desire to destroy anything that smacks of the supernatural. In Freud's materialistic world, God cannot possibly be anything other than a projected father image, holy communion must be nothing but cannibalistic oral introjection, original sin is nothing but a carry-over from some horrible past crime, and religion in general can be nothing but an obsessive-compulsive neurosis.

As Stern goes on to explain, however, the same question keeps coming up over and over again, namely, why must we interpret the given situation in one direction rather than the other? When Saint Teresa of Avila (1515–82), for example, reported that she was pierced through the heart with a red-hot arrow, was this a low-level sexual experience raised to a spiritual height or was it something supernatural expressed in a bodily way because of the union of body and soul in each human being? When Newman asked whether the earth is warmed because the sun just happens to shine on it, or whether the sun was designed to shine in order to warm the earth, he was asking basically the same question. The atheist will assume that the arrangement is an accident of blind natural forces, while the theist will assume that the arrangement is designed by God. Either way, though, the facts are the same: the sun shines, the earth is warmed.

Why could not the relationship between humans and God be looked at in some religious way that remains loyal to the facts? We could say that God (the father) is to his creation as the human father is to his human child. In each case, the creator, at the moment of creation, and ever afterwards, remains separate from his creation. This does not rule out a loving relationship between father and child, but it does serve to clearly distinguish the creator from his creation. There is nothing mentally sick about this. As normal human beings, we employ analogous thinking all the time.

The ancient Jews would say that, because God, as the ever-faithful protector of his Chosen People, really exists, human fatherhood has an objective foundation independent of anyone's imagination. The proper analogy is that God is to the parent as the parent is to the child. But Freud says: Because the human child looks up to his actually-seen earthly father, the human adult looks up to an imaginary heavenly father image, that is, the child is to the parent as the parent is to God. This means that there really is no God and hence no model for ever-faithfulness. This leaves us with nothing but our ever-changing private urges to follow, hardly a satisfactory foundation for any kind of family life.

If practised, Freud's philosophy leads to physical destruction. Are we to believe that there should be no restrictions on man's sex life? Could society survive under such circumstances? Are we really that self-destructive? For example, according to Freud, in the development of human social life the first (totemic) restriction on the choice of a man's sexual object was the prohibition against incest, which he calls the most drastic mutilation that man's erotic life has ever experienced (Freud, 1961, p. 51; also pp. 79, 89, 92).

It seems that, in Freud's case, in order to make sense out of our psychological life, it is necessary to bring in all sorts of things for which there is no place in a materialistic system. Does man really have free choice? Freud says no. Then why bother with ethics? Freud says that the ethical demands on which religion depends for its importance must be given another basis. No doubt, they are indispensable to human society and it is dangerous to link obedience to them with religious faith (Freud, 1965, p. 168). Certainly, though, ethics must be linked to human freedom. But there is no freedom in human nature. Moreover, even if man were free, how could we preserve the heart of Judao-Christian ethics without the real existence of God? As with Bertrand Russell, Freud thinks he can draw water from a dry well.

Even worse, is there really any human nature at all? If not, then how can we talk about something that is common to all human beings? If each passing lump of atoms is really one of a kind, then each individual would constitute its own species. If so, how can a collection of unique things be inhibited by human society? How is the sublimation of prohibited drives in mankind possible if there is no such thing as mankind? The point is that anyone who lacks respect for serious philosophical thinking must pay a high price for his disrespect, which is the death of his own doctrine.

Conclusion

The internal experience of God is a fine thing to have, if you have it. Unfortunately, in a fashion similar to both the as-if approach and the a priori method, the internal experience that any given individual may have of God is sure to vary a great deal with respect to another individual. In one case, there is a strong sense of God as an all-powerful being existing independently of the world. In another case, God is felt to be the world and we are only fleeting aspects of God. So, once again, we must be very careful in our use of the word 'God'. Politicians, teachers, scientists, philosophers, and even theologians, often use the term without any clear understanding of what it means. This then raises the issue of what you are attacking when you attack God. Do atheists really know what they are talking about when they deny the existence of God?

Chapter 8

The For-real Approach: A Posteriori External Experience Method Based on Essence

Natural Theology from 1400 to 1800

The Renaissance was marked by faith without reason. This can be seen in the works of thinkers such as Francesco Petrarch (1304–74), who invented the sonnet, Geert Groote (1340–84) of Deventer, who founded the Brothers of the Common Life, Florens Radewyns (Florentius, 1350–1400), who succeeded Groote as the leader of the Brethren, Nicolaus Cusanus (1401–64), who denied the principle of non-contradiction, Thomas of Kempis (Thomas Hemerken, 1380–1471), a member of the Brethren who authored the famous *Imitation of Christ*, Desiderius Erasmus (Gerhard Gerhards, 1466–1536) of Rotterdam, who attacked Luther's theology, and the great enemy of the Roman Catholic Church himself, Martin Luther (1483–1546).

Whether Catholic or Protestant, however, it was typical for such thinkers to adopt a 'back to the Bible' and 'the Scriptures alone' attitude toward religion. It is no accident that they placed their emphasis upon a moralistic outlook derived to a large extent from the traditions of Plato and the Stoics. In general, they regarded their disdain for reason as a way of becoming more religious. Luther, for instance, regarded the extensive use of logic and reason as the work of Satan.

Later on, after the work of Bacon and Descartes, the status of human reason once again rose to a high level, but this renewed emphasis was almost entirely on essence. The basic attitude was: no essence, no science. Science, especially mathematical physics, was riding high and could not be denied. The emphasis on essence means giving a primary role to concepts, logic, and the process of going from the idea of something to the reality of the thing outside the mind. The emphasis is always on the definition of the thing ('What is it?'). Existential considerations ('Is it?') are played down.

In natural theology, God was gradually removed from the world. Beginning in earnest with Descartes, the view of God most widely defended by intellectuals was deism. This was not atheism. The physical universe of Aristotle was disproved, but God was still needed in order to make the world safe for science. First Descartes created God and then God created just the sort of world needed to carry on science. With Paley, God consulted Newton before creating the world. In effect, the whole reality of God was identified with just one of God's possible actions, namely, the maker of a great clockwork perfectly suited for the science of mathematical physics. God's proper name became the great construction engineer in the sky. And, as expected, the perfect engineer would make the best of all possible worlds.

This universe was regarded as so law-abiding, and therefore so suited to scientific study, that any variation in its structures or procedures, such as might be caused by a miracle, must be ruled out as impossible in principle. Once created, everything must continue as it is. It is as if you are asked what you are and you say that you are a student or a store clerk. In other words, the whole rich being of something is reduced to a tiny part. It was then natural enough, as we see later on with Darwin, to imagine some other means whereby species could have come into existence. Many intellectuals began to think that God, like a factory worker in modern times, might be eliminated if we could find some automatic mechanism, such as natural selection, that could do the same job.

The Orderly World of Newton and Paley

Newton the Genius

Before Paley there was Isaac Newton (1642–1727), who was born on Christmas day (according to the old style calendar) in the same year that Galileo Galilei (1564–1642) died. Newton did not have a happy home life. His father died before he was born and he always felt that his mother, who died in 1679, had rejected him. However, though poor, Newton's genius was recognized early. He attended the local free grammar schools and later entered Trinity College, Cambridge, on a scholarship. He received his BA in 1665, just before the university closed for two years because of the plague. In the same year he discovered the binomial theorem and began work on the calculus. On the reopening of Trinity College in 1667, he was made a fellow, and, in 1669, even though he was not an ordained priest of the Church of England, he was given the coveted Lucasian chair of mathematics at the university. As things developed later on, we cannot even be sure that Newton was a Christian.

During this same period of time, Newton invented fluxions (the calculus), a method of analyzing locomotion by freezing it in space, and tried his hand at unifying terrestrial and celestial mechanics, but without success. He then turned his attention to the study of light, inventing a much-improved reflecting telescope, and discovered that different colours have different wave lengths. In 1675 he proposed his hypothesis on light, saying that light was a collection of particles in the ether. In the same year he joined the Royal Society of London, founded in 1660 by Charles II. The society was devoted to conducting experiments in the inductive fashion recommended by Francis Bacon and was led by its chief coordinator of experiments, Robert Hooke (1635–1703). This work was all done within a religious context. The members by and large agreed with Bacon who, in his essay *Of Atheism*, said that a little philosophy leads to atheism, but that depth in philosophy brings people back to religion (Bacon, 1883, p. 80).

Newton also had an interest in chemistry. His view on chemical combinations was that, in relation to each other, some substances are sociable (sympathetic) while others are unsociable (antipathetic). In 1679 he gave up on the ether (but was to return to it again later), claiming that all physical activities were caused by attractions coming from within the particles of matter. Matter, he thought, was composed of ultimately indivisible particles. On this topic he differed from Descartes, who thought that matter is continuous and infinitely divisible. Today, concerning divisibility, science sides with Descartes against Newton.

In 1678 Newton began showing serious signs of having emotional problems. Some historians say that his nervous breakdown was due to the fact that he had such a hard time getting his fellow scientists to accept his theory of light; he was especially at odds with Hooke. Others attribute his emotional condition to his worsening relationship with his mother. It may also have been due to his interest in chemistry. Unaware of the dangers of heavy metals, such as mercury and lead, Newton would inhale and taste various chemical substances as a way of seeing what results various combinations of chemicals would give. In any event, he withdrew from most public activities for a period of about six years, from 1679 to 1685.

It was during this period of time that Newton was working hard on proving, by a combination of observation and mathematics, his theory of universal gravitation. A short work entitled *On Motion* was written in 1684. Later, in 1687, the same year in which Catholic convert John Dryden (1631–1700) published his *The Hind and the Panther*, Newton's short work was incorporated into his monumental *Mathematical Principles of Natural Philosophy*, a work that immediately made him world-famous as a new-age scientist. There were later editions in 1713 and 1726. His book unified terrestrial and celestial mechanics in conformity with the observations of the German astronomer Johan Kepler (1571–1630). It also spawned some popular myths about its author. Newton certainly did not discover gravity; the story about the falling apple is pure fiction. It was told by Voltaire, who claimed to have heard it from one of Newton's scientific colleagues and relatives, John Conduitt.

The great work also got him into a controversy with Hooke over who thought up the theory first; Hooke claimed that he had the basic idea long before Newton did. At the same time, and until his death, Newton was arguing with the followers of Leibniz over who first invented the calculus. Leibniz had published his work on the calculus in 1684, but Newton claimed to have discovered it much earlier. Throughout all of his many controversies, Newton was very vindictive. If he did not like you, there would be no references to you in his works, even if you really deserved credit.

Following the publication of his major book, the printing of which was paid for by the astronomer Edmund Halley (1656–1742), Newton was elected a Member of Parliament for a year. However, his emotional problems reappeared. From 1693 until 1696 Newton once again experienced mental instability, often acting in an erratic fashion and writing strange letters to people he knew. At one point he accused John Locke of attempting to get him involved with women.

Upon his recovery in 1696 Newton was made warden of the royal mint and later became the master of the mint, for which he received an annual salary of £2,000, a great deal of money in those days. Newton, though, rather than take the position as a sinecure, as was the common practice back then, decided to earn his money. As part of his job was to prevent counterfeiting, he regarded it as important to unmask as many counterfeiters as he could, and to then hang them, which he did with great enthusiasm. He was elected as a Member of Parliament again in 1703. He then turned his interest to clocks. In 1703, following the death of Hooke, which could not have happened soon enough for Newton, he accepted the presidency of the Royal Society and continued to be elected to the post until he died.

From 1696 to the end of his life Newton lived in London. The year 1704 saw the publication of his *Opticks*, with later editions in 1704, 1706, and 1718. In 1705 Newton was knighted by Queen Anne, the first scientist to receive such an honour. Towards the end of his life, Newton was cared for by his niece, Catherine, and her husband, John Conduitt, who later became the master of the mint and continued Newton's pursuit and prosecution of counterfeiters. Newton died in March 1727 of unknown causes and was buried in Westminster Abbey. Always a thrifty person, he left his relatives a sizeable fortune.

Newton's Mechanistic Universe

Newton is known as a genius in mathematical physics. What is often overlooked, however, is the fact that he had an even greater interest in theological matters. He was especially interested in the interpretation of biblical prophecies, thinking that mathematics might throw some light on the subject. Overall, Newton wrote much more on matters of religion than he did on matters of mathematics and physics. As he said in a letter to Richard Bentley (1662–1742), everything his reason had discovered proves the existence of God as the one and only intelligent author of nature. This lesson was not lost on atheists. Later, Hume, for instance, will attack reason in preparation for his attack on religion.

A hint of Newton's interests appears at the end of his *Mathematical Principles* under the title of 'General Scholium', which means a long footnote to the main text. Within a few pages Newton expresses his view that it is proper to discuss God on the basis of science. The existence of God is a part of physics. All good scientists are religious. This section also contains his famous line, *'hypotheses non fingo'*, directed against the Cartesians, about not inventing mechanistic theories just for the sake of having mechanistic devices in order to explain everything about the world. In this regard, as much as he disliked Hooke, Newton agreed with Hooke, who would not give a cent for a cartload of hypotheses. The theory must fit the facts, not vice versa, and there are many things, such as the relationship between God and the world, that cannot be explained by only matter in motion. The vast majority of Newton's religious writings, however, have never been published. This may have been because he was unorthodox. He had no use for saints or other intermediaries between God and man. Newton's religious views were deistic and unitarian (a denial of the Trinity). Nevertheless, what we do have from him in print shows that he had no sympathy for atheists.

For example, Newton, in his *Theological Manuscripts*, declares that atheism is so senseless and odious that few ever defend it (Newton, 1950, p. 48). He thinks that atheism is unscientific. This would be true even without the newest tool of natural philosophy, namely, mathematics. Now (1680s) we know that the more precise is the investigation of nature, as found in mathematics, the more law-abiding are the behaviours and patterns that are discovered by the sincere seeker after truth. We learn of the unity of the universe and of the unity of the laws of nature, which then teaches us the unity of the one creator. This began a long trend in European thought, namely, that to be a scientist is to be a believer.

Newton is most impressed by the organization of the human body. There is so much uniformity, harmony, and symmetry in the human constitution that it could not have come about by accident. It must be due to the counsel and contrivance of a great author. Newton is especially interested in light.

> Whence is it that the eyes of all sorts of living creatures are transparent to the very bottom and the only transparent members of the body, having on the outside a hard transparent skin and within transparent layers with a crystalline lens in the middle and a pupil before the lens, all of them so truly shaped and fitted for vision that no Artist can mend them? Did blind chance know that there was light and what was its refraction, and fit the eyes of all creatures after the most curious manner to make use of it? These and such like considerations, always have, and ever will prevail with mankind, to believe that there is a Being who made all things, and has all things in his power, and who is therefore to be feared. (Newton, 1950, pp. 48–9)

Newton concludes that, in a unified universe, there is only one God who possesses all of the attributes of traditional supernaturalistic monotheism. He must be loved, feared, trusted, prayed to, thanked, praised, and obeyed. We must also set aside time for services dedicated to him.

> These things we must do, not to any mediator between him and us, but to him alone, 'that he may give his angels charge over us', who, being our fellow-servants, are pleased with the worship which we give to their God. And this is the first and principal part of religion. This always was and always will be the religion of all

God's people from the beginning to the end of the world. (Newton, 1950, p. 51; see also pp. 54–7)

Paley the Professor

William Paley was born in 1743 in Peterborough, about 50 miles north of London. He attended Christ's College, Cambridge, and in 1767 became a priest in the Church of England and a lecturer in philosophy at Christ's College. In 1780 he was appointed a member of the staff of the Carlisle cathedral, where he became archdeacon in 1782 and chancellor of the diocese in 1785. His works include *The Principles of Moral and Political Philosophy* (1785), *Horae Paulinae; or The Truth of the Scripture History of Saint Paul* (1790), *A View of the Evidences of Christianity* (2 volumes, 1794), and *Natural Theology; or Evidences of the Existence and Attributes of the Deity, Collected from the Appearances of Nature* (1802). 1802 was also the year in which the term biology was coined. His *Natural Theology* went through several editions even before he died (in 1805) and has been reprinted many times since then.

When Darwin arrived in Cambridge in 1827, Paley's *Principles* and Paley's *Natural Theology* were still required reading. Darwin said later that Paley's book on God showed him how to think in mechanistic terms. In this Paley was following his master, Newton. Although less mechanistic than Descartes, Newton was a thousand times more mechanistic than Aristotle. Moreover, did not Paley himself insist upon the fact that all things are related to each other, especially in the biosphere? As a result, Darwin worked until he finally got himself a machine to manufacture new species.

In his political philosophy Paley was an individualist, reminiscent of Jeremy Bentham (1748–1832), who was also writing on morals and politics about the same time. Paley opposed taking direct votes on everything. He was also against too much leniency in the penal code. In addition, he was opposed to having an established state religion. He was in favour of whatever was useful and expedient for maintaining law and order. He also favoured civil disobedience when citizens are faced with an oppressive government. But how do we know that the time has come to rebel? He said that this is something each man should decide for himself. He seemed to think that human beings are pretty much on their own; that churches and governments do not necessarily represent the will of God to the people.

In his natural theology, however, Paley sounds very traditional. Unlike the deists, he maintains the continuous presence of divine providence. For him, the world is a complicated piece of machinery, which nevertheless has the constant attention of its maker, just as a human artist looks lovingly upon his artwork. Paley is especially impressed by the machinery of the body. For Paley, science lays the foundation for everything religious. His work concludes with the reassurance that our life is passed in God's constant presence and that death resigns us to God's merciful will.

Paley sees Scientific Design

In his *Natural Theology* Paley proceeds to prove the existence of God in a scientific manner. Although not a scientist himself, Paley wants to systematize the religious implications of the work of the great Newton. In chapter 1, 'State of the Argument', he says that, for all we know, a rock found in a field may have been there forever, but not so for a complicated device such as a pocket watch (Paley, 1819). Recall that the pocket watch was a relatively new invention in his day, having been around only since the early 1700s. Today he would most likely stumble across a laptop personal computer lying in the field.

Regardless of the particular device, however, this way of thinking is in keeping with Newtonian science. Paley assumes Newton's mechanistic world-view and then goes on to compare a small mechanical device (the watch) to a large mechanical device (the universe). It is obvious that both demand an intelligent, purposeful maker. What could be more easy and simple to understand?

This approach has one great advantage for those who want to see what is going on in a physical way, namely, we can see bodies falling toward the earth at a certain fixed rate, the clouds forming in the sky, the rain watering the earth, and so forth. The design of contrivances is obvious. We can actually see with our own eyes neat little machines moving along according to their humanly designed plans. Similarly, we can see the bodies of the universe, great and small, moving along according to their appointed places in the divinely established scheme of things. It also has the advantage of being a very easy analogy to grasp. As in the case of three is to six as five is to x, solving for x is as easy as falling off a log.

Paley then immediately goes on to deal with some possible objections.

- The first objection: I personally (the atheist) do not know how to make a watch. Paley's answer: Such ignorance is your problem and irrelevant to the argument.
- The second objection: Watches are not always precise. Paley's answer: Yes, but mechanical devices, even when they do not always work exactly as desired, still require a purposeful designer.
- The third objection: I do not know the exact purpose of each part. Paley's answer: You may not know exactly how the thing works, but the designer does.
- The fourth objection: A watch is a chance occurrence. Paley's answer: Now that is nonsense. This, of course, is the heart of the matter. Which came first, the chicken or the egg, the caterpillar or the butterfly, the road or the wheel? Paley's main point is that, on the basis of chance alone, neither one could have come first. Later on, Darwin will claim that natural selection was in operation for an almost infinite period of time in order to bring about such wonderful things.

- The fifth objection: The operation of the thing can be explained by an internal principle of watch-orderliness, that is, it arose spontaneously out of its parts because of internal tendencies to do so. Paley's answer: No, a formal principle of watch-ness is not enough; it still needs an efficient cause.
- The sixth objection: The watch is no proof of a maker, but only leads the mind to think so. Paley's answer: This is silly. The interesting thing here is that later Darwin will claim that this is in fact a very serious objection. Maybe the human brain has evolved in such a way as to think things that are not in fact true of the world. However, a rebuttal to Darwin's rebuttal is that such a state of affairs would contradict Darwin's own theory of evolution, since a brain out of tune with reality would be a great disadvantage in the struggle for survival and so would not be preserved.
- The seventh objection: Watch-ness is due solely to the impersonal laws of metallic nature. Paley's answer: Yes, there are stable laws of nature, but where did the laws come from? The very existence of the laws themselves requires the existence of God, the supreme lawgiver.
- The eighth objection: But we know so little about the origins of things. Why not adopt agnosticism, suspend judgment forever, and live in perpetual ignorance? Paley's answer: It is irrational to get ourselves into an all-or-nothing situation. Instead of either knowing everything or knowing nothing, the fact is that we know some things and we do not know other things. It may be the case that there are many things we still do not know, but we still know enough to know that the watch demands a maker.

In chapter 2, 'State of the Argument Continued', Paley increases the pressure on the would-be atheist. He asks us to imagine what we would think if the watch were able to reproduce itself. Imagine little baby watches coming out of the big watches. Amazing! Yet this is what we find happening in even the simplest organisms. The creator of such a thing must also be amazing.

Paley recognizes the fact that time is not a cause of anything. How did you get from here to London? It took a long time. In so far as evolutionary theory depends solely upon long periods of time, it explains nothing. Darwin was also aware of this, which is why he had to have a mechanism for change. And even if a living thing were a self-replicating machine, it could not be the cause of itself. Regardless of how far back we go, there has to be a first support for the chain of cause and effect. If this is true of a simple watch, how much more does it hold for organisms.

Most of Paley's book is devoted to giving detailed accounts of organization and harmony in nature. He systematically goes through the mechanisms of plants and animals, the bones, the muscles, the blood vessels, comparative anatomy, organizations peculiar to some classes of things and not to others, such as the oil glands possessed by birds for the purpose of oiling their feathers, contrivances that anticipate the future, such as, in human beings, teeth being held in reserve until there is a use for them later on, the relations among creatures and the parts of creatures, such as the way the teeth and stomach act like mechanical grinding devices, the compensation of one part for a defect found in another part, such as the short neck of the elephant being balanced by its long nose, the relationship of living and non-living nature, instincts, insects, plants, the elements, and astronomy.

Paley thinks that he would have a case even if there were only one example of design. However, there are countless examples and so the cumulative effect is overwhelming. He says in chapter 6, 'The Argument Cumulative', that the contrivance of the eye would be alone sufficient to support the conclusion that there must be an intelligent creator (Paley, 1819, p. 46). The eye is constructed like a carefully designed telescope. It is arranged with things that allow it to move around, with lubricating devices, and with protective coverings. Combine this information with similar information about the ear and other parts of the body and only a complete fool could possibly deny the need for a supernatural designer of infinite wisdom.

Towards the end of the work, Paley goes on to discuss the traits that God must possess in order to account for his creation. In chapter 23, 'Of the Personality of the Deity', he states that the fact of contrivance proves everything he wants to prove. God must be a personal being with intellect and will. Foresight requires the power to know where you are going before you get there. If we have such power, how much more must God also have such power. Moreover, God cannot be some power within the universe itself or some aspect of the universe, as in pantheism. A machine does not design itself from within; the one who constructs the machine must be outside of it. Once in existence it will operate according to certain laws, but the laws themselves cannot be responsible for the existence of the thing in the first place.

It is interesting to see that in chapter 23 Paley is aware of various theories circulating at the time concerning the possibility that the present state of the biosphere might have come about by means of gradual changes over a long period of time. The leading evolutionary-minded theorists at the time were two French naturalists, namely, Georges Buffon (1707–88) and Jean Baptiste Lamarck (1744–1829), both of whom proposed theories allowing for the gradual emergence of new and modern animal characteristics out of previously existing creatures. Lamarck's *Philosophical Zoology* (1809) was too late for Paley, but Buffon's work was well known during Paley's own lifetime, and the idea of appetency (a desire or willing to change on the part of creatures) was also in circulation before Lamarck's work was published.

Paley, however, rejects all such views. He wonders how the same process of latent forms, supposedly inhering in some primordial creature, combined with the inheritance of acquired traits and the willing of traits into existence by the creatures, could have produced such a vast variety of different creatures now. In addition, many features of present-day creatures could not have come about by means of a gradual process. To develop, by any means, they must first get started, but there is no way that Paley can see that they could have begun in the first place. How, for instance, could a creature without the power of sight have willed sight into existence, or how could it have even wanted to will sight into existence? Will plants ever develop eyes, even given an eternity of time?

Later, in 1844, Robert Chamber's (1802–71) *Vestiges of the Natural History of Creation* was published and went through 14 editions. The *Vestiges* outsold Darwin's work by a large number right up until the end of the century. This was due largely to its religious orientation. In this work Chambers agrees with Paley that it is possible for species, under divine guidance, to change over time (Secord, 2001).

In chapter 26, 'The Goodness of the Deity', Paley says that there is no simple and universal solution to the problem of evil. Yet he does make two main points: one is that in the vast majority of cases where design is detected it produces good results; the second is that in the case of sentient creatures the amount of pleasure received is much greater than the pain suffered. We also have the powers of intelligence and will, powers that go far beyond anything needed for mere biological survival and that provide us with a great deal of pleasure in life. Given the overall picture, God must be all-good. This goodness, says Paley, must be infinite in God because of the incalculably great number of objects upon which it is exercised (Paley, 1819, p. 263). Here, of course, is the rub. Regardless of how great the number of things may be, there is still no proportion between the finite and the infinite.

With respect to evil, it is not the result of design, but is due to various accidents of natural processes, to the abuse of free will, and to the misuse of artefacts. A sickle, for instance, is not designed for cutting off the farmer's hand. Nevertheless, it might do so due to carelessness. Similarly, civil evils, such as the inequalities of social life, are accounted for by the natural process of reproduction. Not surprisingly, Paley sides with the Anglican priest Thomas Malthus (1766–1834) against the French deist Rousseau on the question of the origin of inequality. For the priest, inequality is not caused by man-made institutions and conventions, but rather by too many people in the local population relative to the local food supply. The result is a certain degree of poverty, which in turn necessarily imposes a certain degree of servitude upon the poorer people.

One way to remove these problems, thinks Paley, would be to remove free will. But this would be a cure worse than the disease. In general, the strong passions of man serve a good purpose. Passions go wrong when they are detached from their proper ends. In this regard, Paley disagrees with Hume's view that laziness, for instance, is a pure evil. No, says Paley, it is a mixture of good and evil, as are all human faults. In every community, thinks Paley, because it is a corrective for other bad qualities, there is a large class of people whose idleness is the best quality about them (Paley, 1819, p. 273).

Overall, therefore, although we can access only a part of the universe, we know enough to see that good predominates over evil by a large margin. God's design is benevolent. We live in a happy world after all. The air, earth, and water teem with delightful things. On whichever side he turns his eyes, myriad happy beings crowd in upon his view (Paley, 1819, p. 245).

Later, Darwin will call Paley's optimism a naive illusion. According to Darwin, every part of nature is at war with every other part. The meadow that looks so peaceful on a sunny Summer afternoon is in fact a scene of constant competition in which the losers are doomed to extinction.

The Anthropic Principle

The anthropic principle of more modern times carries Paley's view to a more cosmic level. A careful examination of the whole universe shows us that the earth is exactly the sort of place we need in order to live as human beings. In terms of atmosphere, water supply, climate, protection against cosmic radiation and objects flying through space, and so on, the earth is perfectly situated in the universe and in the solar system for us to survive and prosper. For instance, the magnetic field of the earth offers us very good protection against the powerful stream of plasma that is constantly coming at us from the sun. This arrangement of objects and events could not have been accidental, but was instead deliberately designed by God to give us a decent place to live. With respect to supporting intelligent life, our planet is very likely unique (Rees, 2001).

The typical rebuttal to this approach is in keeping with the Darwinian theory, namely, regardless of what situation developed by accident out of the cosmic dust, the anthropic principle could say that the situation we observe in the world today is perfectly suited to the environment in which we presently find ourselves. So, for instance, if we were closer to the sun, and if we lived comfortably in a much hotter environment, the anthropic principle could say that things were deliberately designed that way by God for our comfort.

Unfortunately for the Darwinians, however, the rebuttal can be turned around. The Darwinian theory is also such that, regardless of what emerges from the cosmic dust, it is in conformity with the theory. Put otherwise, there is no way to perform some confirming experiment that would show that the Darwinian theory is true while some competing theory is false. This, though, is much too convenient for Darwin and not at all in keeping with proper scientific methodology.

Critique of Design by Hume

Hume the Cartesian

In 1707 witchcraft was removed from the British criminal code. In that same year, engineered by businessmen, England and Scotland were forcefully united. At the same time, their two flags were combined into the one English flag of today. This was also a time of intensified anti-Catholic legislation. In 1701

Parliament passed the Act of Settlement, declaring that no one professing the popish faith or who marries someone professing the popish faith could become the monarch of England. In 1711, David Hume was born into this new political and commercial climate.

Hume's mother was the daughter of a high-ranking judge. His father was the laird of a large estate called Ninewells near the town of Chirnside, not too far from Edinburgh. However, as the younger of two brothers, David did not have first claim on the family estate. Although his family thought that the legal profession was suitable to him, Hume was much more devoted to a literary career. He attended the University of Edinburgh, studying the classics and philosophy. In 1734 he went to Bristol to work for a sugar merchant and slave trader, but was soon fired for being too critical of the man's crude language and manners.

Before moving to London, he travelled in France (1734–37), staying for a while at Rheims and at La Flèche in Anjou, where Descartes had attended school. While in Anjou he began writing his chief work, *A Treatise of Human Nature, Being an Attempt to Introduce the Experimental Method of Reasoning into Moral Subjects*, which he published in 1739–40. Hume might have said 'the scientific method', but the terms science and scientific, in their present-day meaning, would not come into use for another 90 years. Regardless of the title, though, the work was a big flop. Hume himself said sadly that it fell stillborn from the press.

Deeply disappointed, Hume returned to Ninewells. In 1744 he applied for a chair in moral philosophy at the University of Edinburgh. He was turned down. In 1745 he became a tutor to the young Marquess of Annandale in England. During the Jacobite Rebellion (July 1745–April 1746) Hume supported the English against the Scots. In 1746 he became the secretary to General Saint Clair, who was supposed to capture French Canada, something that was actually done by Wolfe and Amherst in 1759–60. When the Saint Clair expedition stalled, Hume was made a Judge Advocate to keep him busy. The expedition finally set off to attack the French coast of Brittany, where it was promptly defeated and later ridiculed by Voltaire. Neither could Voltaire understand why anyone would fight and die for a few acres of snow in Canada.

In 1747, under the direction of General Saint Clair, Hume went dressed as an officer on a military mission to Vienna and Turin. In the same year the first part of his *Treatise* was reissued in an abbreviated form under the title of *An Enquiry Concerning Human Understanding*. This work was translated into German in 1756, where it had a great influence on Kant. Hume returned to Scotland in 1749 and lived with his brother for two years. While at Ninewells, he again failed to obtain a teaching position. He did, though, write his *Political Discourses*, *Enquiry Concerning the Principles of Morals*, and began his *Dialogues Concerning Natural Religion*.

Finally, in 1751, Hume grew tired of country life and moved to Edinburgh, the city being the proper place for a man of letters. In 1752 his *Political Discourses*, a revision of the second part of his *Treatise*, was published in

Edinburgh. This work, he said, was the only work that proved to be a success at the time of its first publication. In the same year he published his *Enquiry Concerning the Principles of Morals* in London, a revision of the third part of his *Treatise*, and which he considered the best of all his works. At the time, however, it was hardly noticed.

He was, though, given the position of librarian in the University of Edinburgh law school. This allowed him to begin his long *History of England* (1753–61), a work that was very biased in many ways. At the beginning of the first volume of the *History*, Hume published a brief autobiography. Later editions also carried a letter praising Hume written by Adam Smith, written after Hume's death.

By now Hume was becoming known as a literary figure in England, which was his aim all along. However, his growing fame also brought down on him the criticism of those who could see that his views as basically atheistic and dangerous to the state. Among those leading the attack on Hume was William Warburton (1698–1779), who served as the chaplain to King George II (1683–1760), and who was rewarded by being appointed bishop of Gloucester in 1760. Warburton was friends with Alexander Pope (1688–1744), with whom he collaborated in editing the works of Shakespeare. He was also a strong defender of the Church of England and adamant in his rejection of deism.

Needless to say, Hume despised Warburton. In his autobiography he went out of his way to verbally assail the whole clan of Warburtonians, who were lambasted for their illiberal petulance, arrogance, and scurrility. The fact is that Hume had no use for any organized religion, whether pagan or non-pagan. He rejected all shrines, relics, and worship services. He thought that all religion was a 'con game'; a way of extracting money from ignorant people under false pretences. Primarily in the context of Judao-Christianity, despite religion's claim to being essentially a relationship between the people and God, with all of the money aspects being accidental to it, Hume thought that the primary interest of religious professionals was economic. Would religious leaders remain interested if they could not use religion to make money?

In 1763 Hume accompanied Lord Herford, the ambassador to France, to Paris, where he met many of the French materialists, such as Denis Diderot, whom he admired so much because of their deism and atheism. He also met Rousseau, who had been expelled from Bern, Switzerland. In 1766 Rousseau returned to England with Hume, living with Hume at his house in Wotton, Derbyshire. However, the arrangement was short-lived because of Rousseau's mental and physical problems, which were becoming more severe. Their living together in the same house also caused an international scandal for a while.

After a stay in Edinburgh, Hume became an under-secretary of state to Lord Herford in London. In 1769 he retired to Edinburgh, where he became friends with Adam Smith (1723–90), the deistic philosopher of modern capitalism. In the Spring of 1775 Hume became ill with some disorder of the bowels, leading to constant diarrhoea, and died the following Summer (1776).

The exact cause of death is unknown. After his death, Hume was praised by Smith as a man of cheerfulness and of great frugality, but not stinginess. Smith considered him to be a perfectly wise and virtuous man. (See Mossner, 1954.)

In philosophy Hume is best known for his attack on the objective reality of the cause–effect relationship (Hume, 1961). How does one prove an idiosyncratic theory that runs contrary to commonsense experience? One appeals to Descartes. Although he claims to base his conclusions on experience, the experience he is referring to is, following Descartes, the experience of his own ideas. For Hume, the relationship between cause and effect, and therefore the relationship between God and the world, is restricted to the mind. According to Hume, the appearance of one sense impression, because of its long association with others, determines me to bring up another sense impression, from which I get the false impression of a necessary connection between them as something outside the mind. His deduction can be summarized in a series of syllogisms. The first major premise is a restatement of Descartes' Reversal.

- Whatever is logically separated (clear and distinct) intra-mentally is separated extra-mentally.
- All causes and effects are logically separated (clear and distinct) intra-mentally.
- Ergo, all causes and effects are separated extra-mentally.

No knowledge less evident to us than our knowledge of the world can give us a knowledge of causality.

- All knowledge of God is such.
- Ergo, no knowledge of God can give us a knowledge of causality.

- All arrangements of perceptions are only within the mind.
- All knowledge of causality is an arrangement of perceptions.
- Ergo, all knowledge of causality is only within the mind.

- Anything based on the knowledge of causality is only within the mind.
- All reasoning to God is based on the knowledge of causality.
- Ergo, all reasoning to God is only within the mind.

The upshot of his reasoning was a scepticism concerning our ability to know anything about human destiny. Looking to the past (antecedent scepticism), Hume could find no absolutely indubitable first principle upon which to base all reasoning leading to equally secure truths about nature, man, and God. Descartes, with respect to the content of his philosophy, was certainly wrong when he thought that he had discovered an indubitable mind-substance. Looking to the present and future (consequent scepticism), we cannot even be sure about the connection of our sense impressions and things outside the mind. We do not know things; we know only faded sense impressions (ideas) of things. We can never be sure that the idea we have of something is an accurate representation of the extra-mental thing itself.

Hume, however, failed to question his own (Cartesian) presuppositions. His reasoning is not based on actual human experience, but is, instead, from beginning to end, a deduction based upon the authority of previous thinkers. If Hume had not been such an amateur philosopher he would have questioned the approach of going from the idea of something to the reality of something. It is fantasy to claim that mental abstractions can cause real things to happen in the real world. However, in Hume's terminology, only vulgar people reject Descartes' Reversal. As a common person, when your car hits a tree, you (and the insurance company) think that the real front end of your car is smashed in by a real tree. You know that an intra-mental idea of a car cannot be smashed in and that an intra-mental idea of a tree cannot smash in anything. Not so for Hume, who rejected the path of commonsense and facts and adopted instead the path of the Cartesians (Prichard, 1970; see also Centore, 1991, appendix).

Nevertheless, his deductive powers did serve his overall purpose very well. His real love was the atomistic doctrine of Epicurus. Atomism, though, is not a simple doctrine. It does in fact contain many strange twists and turns. The atoms themselves, for instance, cannot be sensed, pictured, or experienced in any way. Quite reasonably, as the explanatory principles of what we do experience, the atoms cannot have any of the properties they are supposed to explain. This is the case despite the fact that the atoms are supposed to be 3D material entities.

Another strange feature of ancient atomism is the way it handles the motions of bodies. As we see from Epicurus' *Letter to Herodotus*, outlining the atomistic view, all atoms move at the same speed. The fact of different speeds for different bodies is a function of the net speeds of all the atoms that compose the different bodies as the atoms constantly collide with each other within the bodies. As they move, the imperceptible atoms must cross in succession units of space, with the result that continuous motion is really a series of imperceptible discrete motions, like a modern-day film strip. In addition to Epicurus' practical atheism, this view of motion matches up perfectly with Hume's contention that all cause–effect connections outside the mind are illusions. In reality, they are merely a series of still-shots as one perception or idea follows another within the mind (Pyle, 1997, p. 34).

Hume and the Superior Being

Paley was caught in a vice. With Hume on one side and Darwin on the other, the combined pressure pulverized poor Paley. The standard rebuttal to the scientific design-type argument was given by Hume even before Paley wrote his famous work. Later on, it was repeated by John Stuart Mill (1806–73). Hume points out that the scientific design argument must fail because it does not arrive at the God of religion. According to Hume's rebuttal, Paley, who wanted to harmonize science with his preaching from the pulpit, could not guarantee the matching up of the two. As far as Hume can see, Paley's creator is much too anthropomorphic, finite, and imperfect to be useful for religious purposes in a Judao-Christian context. To make matters worse, could the world have been made by a committee (polytheism)? To Hume this is obviously not the best of all possible worlds and the God of science need be no more perfect than the perfection of the universe. In addition, maybe the whole world is one great living organism, with God as the world-soul.

Hume's most sustained criticism of the scientific design argument, which he calls the cosmological argument, is found in his *Dialogues Concerning Natural Religion* (Hume, 1947). This work was revised during has mature years, but not published until after his death. Hume is especially concerned with the problem of evil. Nevertheless, as Hume himself admits, if the existence of the Judao-Christian God could be proven by some airtight scientific argument, then he would have to admit that all of his problems with the existence of evil were really of secondary importance. Hume, though, is absolutely certain that such a proof cannot be found. Those who try it are forced to proceed on the basis of cause and effect. They must move from the world of sense perceptions and ideas (which are merely faded sense impressions) to a world that is beyond all such material manifestations. Such a move, however, is rationally unfounded. Even though it may work internally, the principle of causality cannot apply to the world of real things outside the mind.

Certainly in his *Dialogues* Hume has in mind his critique of the principle of causality when he has his mouthpiece (Philo) say that, if the existence and providence of God could be proven by some means other than the cosmological argument, such as by defining God into existence as was done by Anselm and Descartes (the term ontological argument had not yet been invented by Kant), then he would have to admit that evil and God could be reconciled in some mysterious way. However, he is absolutely certain that such a thing cannot be done. The most such an approach could ever accomplish would be a series of intra-mental hypotheses and postulates, perhaps consistent among themselves, which would forever circulate within the mind, leading nowhere as far as anything extra-mental is concerned.

Hume, though, has more to say on the subject. Feeling his strength, he moves the attack into the very centre of the enemy camp. Let's assume, he says, just for the sake of argument, that the existence of God can be proven on the basis of the universe as one large machine. In the end, what sort of God would such a world-machine require? Is the world perfect? Is this really the best of all possible worlds? Are all the parts of the universe in harmony with each other? Is there a perfect adaptation of each and every creature to its environment? Are human beings free of all disease and stress? The answer to all these questions is no. Hence, even if we assume the need for a creator, the creator need not be any more perfect than the product created. The cause need not exceed the perfection of the effect. On the basis of the observed universe, the creator would be non-infinite, non-perfect, and a being limited in power, knowledge, and providence. Such is the God of the scientists. Consequently, the God of religion cannot be found.

All three of the participants (theist, agnostic, atheist) in Hume's *Dialogues* agree that the world is full of war, hunger, poverty, fear, anxiety, terror, weakness, distress, agony, horror, abuse, torture, destruction, pain, misery, oppression, tyranny, contempt, sedition, treachery, fraud, disease, remorse, shame, rage, rape, dejection, woe, and despair. True, there are some good aspects to life, but that is not the point. The main point is that such a limited world does not need a supreme being, but only a somewhat superior being.

Or could we say that the imperfect world was made by a team of gods (polytheism), with various gods working on different parts of the universe? Then again, maybe the universe is comparable to a huge body and God is comparable to the soul of the body, a world-soul, as among the ancient Stoics, for whom the soul, even though made of very fine material, is nevertheless a material substance. Maybe the world is not like a man-made machine at all, but more like a nature-made plant or animal. Maybe orderliness is the result of a self-ordering process built into matter. Or could the material world have been created by an evil demon or god? Hume does not think that this evil demon theory is likely. The material world, after all, is not so much out to get us as it is completely indifferent to us. He is even willing to consider a theory in which God is changing and developing with the world, the view of process philosophy and theology.

In any event, the notion of God as the author of nature, the great engineer and mathematician in the sky, is useless from the viewpoint of traditional religion. The most we can deduce from the evidence of nature is that God is a very anthropomorphic being, a big man who somehow managed to make an imperfect and very finite universe. So in the end the Scotsman thinks that he has emerged victorious over the naive traditional believer. It is not God who is the necessary being, but the material universe as a whole. It is simply a brute fact.

Such a world is governed by the iron-clad laws of nature, revealed to us by scientific investigation. This rules out the possibility of miracles. As soon as we hear anything concerning the miraculous we know that the speaker is either honestly mistaken or, more likely, a lying con artist. This position serves Hume well. It relieves him of the responsibility of investigating individual events claimed to be miraculous. We know from the simplest form of logic that if the universal proposition is true then the corresponding particular proposition must also be true. Thus, knowing that all men are mortal tells us that some men are mortal. Knowing that all perpetual motion machines are impossible tells us that this one is impossible. Likewise, by assuming that all miracles are impossible, Hume can also assert that some miracles are impossible. He can now immediately reject any particular claim concerning a miracle.

Although some people claim that Hume is a thoroughgoing sceptic, in fact he is not a sceptic in every way. He certainly is not a sceptic with respect to the philosophy of nature. He knows for sure what the world really is. Reality is nothing more nor less than a vast collection of atoms moving about in space, just as the ancient atomists, such as Epicurus, had said. The whole of section 11, the penultimate in Hume's *Enquiry Concerning Human Understanding*, is devoted to this view. His main points are that atomism is basically correct, especially as it relates to the denial of God's traditional mode of existence and providence, and that this does not pose any great threat either to personal morals or to being a good citizen (Hume, 1962).

As part of an imaginary conversation between Epicurus and the Athenian people, Hume takes the side of the Athenians, who accuse Epicurus of atheism because he will not agree that the existence and providence of God can be known by reasoning on the basis of the orderliness of the natural universe. The core of the response made by Epicurus is that he is not interested in asserting atheism, but only in showing that the existence and providence of God, when defined in a supernatural monotheistic sense, cannot be established by an appeal to the orderliness and excellence of nature as studied in science, even if we use as our guide the work of the best scientists, such as the incomparable Newton.

At the end of the response given by Epicurus, Hume says that Epicurus, by having Hume stand in for the Athenian people, had insinuated himself into Hume's heart by embracing the very same principles to which Hume himself had always expressed a strong attachment. Thus, by talking to himself out loud, Hume lets us in on his own position. If God exists at all, it is only as a superior being who abandoned the world long ago. As with Protagoras and Epicurus in ancient times, of the gods Hume knows nothing. Consequently, when it comes to morals, we are on our own.

Hume and Morality

Hume also defends Epicurus elsewhere, especially with respect to moral virtue. For example, in Hume's *An Enquiry Concerning the Principles of Morals*, appendix II, concerned with the topic of self-love, he goes out of his way to defend Epicurus against the charge of being a bad citizen because of his practical atheism. Atheism, some say, fosters only self-gratification and is thus bad for society. Not so, says Hume. Even though a materialist, you need not necessarily be selfish and suspected of treason at every turn. In fact, Epicurus and his followers were not strangers to love and honour (Hume, 1938).

Even though all virtue reduces to pleasure and all vice reduces to pain, we can still have standards of morality. Our motive for acting is to gain pleasure and avoid pain. The content of our actions, though, must be determined by what works out well for the preservation of individual life and society. My own continued pleasure depends upon the continued pleasure of others. There is such a thing as enlightened self-interest. Recall that, among all of his works, Hume regarded this *Enquiry* as his best work.

The same point is made by Hume in his *Dialogues Concerning Natural Religion*. Hume will not allow his hero to be smeared with the label of immorality, especially if morality is defined in a Judao-Christian way. Toward the end of the *Dialogues*, in part XII, Philo, the one who loves and who represents Hume himself, argues in favour of the true religion, which is a rationalized religion, in opposition to the usual superstitious stuff of the common (vulgar) man in the street, as represented by the sincere but naive Demea. The conversation comes around to asking about what sort of thing is really most useful for ensuring that people behave well in society. Hume declares that it is not the superstitions of the vulgar masses.

In the opinion of the Scotsman, the vast majority of those who go around asserting their great religiosity are in fact great hypocrites. What really controls social behaviour is not a belief in some unseen God. What really motivates us is the pleasure we derive from participating in the solemnity of the occasion, the regard for one's own reputation, and reflection by the individual on what is best for himself as an individual and what is needed in order to have a society in which he can live safely. These are all natural forces. They are the impression made upon the untutored by pomp and circumstance, the power of public opinion, and enlightened self-interest. He thinks that the state could take away traditional religion and everything would go on as usual. The real forces establishing law and order would continue to operate. Consequently, even though Hume favours the ancient doctrine of the Epicureans over that of the Church of England, he should not be looked down upon as an anarchist fit for public punishment.

Hume had already made the same points in his *Treatise of Human Nature*. Book I (*Of the Understanding*) was devoted to showing that, of the gods, we know nothing. Book II (*Of the Passions*), dealing with the passions, emotions, and will, was devoted to showing the continuity of men and animals, the central role of physical pleasure and pain in determining what is good and bad, and the superiority of the passions over reason. Hume wanted to say that we are all alike in our physical, political, and social needs, and that freedom of choice is an illusion. The human mind and will, just like the rest of the material world, is determined. Freedom can mean only that we are freed of physical constraints, thus allowing the determinations of the will to run their course. As he asserted in Book II, part II ('Of the Will and Direct Passions'), section 1 ('Of Liberty and Necessity'), since the mind is as much a material thing as a falling rock, it would be absurd to say that the one (the rock) acts out of necessity and that the other (the mind) does not. Thinking that the mind is the brain, many today hold the view that religious belief is only some sort of electrical activity in the brain. Can the same be said about science and ethics?

Just as Book I sets up Book II, so Book II sets up Book III, the last dealing with morals. With no certitude concerning God, what can we use as a basis for making moral decisions? Nothing but tradition (custom). What about nature? No, nature cannot be used as a moral guide substituting for God. Nature is the way things are in a factual way. It does not tell us about the way things ought to be. The 'ought' cannot be derived from the 'is'. As we learn from his *Treatise*, Book III (*Of Morals*), part I ('Of Virtue and Vice in General'), section 2 ('Moral Distinctions Derived from a Moral Sense'), there are three possible definitions for nature. Nature can mean

1   that which is opposed to miracles;
2   that which is opposed to the rare and unusual; or
3   that which is opposed to the artificial.

None of these can be used as a foundation for morals. They all have to do with what is the case. Moreover, the first one is too broad to be useful as a definition, while the second and third are too highly variable to be useful for guiding action. Consequently, for Hume, there cannot be any sort of natural moral law governing human behaviour.

The only thing left to do, then, is to simply state the facts. We are creatures of feeling, sentiment, compassion, and sympathy. We plan ahead and act with purpose. Man is the inventive species. Such behaviour is an inherent part of our human constitution. However, although we, as a part of nature, naturally act in certain preordained ways, the exact content of our decisions is not preordained. There are no eternal and unchanging laws of moral behaviour. In this sense, all morality is artificial.

Yet, for Hume, the process of moral decision making, even though a contrivance of mankind for maintaining society, is not completely arbitrary. In his *Treatise*, Book III, part II ('Of Justice and Injustice'), section 1 ('Justice, Whether a Natural or Artificial Virtue?'), Hume says that by 'the natural' he means option number 3 above; that is, something opposed to the artificial. Inventing things, however, including morals, is not itself an arbitrary invention. Hume thinks that, in contrast to what we find in the animal world, concocting artificial things is natural to us. We must invent, but what we invent can vary. Thus, the rules of social justice can be artificial (invented, customary, conventional) without being arbitrary.

For Hume, there must always be some standard to guide human behaviour. You cannot have a moral system that sanctions egotism, selfishness, and do-your-own-thing regardless of its effect on others. Sooner or later our practical needs will assert themselves. Utility is the rule; survival is the law. The constants of human nature are sympathy and cooperation with each other and with the world of nature in order to survive and prosper. The exact way in which these tendencies are actualized, though, will vary. The main point is that human activity will always gravitate towards the same central core of moral values and practices, which happen to be those of his own middle-class English society. Thus, like it or not, Hume finds himself drawn back to a non-subjective nature for some form of social stability.

If we are to have a human moral system conducive to human survival and adaptation, it is obvious that we cannot be completely arbitrary in what we do. By emphasizing this point, many modern atheists, such as the pragmatists, think that they can avoid the charge of being absolute relativists in moral matters. In this regard, they take their lead from the master, who claimed that the major social virtues are meekness, beneficence, charity, generosity, clemency, moderation, and equity. If you want to live well in society, then you had better adopt these virtues. And if the individual cannot bring himself to do so, then the state has every right to force them on him by means of law and education. Given Hume's completely disintegrated view of the world, such coercion is the best he can do in morals.

However, Hume's best is not good enough. Hume is right about the lack of morality in irrational nature. Morality enters in only when there are beings made in the image of God. Such beings possess the powers of intellect and free choice, that is, such beings are personal beings. This is something Hume's system cannot accept. To do so would cause his whole system to fall apart. Consequently, he really has no objective basis for the moral system that he so desperately wants to maintain.

Critique of Paley by Darwin

Darwin the Naturalist

Charles Darwin is one of the leading figures of the Victorian Era in Britain. Named after Queen Victoria (1819–1901), this era is usually described as being marked by prudery, bigotry, and hypocrisy. The Victorians were supposed to be particularly uptight about sex. This, though, is all hindsight. The Victorians saw themselves as living a life of great stability. However, under the surface, things were becoming more and more undone. According to Chesterton, many of the things that existed in the age were anything but 'Victorian'. Its solid respectability was in fact shot full of holes. The Church of England was dying, with the result that people were expected to worship the home without the altar. Morality was quickly becoming arbitrary, which is to say that it was quickly becoming tyrannical. The British Empire was breaking down into many little empires, each one of which was a law unto itself. As expressed by Chesterton in his *Autobiography*:

> Tyrants, religious or irreligious, turn up anywhere. But this type of tyrant was the product of the precise moment when a middle-class man still had children and servants to control; but no longer had creeds or guilds or kings or priests or anything to control him. He was already an anarchist to those above him; but still an authoritarian to those below. (Chesterton, 1937, p. 28)

Darwin was born in Shrewsbury, in Shropshire, near the border with Wales, in February 1809. His family, headed by Robert Waring Darwin (1766–1848), a medical doctor who did not believe in bleeding as a method of treating disease, was well-off. His grandfather was Erasmus Darwin (1731–1802), a very fat and very prosperous physician who had met with James Watt (1736–1819), Joseph Priestley (1733–1804, who discovered oxygen in 1774), Rousseau, and Samuel Johnson. Erasmus Darwin held a view of species development comparable to that of Jean Baptiste Lamarck, which said that animals change by willing themselves to be adapted to their changing environments. All of the naturalists at the time said this because it is obvious that the parts of nature act in a purposeful way. Yet, because he thought it was opposed to the mechanistic philosophy of nature, this is exactly the sort of thing Charles Darwin would later come to reject. Newton's mechanistic view of the material world was, after all, the correct view.

Erasmus was also the grandfather of Francis Galton (1822–1911), Charles's first cousin and the founder of the eugenics movement in England. His grandfather on his mother's side was Josiah Wedgwood (1730–95), a businessman of note. Charles's mother, Susannah Wedgwood (1765–1817), was Unitarian while his father was Church of England. Charles attended services with his mother until, when he was eight-years-old, she died. After that he was cared for by his eldest sister, Caroline (1800–88), nine years his senior, and went to church with his father. Charles was named after an uncle, his father's brother (1758–78), who had died young from an infection contracted while dissecting the brain of a dead child. Darwin always had a great respect for his family, saying that his father was the wisest man that he ever knew.

Darwin attended the local schools and then, starting when he was 16-years-old, spent two years in Edinburgh trying his hand at becoming a physician. Deciding that the medical profession was for him, he transferred in 1827 to Christ's College, Cambridge, where Paley was still very fashionable, and obtained a BA in 1831, even though he enjoyed partying and sports more than studying. While there he corresponded with his cousin William Fox, an entomologist interested in collecting beetles. He thought at the time that he might be happy making a living as a country clergyman. In the same year, he spent three weeks with Adam Sedgwick (1785–1873), a Christ's College professor of geology, on a walking tour of North Wales.

Although his father opposed the trip, Darwin's life was changed forever when he was talked into becoming the unpaid naturalist aboard the ship HMS Beagle by one of his college teachers, John Stevens Henslow (1796–1861), a professor of botany and mineralogy. This trip, ordered by the British admiralty for the purpose of mapping the entire coast of South America, began in December 1831 and lasted until October 1836. The mission ended up sailing all the way around the world. On the trip he read the newly published first volume of Charles Lyell's (1797–1875) *Principles of Geology*, which rejected catastrophism in favour of uniformitarianism. Darwin did not study Thomas Malthus's (1766–1834) *An Essay on the Principle of Population* (1798) until 1838.

Concerning uniformitarianism, today we know that the earth has been visited by periodic catastrophes, resulting in the mass extinctions of life, thus leaving too little time for evolution to take place by means of natural selection. Modern knowledge also raises another problem, this time for environmentalists. The existence of pollution presupposes that the earth is a place that cannot change very much without being destroyed. However, if Darwin were right, there would be no need to worry about pollution. In the long run, everything would adjust and adapt to whatever pollution occurs and so life would continue, on average, getting better and better.

HMS Beagle made numerous stops along the way, allowing Darwin to observe the primitive people living in Terra del Fuego at the southmost tip of South America, the finches with differently shaped beaks living in different parts of the Galapagos Islands, and the many varieties of plants and animals on the mainland. Darwin kept scientific notes, as well as a diary, and one wonders what he was doing ashore during those times when several pages in the diary are blank. Somewhere along the way he picked up an infectious tropical disease that caused him recurring problems for the rest of his life. This, though, he said was a good thing, because it kept him working at home instead of living the high life in London.

A few years after his return home, in January 1839, Charles married his first cousin Emma Wedgwood (1808–96). Emma was superficially an Anglican, but really a Unitarian, Unitarianism being the religion of the Wedgwood family. Emma was well educated, and had even taken piano lessons from Chopin. She was a regular church-goer, whose favourite poem was Tennyson's *In Memoriam A.H.H.* In 1842 the family moved to Down House, in the town of Down, Kent, 16 miles south of London. In order to avoid confusing the postal services, in about 1850 the spelling of the town's name was changed to Downe to distinguish it from County Down in Ireland. The house was a large place, complete with nine servants. Charles was a good husband and father, but, as was the middle-class custom, there was no doubt about who was the boss of the family (Healey, 2001).

Fortunately, the Darwin family had no money problems. Emma already had money given to her while her father (Josiah II, 1769–1843) was alive and that she also inherited after his death. And, when Charles's father died in 1848, he was left a large sum of money, along with some valuable real estate and business stocks, enough for the family to continue living in comfort for a long time. Down House, which Charles continued to expand and improve over the years, has now become a shrine for evolutionists.

True to his theory, within 16 years Emma and Charles had ten children, two of whom died in infancy from birth defects, and one of whom, his second child, Annie Elizabeth, died of scarlet fever in 1851 when she was 10-years-old. Darwin was brokenhearted over his daughter's death. How could God allow such a thing to happen? Nevertheless, to his credit, unlike many modern evolutionists who want both birth control and evolutionary advancement at the same time, Darwin did not attempt to sever sex from reproduction.

How else could the biosphere progress? There must be a large number of living things vying for survival. In this way progress is guaranteed. As the less well-adapted specimens are lopped off through extinction, and the better-adapted ones go on to reproduce in large numbers, the overall average of adaptation is guaranteed to increase. Thus does the biosphere necessarily progress to higher and higher levels of adaptation. Consequently, Darwin was opposed to birth control.

As we see, this was not because Darwin was a Christian. If he was religious at all it was as a deist. How did things get started? Maybe in the beginning God created the world and the first little living cells, but then God abandoned the world. The alternative to God's creative power would be to insist that living things could arise from non-living material stuff, a doctrine known as spontaneous generation. Unfortunately for the strict materialists, this doctrine was being disproved even as Darwin himself was becoming more and more deistic. This advance in science, however, did not prevent some of Darwin's disciples from insisting that spontaneous generation was not only possible in the beginning, but a fact of nature even now in the present (Strick, 2000).

Since there was no sexual reproduction in the beginning of things, Darwin could not admit a God-given purpose for sex. He could, though, admit an unthinking purpose for sex in the form of reproduction. As he says in chapter 1, 'The Evidence of the Descent of Man From Some Lower Form', of his *Descent of Man*, the most important biological function is the reproduction of the species, which is strikingly the same in all mammals, from the first act of courtship by the male, to the birth and nurturing of the young (Darwin, *The Origin of Species, The Descent of Man, and Selection in Relation to Sex*, n.d., p. 397). Darwin sees that natural selection needs something to work on, which is the body of the new creature entering the world. Consequently, a true atheistic evolutionist has many children. The squire of Down House felt strongly the attraction of ripe young women and strong young men itching for sex. Earlier, in his *M* notebook of 1838, p. 71, Darwin asks why both bulls and horses, animals of different orders, turn up their nostrils when excited by love. It must be that the stallion licking the udders of the mare is strictly analogous to men's affection for women's breasts (Gruber and Barrett, 1974; see also Darwin, 1990).

Taking God out of the picture also had the advantage of not having anyone to blame as all those bodies struggled to survive in a world of limited resources. Do we blame the wolf for attacking sheep? Do we blame the car for running out of fuel? Do we blame the computer when we push the wrong buttons? No one is personally at fault for the conflicts among human beings. It is simply nature taking its course.

One must wonder, though, was Darwin philosophically naive? If every living thing, including a human being, is a mistake of the DNA replication process, regurgitated up out of the primeval slime, then why is one person of any importance at all? Judging by the way they keep becoming extinct, even whole species are of no great significance. How much less significant must be an individual within a species. The feeling that someone is important must therefore be peculiar to the subjective emotions of a particular individual.

Why, then, could not someone else regard Annie as a thing of no significance and, with a clear conscience, dispose of her in any way he saw fit? And besides, even though Darwin himself knew nothing of DNA, we today can ask: where did DNA come from in the first place? In the same way we could ask why there are any sexes at all, or why there are only two sexes rather than 22, or 102?

During the 1840s Darwin was thinking evolution, although he refused to use the term 'evolution', for the very good reason that it meant just the opposite of what he wanted to convey. It was an ancient word, meaning to unroll a scroll and read the contents; that is, it meant discovering something that was already there. Darwin wanted a system that would produce something really new. He finally did use the term in the sixth edition (January 1872) of his *Origin of Species* to mean a slow change as opposed to a fast change (a revolution). The important point for Darwin was not the fact of change but the means of change. There was nothing new about the notion of constant change and the constant struggle to survive. Alfred Lord Tennyson (1809–92) had already read some of the pre-Darwinian evolutionists and had incorporated such evolutionary notions into his *In Memoriam A.H.H.*, sections 50 and 51, written in the mid-1840s.

> Are God and Nature then at strife,
>   That Nature lends such evil dreams?
>   So careful of the type she seems,
> So careless of the single life, ...
>
> 'So careful of the type?' but no,
>   From scraped cliff and quarried stone
>   She cries, 'A thousand types are gone;
> I care for nothing, all shall go ...
>
> 'Thou makest thine appeal to me:
>   I bring to life, I bring to death;
>   The spirit does not mean the breath:
> I know no more.' And he, shall he,
>
> Man, her last work, who seemed so fair,
>   Such splendid purpose in his eyes,
>   Who rolled the psalm in wintry shies,
> Who built him fanes of fruitless prayer,
>
> Who trusted God was love indeed
>   And love Creation's final law
>   Though Nature, red in tooth and claw
> With ravine, shrieked against his creed,

> Who loved, who suffered countless ills,
>   Who battled for the True, the Just,
>   Be blown about the desert dust,
> Or sealed within the iron hills?
>
> No more? A monster then, a dream,
>   A discord. Dragons of the prime,
>   That tear each other in their slime,
> Were mellow music matched with him.

Charles was also doing some reading. He had read David Hume and was impressed by his materialistic view of things. After he had returned from his long sea voyage, Charles had also written up notebooks containing his speculations. In addition, in the 1840s and 1850s, he had written up more extensive outlines of his theory. His main problem was finding a mechanistic method that would, without any planning or foresight, automatically lead to the production of new and better species. He wanted nothing to do with mind or with things willing their way to higher levels of perfection.

It is not as if the fossil record was unknown and had to be discovered by Darwin. He himself actually did very little along that line. In fact, educated people were well aware of fossils a long time before Darwin. Indeed, the general pattern of the fossil record was well established in the early 1830s. And, as Darwin himself knew very well, it did not support his theory. He hoped, though, that with intensified searching, the fossil record would support his theory in the future. As a matter of fact, however, as those backing punctuated equilibria know, it has not.

In June 1858 Darwin was forced to act decisively when he received a long letter from Indonesia written by Alfred Russel Wallace (1823–1913) outlining a theory of natural selection the same as his own. The question then arose concerning who should get credit for the theory. The issue was especially important for Darwin because Wallace was much more religious than Darwin. Wallace thought that at least the main divisions of the things in nature (mineral, plant, animal, man) could not have arisen by means of natural selection and therefore required the intervention of God. Some years later, in 1879, Darwin helped secure a government pension for Wallace. Still later, Wallace was one of the pallbearers at Darwin's funeral. (See Fothergill, 1952; see also Raby, 2001.)

Thus, under pressure, Darwin quickly revised an 1844 outline of his own. In July 1858 both Wallace's letter and Darwin's outline were read to the Linnean Society of London and immediately published in its journal with Darwin listed as the senior author, thus assuring Darwin's priority. In November of the next year *The Origin of Species by Means of Natural Selection and the Preservation of Favored Races in the Struggle of Life* was published and sold out quickly. That same year (1859) also saw the publication of Charles Dickens's *A Tale of Two Cities*, John Stuart Mill's *On Liberty*, and Newman's

The Idea of a University. It was also the year in which Claude Monet and Camille Pissarro first met in Paris.

Very soon the *Origin* was criticized by Darwin's old teacher, Sedgwick, who accused Darwin of abandoning the inductive path of true science. In other words, Darwin was attempting to make the facts fit the theory rather than vice versa. Darwin was also guilty of violating the spirit of the great Newton by separating science and morality. Just as quickly, others lined up on the other side. In June 1860 in Oxford, Thomas Henry Huxley (1825–95), known as Darwin's bulldog, got into an argument with the Anglican bishop Samuel Wilberforce (1805–73) over whether or not our ancestors were monkeys. Wilberforce was the son of William Wilberforce (1759–1833), a long-time member of Parliament who supported more freedom for Catholics and who had led the attack against slavery in the British Empire.

Darwin's most able critic, however, was a fellow Englishman with the odd name of Saint George Jackson Mivart (1827–1900), a very knowledgeable naturalist in his own right, whose work *On the Genesis of Species* (1871) showed that Darwin's theory contained internal contradictions. Assuming that some slight change is preserved because it is advantageous to the creature at the time of its first appearance, no complicated organ or process would have ever developed. In cases without number, a complicated organ is only useful when all of its parts are present and working together simultaneously. Anything less and it would be useless. In fact, in its initial stages, the new organ or process would probably be deadly to the creature. Yet Darwin's theory says that the initial tiny variations would have been preserved anyway. Regardless of his talk to the contrary, therefore, Darwin must think in terms of an intelligent planner arranging parts with purpose and foresight. Although Darwin refused to give up his main thesis, Mivart's critique forced Darwin to extensively rewrite and add to his *Origin* in later editions.

Interestingly, this sort of critique has not gone away. In fact, it has become more telling. In our own day, following on from a vast increase in our knowledge of biological processes, more powerful objections to the notion of accidental yet fortuitous developments have been uncovered in organs and processes. The clotting of blood, for example, is something that could not have come about by accident over a long period of time in a series of tiny steps. After a trauma, some chemical changes take place that anticipate other changes that have not yet occurred. The complicated cascade of chemical changes possess foresight. There is no way a rational thinker could explain this fact by means of natural selection. There are many such cases (Behe, 1996; see also Behe, Dembski and Meyer, 2000).

Also, it was obvious to everyone that Darwin's common descent with modification by means of natural selection must apply to everything, including human beings, but no one wrote a book on the subject. So, in 1871, Darwin published his own book, *The Descent of Man and Selection in Relation to Sex*, with a second edition in 1874. The part on sexual selection, a book in itself, is significant because it marks a partial turning away from natural selection as the engine for species change. In the process of sexual selection, it may not always be the case that the new feature is directly related to immediate survival. In fact, in many cases, such as bright and extravagant plumage in a bird species possessed only by the male, the secondary sex characteristic is harmful to the animal. To a predator, the poor thing sticks out like a sore thumb.

For the rest of his life, while he continued to work on other studies and projects related to evolution, Darwin maintained a keen interest in who was converting to his new religion. From May to August 1876 he wrote a brief autobiography. His last work was a study of earthworms. He died quietly at Down House in April 1882, survived by two daughters, five sons, and his beloved Emma. During his lifetime, Queen Victoria, having a higher regard for her dogs than for Darwin, refused to grant him a knighthood. Right after his death, though, Parliament passed a special law granting him an elaborate funeral and allowing him to be buried among England's finest in Westminster Abbey. While in Downe, Darwin became an avid smoker, was active in civic affairs, served as treasurer of the village school and as Justice of the Peace, contributed to Christian charities on a regular basis, attacked slavery and vivisection, and in 1879 wrote a biography of his grandfather, Erasmus. As a gentleman, Darwin was opposed to any form of cruelty towards man or beast.

Being philosophically naive, though, he never appreciated the moral consequences of his work. When Mivart tried to tell him about the moral implications of his theory, Darwin became angry and vowed to never speak to Mivart again. Darwin, you see, was an English gentleman who sincerely believed that, regardless of what he might say, everything would carry on as usual. He was even willing to live with religion. Unlike Huxley, who was rabidly anti-Catholic, Darwin did not believe in open warfare with religion. Being a 'freethinker', Darwin was willing to tolerate even those who criticized his new doctrine, all, that is, except that Catholic convert Mivart. (See Desmond and Moore, 1991, p. 436; see also Browne, 2002.)

Nevertheless, Darwin's mechanism was a sure prescription for social trouble. First of all, the theory is racist; some species are favoured and some are not. With respect to Blacks, for instance, Darwin concludes in his *Descent of Man*, after a comparison of Whites and Blacks, that Blacks are a subspecies of the loosely conceptualized human species. In time, if there is no interbreeding, present-day subspecies would develop into separate species. Moreover, we must become comfortable with the idea of violence as a natural part of life. Darwin himself, in a letter dated 5 June 1861 to his pen-friend, the American Christian medical doctor and botanist Asa Gray (1810–88), strongly asserted that, if the northern states were to wage an unrelenting crusade against the southern states, he would be happy to see a million horrid deaths in order to eliminate slavery. Even though, officially, the Civil War had begun on 15 April 1861, at the time of Darwin's letter to Gray very little actual fighting was going on. In addition, social Darwinism taught that women are less mentally developed than men and was also used to support colonialism and cut-throat capitalism (Darwin, *Descent of Man*, chapter 7, 'On the Races of Man', p. 537).

Being more philosophically sophisticated, Karl Marx realized that Darwin's doctrine had to be altered so as to allow for an anti-reductionistic sort of materialism, which is something akin to Hegel's view, but with an ever-active material base rather than an ever-active spiritual base. Marx liked Darwin's view because of the theory's emphasis on the naturalness of struggle and ensuing necessary betterment of the biosphere as a whole. Such a doctrine could be used to support a social revolution in which the oppressed workers, with a clear conscience, kill off the capitalist oppressors as humanity moves ahead into the glorious future of the classless society. Vengeance was necessary so that a new world order could arise out of the ruins of the collapsing capitalistic system. It was up to the Marxists to help along this inevitable process by brutally eliminating the old system.

We still have with us today various forms of this revenge ideology, encouraged in the 1960s by the Marxist Herbert Marcuse (1898–1979), who emigrated to the United States in 1934 and who taught at Columbia University from 1934 to 1940. Then, from 1941 to 1950, he worked for the United States Office of Strategic Services and for the State Department. In 1951 he returned to teaching at Columbia University and later went on to teach at Harvard, Brandeis, and the University of California at San Diego until his retirement in 1970. According to Marcuse, an even-handed policy toward everyone was repressive with respect to some subgroups in society. He advocated a policy of reverse discrimination, in which the living descendants of those oppressed in the past are given the advantage over the living descendants of the dead oppressors. In other words, children must be whipped for the sins of their parents.

Late in life, Thomas Huxley began to see the moral problems in Darwin's view and wrote *Evolution and Ethics* (1893) in an effort to forestall the consequences of applying Darwin's theory to human society. His basic point was that, now that evolution had done its work in producing human beings, we can abandon the jungle warfare aspect of the theory and concentrate instead on living in peace and harmony. Needless to say, his proposed solution was not convincing. Why should the engine of species production come to a stop here and now? In fact, there is no reason for it ever to stop. It is a process that will go on, according to Darwin himself, until the sun burns out.

Later on, in the mid-twentieth century, Hitler would see in Darwin's theory a justification for an aggressive form of artificial social selection, which was sure to better the human condition in a way that neither Stalin's Russian communism nor Benito Mussolini's (1883–1945) Italian fascism could promise. Nietzsche gave Hitler the moral right to do whatever he wanted and Darwin supplied the content of the action. Hitler saw himself as fulfilling his evolutionary destiny. The result was Hitler's racist doctrine, claiming that one subdivision of the human species was superior in every way to all other subdivisions. The Aryans had the right to do things to others that others could not do to them. In consequence, millions died for the noble cause of species betterment. But Hitler was okay with that. He always acted in good conscience. How could something that feels so good be wrong? Even though his policy of biological engineering was a source of deep ethical conflict, Hitler sincerely believed that the result would be unprecedented biomedical advances. Why should scientific progress be inhibited by archaic ethical and religious views?

Unfortunately, nowadays many scientists share the attitude of Josef Mengele and the Japanese Unit 731. Well-meaning scientists see nothing wrong with the end justifying the means. In eager anticipation of the many cures that are foreseen as a result, biomedical engineering, DNA recombinations, human cloning, and uninhibited stem-cell research, even if developing human beings must die in the process, are regarded as perfectly acceptable programmes.

Darwin's New Religion

For the atheist and deist, Darwin's doctrine was just what the doctor ordered. Many today want people to think in terms of science (evolutionary doctrine) standing in opposition to religion. In fact, it is a case of one religion facing off against other religions. Darwin's special theory of evolution is the final stage in the development of the deistic religious doctrine that began with Descartes. Darwin's immediate intellectual predecessor, however, was not Descartes, but Descartes as he ended up in the hands of Hume.

There is little exaggeration in saying that Darwin completed the theoretical side of Hume's system. The emotional and mental continuity of animals and men and the mechanistic necessity of all things were a part of Darwin's inheritance. For instance, in his 1838 *M* notebook, p. 155, Darwin says that Hume's essay on human understanding is well worth reading. In his *N* notebook, also from 1838, p. 184, Darwin recommends the study of Hume's views on the passions to anyone interested in the mind. For Darwin, as for Hume, free will is to mind as chance is to matter. Because we lack a precise knowledge of the causes operating on the matter of the human being, being free means being unpredictable. If we had an exact knowledge of the causes, we could predict every choice someone makes. What we call freedom is simply an ignorance of the material causes.

Darwin regarded his theory of natural selection as a substitute for all religions containing a doctrine of God's presence. As with Hume, Darwin knew nothing of the gods. This induced Darwin to make some bold assertions. Whatever is actual is possible. Whatever is surviving is capable of surviving. So, obviously, whatever survives has what it needs to survive. For example, some animals have teeth fit for ripping, some for cutting, some for grinding, and some have a combination of teeth. Why must we say that such teeth evolved to fit the needs of the creature? Why not just say that the teeth fit the needs of the creature? Coordination is a fact; the mindless origin of the fact is not a fact.

Why do giraffes have long legs and long necks? Why do sharks have no legs? Why do centipedes have many legs? Why do sea slugs taste so bad and trout taste so good to us? Why do some parasitic micro-organisms kill their hosts quickly, while others allow their hosts to live a long time? Why do both ants, that live underground and crawl around, and bees, that live in the air and fly around, have queens that continuously produce large numbers of workers that are useful to the group almost immediately, while human females take a long time to produce only one offspring at a time? Why do some insects produce many females and few males? Why do some insects produce many males and few females? And why does even one human baby require so many years of nurturing before he is useful to anyone or anything, including himself? Why does anything have anything or do anything? Because it is useful for survival. So should human mothers be twice as big, with four arms and eyes in the back of their head?

Darwin's problem is especially acute with respect to human beings. If it is true that human beings are only naked apes, then the Darwinian origin of human beings cannot be true. Compared to our animal ancestors, we are, physically speaking, inferior in our ability to survive. Being naked to the earth and the elements marks us as being the product of a de-evolution rather than an evolution. Instead of having tough feet, for instance, we are born with tender feet. And what happened to our fur coats? Being naked is dangerous for us. We either freeze to death or we die from sun-caused skin cancer. Rather than adapting to the environment, it seems that nature expects us to wear shoes, clothes, and hats.

We might also inquire about the relative hairiness of human beings. Why do human males have more body hair than human females? According to the evolutionary theory of sexual selection, it is because the males of long ago preferred the less hairy females and so mated with them more often than with the more hairy ones. Over a long time, the female offspring became progressively less hairy. This is in keeping with the theory, but why would less hair be preferred? The males of the various contemporary monkey species do not have any such preference. To this day the great ape females are just as hairy as the great ape males. This sort of inconsistency arises even if we assume that hairlessness is better for us in hot climates. The climate is the same for the primates as it is for the human beings.

In order to make sense of the theory, there has to be something else at work, such as the higher mental faculties of aesthetic appreciation. There is some law of beauty involved. Where, though, did it come from? According to the notion of sexual selection, the females of the species actively choose, generation after generation, certain features (for example, bright feathers) in the males as a basis for mating. Yet, why would females have such preferences, especially when the chosen trait makes the males less suitable for survival and thus less suitable to provide for the offspring?

Furthermore, which is further down on the evolutionary scale: brainless starfish, little newts, sneaky salamanders, or human beings? Yet, which is better suited for survival? Some creatures can regenerate lost limbs, which is a great advantage in the struggle for survival. However, instead of being able to regenerate lost limbs, we must suffer without them. In his *Descent of Man*, chapter 1 (n.d.), Darwin mentions the fact of regeneration in the lower animals and how there is some evidence that human beings in their embryonic phase may possess the same power. He takes this as evidence that man has passed through these lower stages, thereby proving his theory. In fact, though, the conclusion should be just the opposite. Lacking the power of regeneration marks us as inferior to the lower animals; we must have devolved.

Yes, but what about the mind? In that case, Darwin is even worse off. If an appeal is made to man's mental superiority, the question arises as to how such a thing could have arisen out of material cells and non-mind. What of the brain? Is the mind the same thing as the brain? Once again Darwinism fails. If the development of the large brain was gradual, the organ would have been of no use in its early stages. Yes, but maybe the growth of the brain and the shedding of hair kept pace with each other? Maybe so, but we must still wonder why one grew stronger while the other grew weaker. The combination of a big brain and a strong gorilla body would be much better for survival than what we have now.

And just to make things worse, we know today, as the result of scientific investigation, that we do not even require a large brain in order to be intelligent. Children can be smarter than adults. In addition, women, with smaller brains, are just as smart as men, who generally have bigger brains. Moreover, members of both sexes can be intelligent even when the vast majority of their brain is missing. As we now know from actual cases of people who have survived 'water on the brain', someone can graduate with honours in mathematics even though the person has only 5 per cent of the normal amount of brain tissue. And the missing brain tissue is exactly in that area where intelligence is supposed to reside. So, then, what are we left with? Either having a big brain or not having a big brain is good for survival.

To sum up, why does an elephant have a long nose? Because it needs it in order to obtain food and drink. Why does a human being have a short nose? In order to be able to wear eyeglasses. For Darwin, no matter what trait something possesses, it is accounted for by natural or sexual selection. Darwin's approach is comparable to someone who proposes a theory in which substance X is held responsible for causing various physical problems. The theorist then lists 30 symptoms, two or three of which practically everyone will exhibit at one time or another. Is this scientific? Hardly. It means that there is no way of testing this one theory in comparison with other theories. With respect to species change, maybe it is all a matter of chance. Maybe there are quantity-quality leaps. This inability to test the theory is therefore an indication of the Darwinian theory's lack of scientific status (Adler, 2001, pp. 53–4).

Darwin and Morality

For Darwin, even though God has nothing to say to us, nature still speaks to us. Nature, though, is promiscuous. There are no species in nature; a species is only a convenient label that a naturalist chooses to apply to a certain set of traits belonging to a certain number of specimens. In fact, all reality is merely a vast collection of tiny atomic particles moving about in space. Furthermore, since there are no real separate species, there is nothing preventing individuals from going through a process of altering their traits until a new set of traits becomes more or less fixed. This is how we came into existence.

Darwin sought out the origins of modern man among the higher primates. He says in his *M* notebook, p. 84, that we can learn more about metaphysics by studying the ape than by studying the philosophy of John Locke. In Darwin's day, the subject-matter of metaphysics was the soul and God, a definition he inherited from a long line of European thinkers going back to Bacon and Descartes. It follows that, if we want to learn something about the human mind, spirit, or soul, says Darwin, we should not study those old philosophers who purported to tell us all about our mental and moral developments outside of a naturalistic context. Rather than being handed down to us by God, our ideas about such things have emerged gradually from our primitive past. The transition from the animal mind to the human mind has been slow but steady over a very long period of time. In both the intellectual sphere and the moral sphere there has been an ascending development to higher and higher levels of perfection.

Revenge and anger, for example, useful to animals fighting to survive in the jungles, have now given way to more noble sentiments. Our moral sense has arisen out of the experiences of our animal and semi-human past. From a confused idea of the 'ought' in ancient times we have advanced to the Golden Rule. From the crude notions of dreams, ghosts, and many gods, in conjunction with an imagined notion of some necessary being, such as in monotheism, we have arrived in modern times at the wonderful Sermon on the Mount. Certainly today some people continue to behave in a crude and primitive fashion. However, we now at least are in a position to see the difference between good and evil behaviour more clearly. Nowadays we have much higher standards against which we can judge proper and improper behaviour.

Therefore, for Darwin, the present-day cruelty and sinfulness of the average man have nothing to do with some sort of deliberate turning away from God at the beginning of human history. First of all, there never was an Adam and Eve and there never was an original sin. In addition, there is no need for such a doctrine. When we see today the propensity of human beings to torture, maim, abuse, and kill each other, we need not refer such behaviour patterns back to an original disorder introduced into human nature by our first parents. The remaining inherent disposition of human beings to take pleasure in the sufferings of others, and their unwillingness to help their fellow man, should instead be explained by our animal past.

In his *Descent of Man*, chapter 4, Darwin states that the human moral conscience is the most important difference between humans and animals. By conscience, Darwin means our ability to feel remorse, repentance, regret, and shame. Such feelings are based almost exclusively on the judgments that are passed upon us by other people. In turn, the foundation for such judgments is found in our social instincts, our sense of the greater good of our fellow human beings, and our sentiments and sympathies for other people. In the long run, survival demands that certain moral values come to dominate. Courage, temperance, chastity, and a universal respect for other human beings and animals, must come to the surface. As we see when we compare savages with civilized people, the best of which is the English gentleman, our nobler instincts must move ahead while our baser instincts must recede. The evil that surrounds us cannot be denied, but it cannot be attributed to sin. It is due to the gap that still exists between the savages and the civilized people of the world. As with Hume, God is not needed to carry on a civilized society of law and order.

Following the lead of Hume, Darwin distinguishes between the standards of morality and the motives for acting morally. The standards are those virtues that have been carried on over a long period of time and that lead, first, to the overall welfare of the human society and, second, to the happiness of the greater mass of mankind. For Darwin this means the rearing of the greatest number of individuals in the fullness of bodily health, with all of their faculties fully developed given the environment in which they happen to live. On the other hand, the motive for proper human moral behaviour is our sense of sympathy with others and, generally, the approbation or disapprobation we receive from others. Fortunately, we can count upon the fact that the fulfilment of our own individual desire for self-preservation and self-development will coincide, by and large, with the needs of the wider society of which we are a part.

There is, though, a major problem with Darwin's view, something that Darwin himself never saw. The fact is that animals are not sinful. It is true that some subhuman creatures will lay their eggs inside the living bodies of other creatures, that cats will play with mice before eating them, that spiders wrap up flies, that male animals will fight with each other to a certain extent in order to secure a larger group of females with which to mate, that male mice will kill the male offspring of their neighbouring mice, that chimpanzees will kill and eat their own offspring, and the like. Such behaviour, however, is a far cry from what human beings do to each other. Animals kill for food and for survival, not just for the fun of it.

Even assuming that animals are moral agents, the trend could not have been from cruel animal behaviour to charitable human behaviour. If there were any sort of transition, it must have been the other way around. When human beings sin they are much worse than animals. The pseudo-liberals keep forgetting about original sin. Human beings are especially susceptible to temptation. Given half a chance, they go crazy committing the seven deadly sins of pride, envy, anger, gluttony, lust, sloth and avarice. If all we ever had to worry about with respect to human behaviour is the search for food and the struggle to reproduce in accordance with a fixed mating season, there would be no more need for the Ten Commandments, the Golden Rule, the Sermon on the Mount, and the New Commandment (John 13:34) among humans than there is now among chimpanzees.

One must also wonder how Darwin can say the things he says at the end of his *Descent of Man* and *Selection in Relation to Sex* (n.d.). He recommends that monogamous marriage be eliminated so that the best-adapted male specimens can mate freely with the best-adapted female specimens. He thinks that such a fundamental reorganization of sexual relations would encourage the production of better-adapted offspring, thus advancing the species. How, though, does this constitute an advance over our primitive animal ancestors? Monogamy is extremely rare among animals. Darwin, it seems, is contradicting his own theory of moral development by making such a recommendation. Instead of wanting us to go forward, he wants us to go backward (Darwin, *Selection in Relation to Sex* (n.d.), chapter 21, 'General Summary and Conclusion', p. 919).

Nevertheless, Darwin's doctrine does preserve some of the main points of the natural moral law doctrine as taught by Aquinas. With respect to sexual matters, Aquinas taught that sex has a God-given purpose, namely, the reproduction and care of new human beings within a lifelong, loving, secure family setting. Because of this, certain practices are ruled out. With some overlapping of categories, there can be no abandoning of one's spouse and children, abortion, adultery, conflict over family leadership, contraception, divorce and remarriage, fornication, homosexuality, incest, masturbation, necrophilia, paedophilia, pornography, prostitution, rape, sodomy, and sterilization. Needless to say, many today are overwhelmingly opposed to such a view.

For example, according to the pro-choice position on abortion, in effect a mother is to her offspring as a master is to her slave, a slave that can be treated kindly or killed. Consequently, whereas some people say that all forms of racism and slavery must be outlawed, the pro-choice people say that some forms of racism and slavery are permissible. Such people, who are often politicians, like to think of themselves as being open-minded and tolerant. What they really are, though, are pseudo-liberals, people who refuse to swallow the same sugar-coated poison pill they so generously offer to others. If, for instance, a pseudo-liberal's daughter is raped, he does not say: 'Oh well, that is a consequence of my own dogma.' Instead, he becomes angry and condemns the rapist to hell. If the criminal responds by saying that he is only practising what the father preaches about morality being only in the eye of the beholder, the father refuses to admit that he himself has justified the very action he is condemning.

Another example of modern thoughtlessness is the way we think about the relationship between sex and love. In fact, sex and love are not connected in any intrinsic way. We cannot say that all sex is love, for that would make rape an act of love. We cannot say that all love is sex, for that would make it necessary for loving parents to have sex with their children. For purposes of definition, sex and love do not belong together in the same proposition. Sex is a physical arrangement of bodily parts. Love is one person sincerely wishing well to another person. Sometimes, as in marriage, sex and love go together, but there are many circumstances in which they do not go together.

And what about reproduction? Nowadays, the severing of sex and reproduction is something everyone is supposed to take for granted. This, however, was not always the case. For Darwin, natural selection demands massive reproduction and a never-ending struggle that continuously weeds out less well-adapted specimens. Ideally, inferior specimens will not survive long enough to reproduce themselves. In this way, new species will evolve from the original stock and future generations will look back on us in the same way we look back on our monkey ancestors. Consequently, insists Darwin, practices such as incest, contraception, and sterilization must continue to be ruled out. Everything else, though, is in.

Nowadays, however, even the few restrictions found in Darwin have been removed. Today, the only purpose of sex is fun. The playboy always has fun. Quite logically, once the connection between sex and reproduction is completely severed, all of the things ruled out in Aquinas' Catholic religious context are ruled in. As a result, the position that some actions are intrinsically evil, and are therefore never to be done freely, is now widely rejected by the popular media and the state.

Whitehead's Compromise

Whitehead the Mathematician

Alfred North Whitehead was born in 1861 in Ramsgate, on the English coast east of London. His grandfather was a Quaker and his father was an Anglican priest who ran a private school in Ramsgate. After learning his Greek and Latin in his father's school, he went on (in 1880) to study mathematics at Trinity College, Cambridge, where he later took up a teaching position in mathematics from 1885 to 1911. He then took up a teaching position at the Imperial College of Science and Technology at the University of London (1911–24). In 1890 Whitehead married Evelyn Wade, with whom he had three children, one of whom died in World War I. The death of his son had a great effect on his philosophical thought. In 1924 he retired from his duties in England and immediately moved to a teaching position in philosophy at Harvard University, which lasted until 1937. Whitehead died in Cambridge, MA, at the end of 1947. There was no funeral service, his body was quickly cremated, and, in conformity with his last wishes, all of his unpublished manuscripts and letters were also burned.

Whitehead said that while at Cambridge his education was very narrowly confined to mathematics. He was not happy about this. The only education he got in philosophy and the liberal arts was by talking to other students in the common room. An interdisciplinary group of 'Apostles' would meet for wide-ranging discussions from Saturday evening until any time the next day. He also enjoyed reading on his own, especially the romantic poets Shelley, Wordsworth, and Tennyson.

For-real Approach: Essence-based A Posteriori External Experience 153

During 1910–13, Whitehead, along with his former student, Bertrand Russell, published the *Principia Mathematica* in three volumes. This work was an attempt to show that all of mathematics can be reduced to a few basic axioms in logic. Among his other works are *A Treatise on Universal Algebra* (1898), *An Introduction to Mathematics* (1911), *An Enquiry Concerning the Principles of Natural Knowledge* (1919), *The Concept of Nature* (1920), *The Principle of Relativity* (1922), in which he disagrees with Einstein on some points, *Science and the Modern World* (1925), *Religion in the Making* (1926), *The Function of Reason* (1929), *Process and Reality: An Essay in Cosmology* (1929), *Adventures of Ideas* (1933), *Modes of Thought* (1938), and *Essays in Science and Philosophy* (1947), the last containing a brief autobiography.

Process Philosophy and Theology

Whitehead is known as the father of process philosophy and theology in the twentieth century. He called his doctrine *panentheism*, which is pantheism with an extra syllable in the middle to indicate that his doctrine was not the usual sort of pantheism. He offered his doctrine, not as a logical proof that examined its own first principles and factual foundations, but rather as a hypothesis, something that would satisfy the inner desire he had to bring the idea of God up-to-date. For Whitehead, as for Paley, God is needed in order to have the orderly, law-abiding world studied by science. However, unlike Paley, there must also be something about God that accounts for the disorderliness of the world. Ultimately, this desire for a dual-natured God will land Whitehead in a contradictory situation.

Nevertheless, Whitehead must be given credit for being more astute than his old colleague Russell. Unlike Russell, while admitting the great value of science, Whitehead knew very well that science is not the ultimate form of knowledge. Science requires the more fundamental context of philosophy in order to be fully intelligible. Whitehead says:

> But the claim of science that it can produce an understanding of its procedures within the limits of its own categories, or that those categories themselves are understandable without reference to their status within the widest categories under exploration by the speculative Reason – that claim is entirely unfounded. Insofar as philosophers have failed, scientists do not know what they are talking about when they pursue their own methods; and insofar as philosophers have succeeded, to that extent scientists can attain an understanding of science. With the success of philosophy, blind habits of scientific thought are transformed into analytic explanation. (Whitehead, 1958, pp. 58–9)

As with Darwin, Whitehead is optimistic, believing in necessary progress. And, as with Hegel, his language retains much of the traditional religious terminology of Judao-Christianity, even though the meanings of the words have been radically altered. In his lectures on *Religion in the Making* (1926), Whitehead says that religion must be rational, not just emotional, and that

Buddhism is a philosophy in search of emotional religious feelings, while Christianity is basically an emotional religion in search of a philosophy. By evil Whitehead means a lack of perfect adaptation, things working at cross-purposes, disharmony in the world, physical and moral turbulence, and internal inconsistency. Evil occurs when things do not harmonize and match up, as already said by Darwin.

He goes on to note that moral snobbishness, that is, claiming that you suffer because you are evil, is itself evil, that every cosmology (world-view) is capable of generating a religion, and that process thinking must reject both the extreme of God as the impersonal order of the world and the extreme of God as a personal creator separate from the world. According to Whitehead, traditional theology is much too static. It does not explain why, if God is perfect, there is evil in the world.

In order to account for the presence of both adaptation and the lack of adaptation, for both good and evil, Whitehead thinks we need a more progressive and evolutionary religion, a new way of combining permanence and flux, God's transcendence and immanence, a doctrine adapted to the experience of imperfection and constant change. Religion, after all, is a personal matter. Christ, for instance, gave his life for the world, but only individual Christians can determine what that means. Religious dogmas are the external modes of expression of one's inner thoughts. At no time should dogmas be made into something absolute and unchanging. According to some people in the know, process thinking has now become the predominant natural theology in North America, especially among Liberal Protestants (Peacocke, 1985, pp. 101–30).

His main theological point, as stated in *Religion in the Making*, is that to be an actual thing is to be limited. God is real as an actual entity and so God is finite. God is not altogether perfect, but is rather in the process of becoming more perfect, just like all other things. For Whitehead, too much of a good thing is no good. Even goodness must be limited. God must share in our disorganization and weaknesses. In Whitehead's view, in order to have God avoid knowing evil, God is gaining knowledge, just like other things. In order to avoid having to conquer evil, God is gaining in power and strength, just like other things. Therefore, to account for the continued presence of evil, God must be imperfect. If God were all-knowing, he would know about evil and would do something about getting rid of it. If God were all-powerful, he would be able to get rid of evil. By having imperfect knowledge, God avoids knowing all about evil. By having imperfect power, God avoids having to conquer all evil.

By the same token, the notion of evolution must also be modified in order to fit the new dispensation. Instead of meaning that new things must arise by the mechanical process of natural selection, evolution is broadened to mean that everything is related to everything else in the biosphere. Organic unity is the key feature of the biosphere. Yes, everything new is the result of a development out of older things, but the precise mechanisms are of secondary importance.

Therefore, God, like the world, is imperfect. God is growing and developing along with the things in the world, including human beings. Thus God progresses along with the world and its people. God may know what I did this morning, but he does not know what I am going to do this afternoon. This means that evil is inherent in the world process. Evil is natural, a necessary aspect of the world process. Nevertheless, even though there is a lack of perfect adaptation among things in the world, as the world progresses the mismatch of parts will be lessened and we will move into a better world in the future. Reminiscent of Mary Baker Eddy (1821–1910), every day in every way things get better and better. The creative advance into novelty is an ever-ongoing process.

According to Whitehead, this is achieved by regarding God as bi-polar, as having a mental and a physical pole. The whole universe is organic rather than mechanistic. In this regard, God is the same as everything else in reality. In order to have science we need unity and stability. This is explained by God's primordial nature, which is Plato's world of divine ideas incorporated into God. These ideas give developing actual entities something to strive for; aims and goals that they freely choose for themselves. Every actual entity is empowered to pursue its own destiny. In this primordial aspect, God is eternal and unchanging.

God, though, also possesses a consequent nature, which is the accumulation of all the best of all the developing entities that have lived and died. In this sense, but only in this sense, can things be said to have died and gone to heaven. This aspect of God is temporal, forever changing, growing, developing, and responding to unforeseen entities and events of the future. In this way, thinks Whitehead, the human desire for God's love and the preservation of what is good and valuable will be satisfied. He says:

> The present type of order in the world has arisen from an unimaginable past, and it will find its grave in an unimaginable future. There remains the inexhaustible realm of abstract forms, and creativity, with its shifting character ever determined afresh by its own creatures, and God, upon whose wisdom all forms of order depend. (Whitehead, 1969, p. 154)

In his major work, *Process and Reality: An Essay in Cosmology* (1929), Whitehead reinforces his earlier stated view that God is implicated in every part of the world. He says that the philosophy of nature is first philosophy or metaphysics, that religion is the ultimate craving to rationalize our emotional feelings, that the separation of flux and permanence is vicious, that reducing the world to mere appearance is vicious, that everlastingness and temporality must go together in all things, that God is the world and that the world is God, that all opposites are elements in the very nature of things, that there is no personal immortality, but the best of everything is preserved in the consequent (physical pole) nature of God, and that everything is in the grasp of the creative advance into newness. In other words, reality is process (Whitehead, 1960).

The Church of What's Happening Now

When all is said and done, though, one must still wonder how it is possible for Whitehead to talk intelligently about progressing toward perfection without knowing here and now what constitutes the perfection he is anticipating. Whitehead denies personal immortality, so what is there for me personally? How can I claim to have arrived at my destination if I do not know where I am going? Where are you going? To New York City. Where, after travelling all day, are you now? Alaska. Well, at least you know that you are not making progress. Even if we assume that the traveller is taking the long way around the old barn, he still has to know that he is heading for the other side of the barn. The upshot of this for Whitehead is that he cannot talk about progress until he specifies the traits possessed by the ideal to be achieved. What is perfect harmony? Even if there is more than one ideal, we still have to know what characterizes each of them.

In addition, Whitehead's idea of God is contradictory (Centore, 1970, pp. 149–71). Something cannot be both eternally unchanging and forever changing at the same time. The two traits are mutually exclusive. What Whitehead tried to do was to combine Plato's two incompatible worlds, the world of Greek being (the ideas) and the world of becoming, into one thing. However, this is impossible. As I pointed out some years ago:

> Whitehead was totally opposed to the Cartesian type of dualism. What Whitehead was prepared to allow into his system was a unified type of dualism; one in which there exists two aspects of the same principle and not two irreconcilable principles. However, what he intended and what he accomplished are at variance. What Whitehead has done has been to replace the Cartesian duality with a Platonic duality – that is, with an immutable world of Ideas and a transient world of generation. (Centore, 1970, pp. 169–70)

Whitehead was of the opinion that a speculative thinker works best when freed of concerns about the effects of his views on social and political affairs. Nevertheless, Whitehead's doctrine does have social implications. Naturalistic theism has no use for institutional churches claiming to have a lock on truth. All hierarchies must be levelled and all those at the margins must be taken into the centre. As we constantly reinvent the church, everything must be adjusted to what is new. New times demand new theologies. Those resisting change are regressive, authoritarian, and insensitive.

Consequently, talking about something as being 'from the beginning' (Matthew 19:5) makes no sense. Neither can we nowadays take seriously the words of Saint Paul when he says that we must not fall in with the manners of the world (Romans 12:2). Today, falling in with the ways of the world is precisely what you are expected to do in order to be good. In Whitehead's book, the Bible is at best only an interesting story, containing many useful insights into human life. It is not, though, a revelation from God. In the early twentieth century, all of the traditional religions are dead.

For Whitehead, religion must be modernized by emphasizing the creative advance into newness. There is no single ideal to which each developing being must adhere. With respect to human relations, for instance, there is an endless number of possible permutations and personal destinies. Objectively speaking, none of the possible, self-selected, goals is superior to any other one. The family, for example, can be anything people want it to be. Morality, like religion, is a matter of personal interpretation. So, for example, if divorce, homosexuality, sex before marriage, multiple partners, mothers working outside of the home, or wives refusing to have children, is what happens to be culturally avant-garde, then modern religion must 'get with-it' and create new rites, rituals, liturgies, and ceremonies sanctifying any and all such behaviour patterns. Religion and the state must be creative in giving modern believers what they want. In the Catholic Church, for example, the only real heresy is claiming that the Church cannot change.

This lack of objective moral standards is in keeping with Whitehead's modified pantheism in which he attempts to combine Plato's fixed ideas with an atomistic view of the natural world. In a pantheistic setting, everything is holy. There can be sacred wars as well as sacred prostitution. To raw nature, there is no difference between the 'is' and the 'ought'; no difference between the sacred and the secular. Starting a forest fire is an imitation of natural lightning. Dowsing a forest fire is an imitation of natural rain. In the woods, water, and air there cannot be any such thing as pollution, prostitution, perversion, abuse, or injustice. As said by Schopenhauer in the century before Whitehead, pantheism is the polite form of atheism. For the atheist, the only unnatural act is one that it is impossible to physically perform. In this way, Whitehead's process thinking very nicely reinforces the cultural relativism derived from Hegel's process philosophy and Darwin's evolutionary thinking.

Chapter 9

The For-real Approach: A Posteriori External Experience Method Based on Existence

Aquinas the Angelic Doctor

At the time Thomas Aquinas was born interesting things were happening in England, France, Italy, and Spain. New religious orders were being formed. Notre Dame Cathedral in France was being built (1163–1257) and Salisbury Cathedral in England was started in 1220. The archbishop of Canterbury, Stephen Langton (1160–1228), an Englishman, was subdividing the books of the Bible into chapters and, by writing the Magna Carta (1215), also siding with the English barons against the king. The Magna Carta marked the beginning of the parliamentary system of government in Europe. The battle between Church and state was continuing, with Langton himself agreeing to take office in 1213, but only after King John (Lackland, 1167–1216) agreed to become a vassal of Pope Innocent III (1160–1216). And the Fourth Lateran Council, which did so much to establish Church discipline and practice, was held in Rome in 1215.

On the academic front, in 1209 Cambridge University was founded. And of greatest significance, the complete works of Aristotle, which contained an account of everything worth knowing in logic and science, along with their Arabic commentaries, were being translated in Spain and Italy.

On the political scene, the semi-Christian, semi-Muslim Frederick II (1194–1250), the grandson of Frederick I (Barbarossa), was the Holy Roman Emperor (1220–50). Although a member of the German Hohenstaufen family, he preferred living in sunny Sicily rather than cloudy Germany. Frederick II was known as the 'wonder of the world' because of his many and varied interests. He loved to experiment, for instance, by rubbing a newly deceased man between two prostitutes to see if the corpse could be revived, or by sealing someone sentenced to death up in a barrel, allowing him time to die, and then carefully opening the barrel so as to perhaps hear the man's spirit escaping through the opening. He also took some children from birth and had them raised in isolation with no words being spoken in order to see if they would speak spontaneously, and in which language.

In 1224 Frederick II established a school in Naples, which taught Aristotle's works, including the books on nature. At the same time, universities were beginning in earnest. In April 1231 the University of Paris, which had already been in operation for more than 30 years, was officially recognized by the long-lived Gregory IX (1145–1241, a nephew of Innocent III) and the role of the bachelor's degree formalized. This action ended a strike by the masters that had begun in March 1229. At that time, the Dominicans held two of the 12 chairs in theology in the university. Paris, named after a Celtic tribe, the Parisii, with thousands of students living in the area, quickly became the most important city in northern Europe.

Aquinas' father, Landolfo, was a respected knight with a castle named Roccasecca, located north of Naples and outside of the Papal States. Aquinas was born at the castle either in late 1224 or early 1225. Aquinas' family owed its allegiance to the emperor of the Holy Roman Empire, who always seemed to be at war with somebody, especially the popes. From 1231 to 1239 the young Thomas was sent to live and study with the Benedictine monks at Monte Cassino, most likely as a hostage in order to ensure that Landolfo would not attack Church property. But early in 1239 Frederick II, in an antipapal move, evicted all non-native monks from the monastery and Thomas was forced to return to the castle. In the autumn of 1239 he was introduced to Aristotle when he went to Naples to continue his studies. (See Weisheipl, 1974.)

Aquinas' father died in 1243 and, in May 1244, at age 20, Thomas decided to join the Dominicans (Order of Preachers), which, along with the Franciscans (Order of Friars Minor, the Little Brothers), was a new type of religious order, a hybrid, sharing the traits of both the cloistered monks and the secular clergy (canons, parish priests). The new hybrids were called mendicants because they travelled about, living on hand-outs. His family objected, thinking that he should become instead a knight in the service of the emperor. So, while on his way to Paris for further studies, he was kidnapped by his brothers and held a prisoner at the castle until July 1245.

At that time, Frederick II was deposed by the First Council of Lyons. Since they no longer owed allegiance to the emperor, Thomas was freed by his family. He went to Paris, where he studied from 1245 to 1248. From 1248 to 1252 he went to study with Albert the Great, OP, at the University of Cologne in Germany. Albertus Magnus (1206–80, of Bollstaedt, bishop of Regensburg), who had only recently (1245) himself received his theology degree in Paris, was the first German scientist. He talked about the affinity of sulphur and various metals with one another, used the term vitriol to describe various acids, and thought that every metal was a combination of water, sulphur, and mercury. He also worked on the processes for purifying gold and arsenic (Weisheipl, 1979).

In 1250, following the death of the emperor, Aquinas was ordained a priest in Cologne. While in Cologne, he also picked up the nickname of 'the silent ox' because of his long periods of contemplation. After his studies in Cologne he headed back to Paris (April 1252–June 1254) for graduate studies in theology.

Unlike today, where anyone taking a few courses in religious studies is called a theologian by the popular media, becoming a theologian in 1250 was really hard work. Compared to the large undergraduate faculty of arts and the large graduate schools of medicine and law (ecclesiastical and civil), theology was tiny. The course of studies was long and expensive, requiring the renting of many books. In order to encourage more people to study theology, Robert de Sorbonne (1201–74), in 1253, established a residence (college) for poor students who could not afford the expenses, that is, mainly those who were not attached to a religious order that subsidized their studies. Robert was the chaplain to the court of King Louis IX (1214–70, the famous Saint Louis), who was at the time away on the sixth crusade (1248–54).

Becoming a theologian required going through the undergraduate programme in logic and philosophy in order to obtain the bachelor of arts degree. Then it took two more years for the master of arts degree. Then you had to go through at least eight more years of studying the Bible, obtaining the bachelor of biblical studies. Then you had to become well acquainted with the outstanding thinkers of the past, which meant studying the *Sentences* of Peter the Lombard (1100–64, archbishop of Paris 1158–59, known as The Master). This work was a lengthy anthology of commentaries on the Scriptures, gathered from all the outstanding thinkers of the past. This period of study resulted in another degree. Finally, you had to write and defend your own contribution to theological studies, obtaining the final degree. You could then, at an age no younger than 34, receive your master of theology degree.

During this period (1252–57) there was an attack in Paris on the new religious orders (the Dominicans and the Franciscans) led by William of Saint Amour, who preached that the wandering monks (mendicants) marked the end of the world. Jealous of the growing influence of the new orders, there was a strike by the masters from April 1253 to June 1254. The seculars also resented the new members because they were 'scabs', that is, people who continue to work while others are on strike. This was a dangerous time for the new religious orders, so much so that the civil authorities placed guards around their residences in Paris to prevent violence. Under pressure from the secular clergy, Pope Innocent IV (?–1254, pope from June 1243) rescinded the teaching privileges of the new religious orders in November 1254. But a month later Pope Alexander IV (?–1261, pope from December 1254), a religious man committed to the Franciscan ideals, restored them and reaffirmed them in April 1255. In October 1256 the pope criticized William of Saint Amour for being a fanatic and ordered him back to his home town.

In the meantime, in 1255, Aquinas had written *On Being and Essence* at the request of his fellow Dominicans residing at their college in Paris. In May 1256, even though underage, he was accredited as a master of theology by the order. Finally, in September 1257, he was accepted as a master of theology by the whole university. From his inception in 1256 to the spring of 1259 Aquinas taught theology there. From this period date his *Commentary on the Sentences* (1257), *Disputed Questions on Truth* (1258), and *An Exposition of Boethius' De Trinitate* (1258).

In the autumn of 1259 Aquinas was appointed Preacher General for the Order and left Paris for Italy. In 1260, Reginald of Piperno (died 1290) became his *socius*, that is, his chief secretary. Even though Aquinas' work involved a great deal of travelling, it did not stop him from writing. From 1258 to 1264 he wrote the *Summa Contra Gentiles*, a book to be used by Dominican missionaries working in Spain. Previous to this, he studied various Jewish books and the Koran, works of great importance to the Christian intellectuals of the time. Many contrasts and comparisons are made by Aquinas among Jewish, Islamic, and Christian doctrines. Much earlier, in 1141, Peter the Venerable (1092–1156), the abbot of the Benedictine monastery at Cluny in Burgundy, had commissioned a translation into Latin of both the Talmund and the Koran. These works then became required reading for all those working around the Mediterranean Sea.

Recognized as a genius, Aquinas' advice was in demand at the papal court of Urban IV (?–October 1264, a Frenchman, pope from 1261) in Orvieto. Urban IV is noted for increasing the College of Cardinals from eight to 22 members, divided about half-and-half between the Italians and the French. Aquinas was also favoured by Clement IV (?–November 1268, another Frenchman, pope from 1265) in Viterbo, who sought his advice on East-West relationships. In 1264, for the Cantor of Antioch, Aquinas wrote a letter entitled *On the Reasonableness of the Faith* in which he says that philosophy should not try to prove the articles of faith, but only aim to show that they are not inherently irrational. From the autumn of 1265 to the autumn of 1268 Aquinas, in remission of his sins, served as the master of a new house of theological studies in Rome. In 1267 he wrote the *Disputed Questions on the Power of God*.

Also in 1267, the English Franciscan Roger Bacon (1214–94, the Doctor Mirabilis) sent Clement IV his *Opus Majus*, on the importance of observation and experimentation in natural philosophy. Undoubtedly Aquinas was aware of his work; Bacon was noted for drawing attention to the errors in the Julian calendar, giving the correct formula for gunpowder (saltpeter or potassium nitrate, sulphur, and pulverized carbon), investigating the structure of the eye, inventing eyeglasses, doing work in optics, showing that air is needed for burning, imagining that some day human beings would fly through the air in vehicles imitating the motions of birds, and for writing a work (*On the Non-Existence of Magic*) insisting that all magic tricks can be explained by natural means. He also denied the possibility of transforming base metals into silver and gold. Unfortunately, some people were suspicious of his work and he ended up in prison for ten years (1278–88), where he nevertheless continued with his research and writing.

About this time (1266–71) anti-mendicantism was again becoming active in Paris, led by Gerard D'Abbeville. In order to combat the renewed attacks, Aquinas was sent back to Paris from the autumn of 1268 to the spring of

1272. By now he was well known and his views in philosophy and theology could not be ignored by those many diocesan clergymen, Franciscans, and even Dominicans, who disagreed with him. In October 1268, Stephen Tempier, a diocesan priest, became bishop of Paris and, on 10 December 1270, condemned 13 propositions as heretical, several of which sounded like things Aquinas had said. Later, on 7 March 1277, after Aquinas' death, 219 propositions were condemned, with even more sounding like things Aquinas had said. Somewhat later, on 18 March 1277, the Dominican archbishop of Canterbury, Robert Kilwardby, proscribed 30 propositions. (Weisheipl, 1974, chapter 7; see also Torrell, 1996).

By the spring of 1272 the anti-mendicants had lost their case. Aquinas left Paris in May 1272, went to Florence, and then to Naples as the master of a new house of studies in theology. Throughout this time (1266–73) he was writing his major work, the *Summa Theologiae* (1894b), as well as commentaries (1268–73) on the works of Aristotle, often dictating to his several secretaries for hours on end, and even in the middle of the night. Writing commentaries on Aristotle was not something Aquinas had decided to do on his own; rather, he had been asked to do so by the popes. Assisting him was William of Moerbeke (1215–86, bishop of Corinth, Greece, from 1277), who was hard at work doing new translations of ancient works from Greek manuscripts in an effort to give Aquinas better texts with which to work. The commentaries were important because 'the master of those who know' (as Dante called Aristotle) was as impossible to ignore in the 1200s as Darwin and Einstein are today. Aquinas' mandate was to interpret Aristotle in a way as favourable as possible to the Catholic Faith, something he did all too well. Contrary to the real Aristotle, Aquinas had 'Saint' Aristotle espousing the creation of the world and the personal immortality of the human soul.

Things appeared to be going well, when, on Passion Sunday 26 March 1273, strange things began to happen. While saying mass, Aquinas froze up and started crying profusely; this recurred over the following months. He later claimed to have had conversations with people long dead and, on one occasion, was seen levitating a few feet above the floor. On Wednesday morning 6 December 1273 he ceased writing the third part of the *Summa Theologiae*, saying that, after experiencing what had been revealed to him, everything he had written seemed to him like chaff. He also ceased writing a simplified handbook of theology (*Compendium of Theology*) that had been requested by Reginald of Piperno. Aquinas then, for about two weeks, visited his sister, the Countess Teodora of San Severino. He then returned to Naples. (After Aquinas' death, the third part of the *Summa* was completed by Reginald with material taken from Aquinas' *Commentary on the Sentences* (1929–47).)

About that time, Gregory X (1210–76), a layman who was living in the Near East and who was elected pope in 1271, called the Second Council of Lyons in order to deal with the eastern Schism. Aquinas, along with others, such as the Franciscan Bonaventure (1221–74, the Seraphic Doctor), was requested to attend. At the beginning of February 1274, about the same time the Venetian Marco Polo (1254–1324) was finally arriving in China, Aquinas and his entourage set out for Lyons. At the time, Aquinas worried about being made a cardinal, whether he liked it or not. He said that he preferred death to receiving such an office, which would require that he give up teaching.

While on his way north, near the little town of Teano, Aquinas hit his head on a low-hanging tree branch and was knocked out. After a while he seemed to recover and the party moved on, stopping along the way to visit some of Aquinas' relatives. Later, though, he became too weak to move. At that point he was taken to the nearby Cistercian monastery of Fossanova where, after a five-week period of being bed-ridden, he died on Wednesday 7 March 1274. What actually killed Aquinas is unknown. Certainly, though, Dante (1265–1321) was wrong when, in his *Divine Comedy*, he said that Aquinas was poisoned by the emperor Charles of Anjou in order to keep him quiet about something bad Charles had done.

After Aquinas' death, things became even stranger. In Catholic tradition the body is of great importance, which is why physical relics of the saints are important. As the situation is described by Vernon J. Bourke, at the time Aquinas died he was recognized as a saint and, as a result, everyone, literally, wanted a piece of him. At first Aquinas' body was entombed in front of the main altar of the monastery church. A short time later, fearing that the corpse might be stolen, it was moved to another part of the monastery. But then, about seven months later, reportedly after a request was delivered by means of a vision to the prior by Aquinas himself, the body was returned to its original site. In 1276 a Dominican (Innocent V) became pope and the Cistercians feared that he would claim the body for burial in a Dominican church. So, they opened the tomb, cut off Aquinas' head and hid the body elsewhere in the monastery, where it stayed for 12 years (Bourke, 1965).

In 1288, at the request of his sister, the Countess Teodora, for a relic, the tomb was again opened and a hand removed from the body. The thumb was then removed from the hand by Reginald of Piperno and given to the bishop of Ostia. In 1303, when another Dominican became pope (Benedict XI), the body was again moved to a safer hiding place. Finally the monks decided to play it really safe. Some time before 1319 they boiled the body down to its bones, which were then kept in a special box in the sacristy of the monastery church. This is not as ghoulish at it may sound to us today. In the days before modern embalming, boiling was the best way to transport a body from one place to another place far away.

In 1349 a descendant of the Aquino family gained possession of the torso bones. In 1368 Urban V gained possession of both the head and the body, sending the head to the Dominican Master General and the bones to the Dominican monastery in Toulouse, France. At the time of the French Revolution the bones were transferred to the Dominican Church of Saint Sernin in Toulouse. Today, the cathedral in Naples claims to have the left arm, while the Minerva Church in Rome claims to have the right arm. If you are of a mind to see Aquinas' remains, what is left of the bones can still be seen today at Saint Sernin's. In 1282 Aquinas was adopted as the official theologian of the Dominicans. He was canonized by Pope John XXII in 1323 and the Paris ban on teaching anything Thomistic was lifted in 1325.

Later in history, Aquinas' works were the chief theological source used during the Council of Trent (1545–63, Trento, in northern Italy), called to reform the Church from head to toe. A short time later, in 1567, he was recognized as a Doctor of the Church by Pope Pius V. In modern times, Vatican Council II (1962–65) recommended that Aquinas serve as the worldwide model to be followed in all Catholic educational programmes, the central attraction being the way Aquinas was able to harmonize faith and reason.

Aquinas' Troubled Times

During the thirteenth century in Europe, feudalism was rapidly decreasing, even while technology was rapidly increasing. Between 700 and 1300 there occurred the introduction of paper-making from cellulose, the development of the organ for making music, the lateen sail, the magnetic compass, a much-improved plough, the use of animal fats for candles, stamp mills, windmills, the hinged rudder, cog wheels, great improvements in the making of glass, eyeglasses, plate armour, gunpowder, standard measures in business and commerce, and the use of the Italian Florin as a common basis of monetary exchange. By 1300 business was booming, trade guilds had been formed, and cities were growing rapidly.

With respect to the Church, the 1200s were years of great conflict both within and around the Church. These conflicts included the constant threat of military defeat by Islam. The Church was surrounded on three sides by Islamic warriors. When, in 1071, the Sunni Seljuk Turks, under Alp-Arslan, declared war on Jews and Christians in the Holy Land, the popes decided that the best defence was a strong counter-attack. This gave rise to the Crusades. By the end of the thirteenth century, however, the Crusades ended in failure and, as late as 1683, the Ottoman Turks besieged the city of Vienna. In addition, there was the military threat from the north-east in the form of the Mongols, under the leadership of Batu Khan (?–1255, grandson of Genghis Khan).

These external military threats were equalled only by a long series of internal military threats. Since the beginning of the Holy Roman Empire in the tenth century, the Church was under constant attack by the very people who were supposed to protect her. Otto I (Otto the Great, 912–73), the first emperor, in 963, attempted to depose Pope John XII and replace him with his own man. In 966, Otto practically destroyed Rome in order to stamp out a rebellion against his rule. It was Otto's view that the Church should be subordinate to the state. Frederick I (1125–1190), known as Barbarossa (red beard), burned down Milan in 1162 and sacked Rome in 1166 in order to teach the pope a lesson about resisting his rule. His grandson, Frederick II, attacked Lombardy in northern Italy, seized the Papal States by means of a largely Muslim army, drove Pope Innocent IV out of Rome, and was excommunicated and reinstated three times.

In 1302, Pope Boniface VIII (1235–1303), in the spirit of Pope Gregory VII (the great Hildebrand, 1020–85), had to issue a very strong letter directed against King Philip IV (Philip the Fair) of France warning him not to try to take over the Church. Since the spiritual is superior to the material, insisted the pope, if anybody is going to take over anything, it is the Church that should rule over the state. As usual, in the long run, the pope was proven right. Following the death of Boniface VIII, the French monarchy almost did succeed in its aim. From 1309 to 1378, during the 'Babylonian Captivity', a phrase designed to bring to mind the Babylonian captivity of the Jews, the popes moved from Rome to Avignon in southern France where they came more and more under the influence of the king. As late as the 1800s, Napoleon imprisoned the popes (Pius VI, 1717–99; Pius VII, 1740–1823) and had them carried back to France.

Finally, the popes came to their senses, largely due to the constant preaching of two of the most remarkable real reformers in history, Saint Bridget of Sweden (1303–73) and the Benedictine Saint Catherine of Siena (1347–80). Because of these two strong and faithful women, the popes returned to Rome and have remained there ever since. One might say that these powerful women put the pope in his place. Moreover, one of them, Saint Catherine, predicted the future. At the time, corruption was so bad in the Church that God himself, in his *Dialogues* with the saint, told her that if the Church did not cleanse itself he would create a 'whip of men' to do the job. This was 150 years before the Protestant Reformation.

As a general rule, the state always wants to gain control over everything within its territory, including religion. In the past, kings often tried setting up anti-popes as a way of gaining control. If the state succeeds, religion is reduced to being just another branch of government with an office down the hall and the religious leaders become bureaucrats. As Søren Kierkegaard noted with respect to the Lutheran State Church in Denmark, rather than taking Christ as its teacher it had switched to the politically acceptable Georg Hegel, with disastrous results for religion.

The internal wars continued for many years on many different fronts. The Albigensians (Manichaes) in southern France posed a threat to morals and civilization equal to that of the earlier barbarian invasions. The Albigensians were both a moral and a military threat, which led to the politically motivated adventures of both Spain and France in an effort to defeat the Manichaes militarily and to gain territory in the area. The threat also led to the establishment of the Inquisition in 1233 by Pope Gregory IX. Although usually badly misrepresented, in principle it was for its time a reasonable and restrained response to a very serious situation, a situation comparable to the spread of illegal drugs and military terror tactics in our own time. As long as the Inquisition remained under the control of the popes it was a relatively moderate response to the crimes of the times.

Often, though, something restrained in principle, as explained by Ronald Knox and Arnold Lunn (1888–1974), can be abused in practice, but that does not negate the need for grand juries, prosecuting attorneys, and strong anti-terrorist legislation. Even today there is legislation with respect to suspected terrorists depriving them of many of our normal civil rights (Lunn and Knox, 1958).

Even later the warfare continued. In 1519, by handing out large bribes, Charles I of Spain (1500–58) was elected as Holy Roman Emperor (and then became known as Charles V) over Francis I of France and Henry VIII of England. King Henry really wanted the position and was very much upset over losing out. Although, when the three of them met near Calais, France, in 1520, they put on a friendly show, under the surface lay serious problems. Soon after (1524–26) there followed the Peasants' War, in which the German serfs and peasants, brutally crushed by the soldiers of the mainly Lutheran Great Swabian League, learned that with a friend like Martin Luther they had no need of enemies. This was followed by a revolt by France, in alliance with Pope Clement VII (1478–1534), against the emperor Charles V.

The 1527 response of the emperor, supposedly the protector of the Church, was to send an army, composed mainly of Spanish soldiers, German Lutherans, and some Italians, to attack Rome. One of the leaders of the Italian gang was Pier Luigi, an illegitimate son of the future Pope Paul III (1468–1549, pope from 1534), the pope who established the Jesuits and who excommunicated Henry VIII. Luigi was later made a cardinal and was assassinated in 1547. From May to July of 1527 this armed force proceeded to pillage Rome, raping, robbing, torturing, and killing large numbers of people. Bishops, monks, sisters, and clergy were systematically tortured in order to extract from them all of their earthly goods and valuables. In addition to teaching the pope a lesson, the sack of Rome also served as a way for the emperor to pay the back wages of his army, which had gone for a long time without pay. Thereafter in Rome the invasion was referred to as the 'German Fury'.

Even David Hume, no friend of the Roman Catholic Church, comments that the pope, who mistakenly thought that he would be shown some respect because of his religious office, was instead taken captive by the invaders. Hume relates in the second of his two chapters on Henry VIII that:

> Whatever was respectable in modesty or sacred in religion, seemed but the more to provoke the insults of the soldiery. Virgins suffered violation in the arms of their parents, and upon those very altars to which they had fled for protection. Aged prelates, after enduring every indignity, and even every torture, were thrown into dungeons, and menaced with the most cruel death, in order to make them reveal their secret treasures, or purchase liberty by exorbitant ransoms. Clement himself, who had trusted for protection to the sacredness of his character, and neglected to make his escape in time, was taken captive; and found that his dignity, which procured him no regard from the Spanish soldiers, did but draw on him the insolent mockery of the German, who, being generally attached to the Lutheran principles, were pleased to gratify their animosity by their abasement of the sovereign pontiff. (Hume, *History of England*, n.d., vol. 3, pp. 158–9)

As already noted, there was also widespread spiritual warfare within the Church. A great controversy arose over the existence of the new mendicant religious orders, which were a hybrid of the monks of the monastery, who avoided the world and who did not move about, and the parish priests, who worked in the world and who could move from parish to parish. One of the new orders was founded in 1209 by the Italian Giovanni Francisco Bernardone (1182–1226), better known as Saint Francis of Assisi; the other in 1215 by the Spaniard Domingo de Guzman (1170–1221), better known as Saint Dominic.

Many members of the secular clergy were opposed to these new orders and at one point the Dominican college in Paris had to be guarded by soldiers in order to prevent violence. Imagine the scandal today if a large number of parish priests and their parishioners ganged up to attack a group of Jesuits living in Washington, DC or London. Some of the secular clergy even regarded the new orders as a sign that the world was coming to an end and claimed that the members of these new hybrids were Anti-Christs. The situation was made worse by the fact that the secular clergy were often more loyal to their political state than to the pope, whereas the members of the new orders were just the reverse. The same thing can still be seen today. Are you Ukranian first or Catholic first?

There was at the time also warfare in terms of 'town and gown'. Drunkenness and fighting were common occurrences among the students, often because they hailed from different ethnic groups. And the students, of all nationalities, often fought with the townspeople, who had to hire constables to beat the students with clubs. There was also widespread corruption among the clergy, especially the secular clergy, and among the students who were all, theoretically at least, on their way to holy orders. And even within the new orders, especially the Franciscans, there was disunity. The Franciscan Spirituals thought that the mainline Franciscans were too worldly and made their views known in widespread public campaigns.

The corruption among the clergy was so bad that it was necessary for the theologians of the time, including people such as Aquinas, to frankly and openly face the various issues involved. As discussed by Bourke, the corruption of the clergy was a serious problem at the time from the viewpoint of the layman. Could a homosexual priest or a priest living in sin with a woman (or women) still continue to offer the sacrifice of the mass? Would it be a mortal sin for a layman to receive communion from the hands of such a sinful priest? What should be the punishment for bishops who allow immoral priests to continue operating in their dioceses? Not surprisingly, the widespread corruption of the clergy was also a common theme of many sermons preached at the time. One need only read some of the sermons of Saint Bonaventure to see what I mean. Criticism of the clergy was also a common theme of messages delivered to the pope by saintly women (Bourke, 1965, pp. 97–9).

As if all this were not bad enough, there was also intellectual warfare to contend with. The newly reintroduced works of Aristotle were causing no end of trouble on the intellectual front. Which Aristotle was the true Aristotle?

Was it the Aristotle as interpreted by the Arabic-speaking commentators? Was Christianity committed to Platonic philosophy? Could Aristotle and Plato be reconciled? Was Aristotle a friend or enemy to religion? If Aristotle represented the last word in science and Plato the last word in philosophy, and they both disagreed with each other, how could they be reconciled with Judao-Christianity? The parallel situation today would be the conflict between science, as represented by those who regard Charles Darwin as the last word in science, modern philosophy, as represented by thinkers such as Martin Heidegger and Hans-Georg Gadamer, and religion, as represented by the Roman Catholic Church.

Members of monastic orders, the secular clergy, and even of the new religious orders, were not of one mind on the relative merits of Plato and Aristotle and often engaged in hot debates over who was the final master of those who know. Although tentatively following Aristotle's philosophy of nature in most matters, including his bad biology, which for instance taught doctrines such as spontaneous generation, the inferiority of the female body relative to the male body, and the progression of souls in the foetus, Aquinas could not accept the Greek's philosophy of being. Although Aristotle had been successful in accounting in a general way for both change and permanence in the material world, he had not solved the problem of being. Doing that required 'boldly going where no Greek had ever gone before'.

As the century progressed the genius of Aquinas went to work on the problem of being and ended up rejecting the metaphysics of both Plato and Aristotle, replacing them with a uniquely existential philosophy of his own. Furthermore, as we can see from our present-day perspective, those 'scientific' teachings of Aristotle that Aquinas accepted, but that have since been proven wrong, in no way affect Aquinas' basic contributions in philosophy and theology. If anything, by eliminating Aristotle's bad science, Aquinas' insights are more cogent now than they were back then.

If some people today persist in looking back on the high Middle Ages as a time of great harmony and universal orthodoxy, it is only because they are suffering from an illusion of perspective. The reason it appears to be so orthodox is because, in the long run, it is always orthodoxy that survives and prospers. Very likely, 500 years from now, future dissidents will look back upon the condition of the Church in our own time and marvel at her wonderful tranquillity, homogeneity, and self-assured orthodoxy. As we are reminded by Ronald Knox, God's view is longer than ours. For all we know we may still be living in the early Church. As we pass though our modern troubles, he reminds us, we must not lose heart (Knox, 1963b, p. 121).

Aquinas' Unique Philosophy

> My only point is that a decisive metaphysical progress or, rather, a true metaphysical revolution was achieved when someone began to translate all the problems concerning being from the language of essences into that of existences. From its

earliest origins, metaphysics has always obscurely aimed at becoming existential; from the time of Saint Thomas Aquinas it has always been so, and to such an extent that metaphysics has regularly lost its very existence every time it has lost its existentiality. (Gilson, 1941, p. 67)

According to Gilson, to advance philosophy Aquinas had to achieve the dissociation of the two notions of form and act. And this is exactly what he did, thus achieving the greatest contribution ever made by any single human being to the science of being (Gilson, 1952, p. 174).

From the historical viewpoint, one of the most important things to realize about Aquinas is that he is not an Aristotelian. The same can be said about others, such as Moses Maimonides (Moses ben Maimon, 1135–1204), who was born in Cordoba, Spain. He was home-schooled by his father, a distinguished rabbi. While he was still young, in 1148, the Almohad Muslims captured Cordoba and began forcing everyone to convert to Islam. His family fled to Cairo, Egypt, where he eventually became the chief rabbi of the city and the court physician to the great Muslim leader Saladin (1137–93). As the 'second Moses', Maimonides is noted for writing the highly authoritative 14 books of the *Mishnah Torah*, for a set of principles of faith consisting of a 13-point 'creed' of Orthodox Judaism, and for his lengthy *Guide for the Perplexed*, which was written in Arabic.

Just as the *Guide for the Perplexed* was not a book written by a philosopher for other philosophers, but rather a book written by a distinguished member of the Jewish community on behalf of his religious colleagues, so too it is correct to say that Aquinas was first and foremost a theologian. Hence, any effort to find in his writings an autonomous philosophy is futile. Nonetheless, to admit that he had no completely independent philosophy is not to maintain that he had no philosophy whatsoever. In Aquinas' view, revelation is to philosophy (natural knowledge) as divine grace is to nature. Revelation and grace do not replace nature but rather bring nature to perfection. It was precisely the extra-philosophical elements in his life that enabled Aquinas' philosophy to reach its zenith. This approach dominates in his two major works, to wit, the *Summa Theologiae* (sometimes spelt *Summa Theologica*) and the *Summa Contra Gentiles* (Aquinas, 1894a, 1894b).

Saying that Aquinas was not an Aristotelian is not to deny that he used the language of Aristotle. To engage in philosophy in the thirteenth century was to enmesh yourself in terms such as substance, potency, essence, and being. Nonetheless, the meanings given to such terms by Aquinas were decidedly not the meanings found in Aristotle. The wax nose of authority enabled Aquinas to force Aristotle to state things that in fact the Greek had never dreamed of saying. In addition, to earmark Thomas as an Aristotelian because he used, for example, the term being would not make much sense, if for no other reason than that this same word was also extensively used by many other thinkers, such as Parmenides, Plato, Plotinus, and Augustine. In parallel fashion, all of the traditional religions of the world use terms such as knowledge, insight, and enlightenment. Does this mean that all religions are the same?

More to the point, Aristotle's contributions belong to pagan Greek philosophy, not to Judao-Christian philosophy. Hence, any inclusion of Aquinas in philosophy necessitates finding in him something that does not belong to pagan Greek philosophy. Long ago, did not Parmenides realize that things do not differ by what they have in common? Consequently, while there is an Aristotelian moment in Aquinas' philosophy, it is only a moment and the next moment is radically different.

Granting, then, that Aquinas' philosophy included an original insight, how are we to discover its novelty? Perhaps history itself supplies the answer. For both Plato and Aristotle, the most basic part of philosophy is metaphysics. As 'first philosophy' (the title is Aristotle's), metaphysics, the subject-matter of which is being itself (being as being), supplies us with the principles that are at the foundation of all of the other branches of philosophy. Aquinas accepts this. Should we conclude from this fact that he is an Aristotelian? Or is this proof that he is a Platonist?

Pursuing this analysis, we find that Plato understood being to mean that which is entirely immutable and hence intelligible. Intellectual knowledge demands perfect stability. In his two-world theory, this intelligibility was located in the separate world of ideas or forms, the really real world. The world of sensible, changeable things was merely a copy or shadow of the real world. Sensible things are what they are by having different degrees of participation in these separated forms. The same sort of thinking can be found in Aquinas. In his 'fourth way' for proving the existence of God, for instance, we find him appealing to the gradation of beings. Beings are more or less good, true, and noble. This would not be possible without the existence of something that acts as the cause of everything further down the scale in its category of being. By extension, there must really exist a being responsible for causing all being, regardless of its degree of perfection. This doctrine of participation aligns Aquinas with Plato against Aristotle, who rejected participation as empty words and poetic metaphor (Aquinas, 1894b, I, 2, 3; Aristotle, 1941, *Metaphysics* I, chapter 9).

At any rate, for Plato, being represents the intelligible, something literally out of this world. Accordingly, all knowledge pertains to the forms, never to matter. Matter is unintelligible. On this point, Aristotle is in agreement with Plato. Although a corporeal thing is sensible and can act as a basis for our sense knowledge, its matter renders it unintelligible in so far as the mind is concerned (Aristotle, 1941, *Metaphysics* VII, chapter 10; *On the Soul* III, chapter 6). Even Plotinus, who culminated Hellenic philosophy, remained in the tradition of Plato's *Phaedo*, a meditation on death, which described salvation as an escape from matter. After all, had not Plato himself described the body as a terrible tomb, a ball and chain dragging down the soul?

Aquinas, however, could not accept this Greek doctrine of the unintelligibility of matter, for the very simple reason that it conflicted with the biblical book of Genesis. If God produced the universe, then matter (which includes the human body), in addition to being good, must also be knowable, because God knows what he makes. In short, the doctrine of creation prohibits a reduction of Aquinas to any Greek philosopher who regarded matter as evil or unknowable.

When we come to Aristotle's doctrine of being, we see that it is not so far removed from Plato's. For both thinkers, being refers to the supra-sensible. As Plato located true being in a form, so did Aristotle. For Aristotle, only substances separated from matter (the pure forms, the gods) are intrinsically beings. It is no accident, therefore, that Aristotle also described his *Metaphysics* (his treatise on being) as theology. Whereas physical things are subject to change, things beyond the physical are immutable. Accordingly, for Aristotle, metaphysics studies the separated forms and especially the Prime Mover, the highest of the separated substances.

When we consider Aquinas, however, we find that his view on being differs radically from both of the two Greeks. In the first place, Aquinas' utilization of the real distinction (essence is not existence) enabled him to view the analogy of being in terms of proper proportionality rather than mere attribution. For Aquinas, all levels of beings are truly beings, whereas, for Plato and Aristotle, only the forms are true beings. For the Greeks, being is only attributed to other things because of their relation to form and, with Aristotle, especially to the highest form, the Prime Mover. It is the difference between saying 2:4::3:6 (a proper proportion) and saying 'the rosy-fingered dawn' or 'a heavenly smile' (metaphors). All proper analogies are comparisons; some comparisons are proper analogies.

This means that Aquinas' entire metaphysical orientation differs from Aristotle's. For Aquinas, metaphysics properly studies all beings whatsoever. For Aristotle, though, material things are properly studied in the philosophy of nature, not metaphysics. Hence, while both thinkers agree that no science proves the existence of its own subject-matter and first principles, they disagree about the application of this fact. For Aristotle, the existence of separated (immaterial) substances is established in the *Physics*. The *Metaphysics* then goes on to deal with these immaterial beings.

So, how do you know an Aristotelian when you see one? He will always go through physics before arriving at metaphysics. Logic and mathematics, because they do not require extensive experience of the world, can be learned while one is still young. Then comes the philosophy of nature, which deals with the changeable things of the physical world. Physics culminates in the discovery of the Prime Mover as the cause of eternally uniform circular motion. Only later, after much experience and the quieting down of the bodily appetites, is one ready for the study of moral philosophy. Finally, when one is over 50, one is ready for the study of the gods. This, though, is not Aquinas' sequence of learning.

For Aquinas, more in agreement with Avicenna (Ibn Sina, 980–1037, the Prince of Physicians), God is properly studied in sacred theology, where the thinker has the advantage of revelation. Therefore, if and when the existence of God is to be rationally proven, it must be proven elsewhere, namely, in the lower science of metaphysics (natural theology) and not in the even lower science of physics. Hence, God is not the subject-matter of metaphysics, but the cause of the subject-matter, which is then studied in the philosophy of being (Aquinas, 1894b, I–II, 66, 5, ad 4).

More interestingly, no Greek ever transcended the realm of essence in metaphysics. For Plato, being refers to the forms and especially to the five highest forms (essence, sameness, difference, motion, rest), while, for Aristotle, being ultimately refers to the highest form, the Prime Mover. 'To be' is to be a 'what', an essence (Aristotle, 1941, *Metaphysics* VII, chapters 7, 10, 11).

There will thus be as many beings as there are essences and to know an essence is to define it. In as much as an essence refers to what is enclosed within a definition, every being will be limited. As Whitehead says in his *Religion in the Making* (1969), to be is to be finite. Aristotle states that to be a man, to be one man, and to be an existing man are all the same thing. There is only a verbal difference among the terms. Unity and being are the same thing (Aristotle, 1941, *Metaphysics* IV, chapter 2). In such a view, any notion of infinity is on the side of matter, the indeterminate. Perfection, on the other hand, stems from the form. The notion of an infinite being is thus a contradiction in terms and in fact it is not found in Aristotle. It is, however, manifestly found in Aquinas, for whom being itself (God) is infinite. In a fashion just the reverse of the Greeks, for Aquinas, where being is limited, the principle of limitation is essence, something other than existence.

Very decisively, Aquinas dealt a fatal blow to Greek philosophy by rejecting the thesis that being is an essence. As he says in his *Commentary on the Sentences* (1929–47, II, I, 1, 5, ad 2), essences, of themselves, are nothing (non-beings). In effect this says that no Greek ever discussed genuine being. Indeed, it is so impossible for an essence to exist by itself as an essence that not even God could create one. Aquinas himself thought that he had learned this, not from Aristotle, but from the Scriptures (Exodus 3:14). Since God is being and since a thing can give only what it possesses, God, if and when he freely chooses, gives being, thus making things exist. But to give being is to create in the proper meaning of the term, as we see in Genesis 1 and in 2 Maccabees 7:28 (Aquinas, 1997, p. 102).

Averroes (Ibn Rushd, 1126–98, The Commentator), the most Aristotelian of all commentators on Aristotle, rejected creation as nonsense. Science is the final truth and the Koran is mostly myth. The First Cause causes uniform motion, not existence. The Prime Mover keeps things moving in perfect circles; he is not the cause of the being of things. He gives being only in the sense of preserving substances (essences) in their orderly activity. In contrast, for Aquinas, the doctrine of creation is not only true, but can be proven philosophically, even if the creation process is viewed as taking place from all eternity (Chroust, 1978, pp. 268–79).

Continuing, Averroes noted that, since being is not one of Aristotle's ten categories, it is nothing above substance and the nine accidents. Into what category could being possibly fall? A changeable substance is matter (potency) and form (act) and one or more of the nine accidents. An efficient cause gives being only in the sense of bringing about a new example of an eternal form in a particular sample of eternal matter. Clearly, however, even though in several places he bends over backwards in order to attribute a doctrine of creation to Aristotle, Aquinas' teaching on creation is divergent from Aristotle's.

Observe also that Aristotle certainly believed in the eternity of the world. Maybe not so for Plato, who thought up a creation myth for the world. This means that, while Aristotle wrote treatises on the cosmos, he had no doctrine of creation. In as much as the reverse is true of Plato, Aquinas is more akin to Plato than to Plato's star pupil. Interestingly, when Moses Maimonides examined the 26 propositions used by Aristotle to prove the existence of the Prime Mover, he rejected only the one concerning the eternity of the world. In turn, Aquinas will declare that neither the eternity nor the non-eternity of the universe is demonstrable by the use of human reason alone. And then, as a commentator on The Philosopher (Aristotle), he will assert that Aristotle's reasoning on the subject was quite correct.

However, Aquinas does not say that Aristotle was right. If at least one premise is false, logically correct reasoning need not yield a true conclusion. Aristotle's deductions are based on the supposition that all coming into being is by way of something coming from something else that is already there. Maintaining that the process of generation (birth, growth, death; the chicken and the egg) is eternal, Aristotle logically concluded that the universe is eternal. If all coming to be is by means of generation, then the universe is eternal. All coming to be is by means of generation. Therefore, the universe is eternal.

The Italian (Aquinas), though, reasons as follows: If all coming to be is by means of generation, then the universe is eternal. But the universe is not eternal. Therefore, all coming to be is not by means of generation. That is to say, some coming to be is by generation and some is not. How did Aquinas know that the universe is not eternal? From Holy Writ. This is not a theological subterfuge. On the contrary, the possession of this tenet enabled Aquinas to realize that Aristotle, not only never proved the antecedent, but also that the mere acceptance of the antecedent prohibited Aristotle from attaining an existential metaphysics.

Having severed himself from Aristotle, and capitalizing on the insights of Boethius and Avicenna, Aquinas was able to view all things as possessing their existence as something other than their essence. For the first time in our intellectual history, someone was positing existence above essence. Yet, because he did not reject essence, Aquinas was able to use Aristotelian notions such as potency and act. However, these notions always occupy a peripheral position, revolving about existence as the nucleus of things. For Thomas, being is basic to both the things that are and to our knowledge of the things that are. It is absolutely impossible to leave out existence in anything that is real or in knowing about anything. We cannot contemplate an essence as though existence were something to be added to it later on. An essence without existence is simply a non-being; it simply does not exist, even in thought.

Aquinas' departure from Aristotle is very conspicuous in the domain of natural theology. Leaving aside the fact that Aristotle's Prime Mover was not one of the popular Greek gods, such as Zeus, let us recall that Aristotle defined his First Cause of motion as pure act because the Prime Mover was a pure form. Thomas, although he could accept the notion of God as pure act, could not accept God as pure form. This is because, for Aristotle, every act is a form (an essence) and every form is an act, act and form are the same thing. But, for Aquinas, existence is precisely an act that is not a form. With Aquinas, every form is an act; some act is a form.

This then leads to another important difference between the Greek and the Italian. Our mental grasping of a thing is by means of a concept, which is the essence (form) of the thing in the mind. What happens, though, when there is no concept of the thing being grasped? As a consequence, we can have no idea of existence as an act; we never have a concept of existence. As an object of predication, that is, when used as a subject in a proposition, existence is as existentially barren as any other idea, for example, dodo bird, unicorn, dinosaur, Mickey Mouse, polygram, and so forth. This means that we can know that God is but not what God is. Far from being unreasonable, such a situation is eminently reasonable.

In other words, although Aquinas was willing to grant that form is an act within essence, he insisted that over and above the entire order of essence there resides the most important aspect of any individual thing, to wit, its act of existing. For him, existence is the actuality of every form and is related to essence as actuality is to potency. Existence is the most perfect reality, related to everything else as its actuality; it is the actuality of all beings, even of forms (Aquinas, 1894b, I, 3, 4; I, 4, 1, ad 3).

The real distinction of essence and existence applies to all beings except God. These beings include angels, beings that the Greeks would have regarded as gods. For Aquinas, though, angels are not gods. This is because even in immaterial angels there is a real distinction between essence and existence. Gilson expresses Aquinas' problem and its solution in the following way:

> Here as elsewhere the hardest obstacle to remove was the Platonism of essence. Aristotle himself had failed to brush it aside, or, rather, had not even tried. For him, as for Plato, being was ultimately identified with the immovable. What he called 'being as being' was accordingly 'being as not becoming' ... If the divine is identified with the purely immaterial, and being with essence, then all being whose essence is purely immaterial has a right to be called a god. But if the reality of essence is rooted in its act-of-being, it is at once evident that further distinctions are to be introduced among immaterial beings. (Gilson, 1956, p. 167)

Also in the area of natural theology, Aquinas aligned himself with Augustine against Aristotle in maintaining that there are divine ideas, that there is divine providence, and that God is immanent to things, although God is not in any way identified with the world or any part of the world. For Aristotle, in contrast, God is a cold thought thinking only of himself (Aristotle, 1941, *On Generation and Corruption* II, chapter 10, *Metaphysics* III, chapter 3, XII, chapter 7). Thus, while Aristotle's God is only a non-creating final cause, the object of desire of lower forms, Aquinas' God is a loving being who is also the efficient cause of the world. God is a creator in the proper sense of one who gives existence (Aquinas, 1894b, I, 3, 5).

Discarding the eternity of the world on the basis of scripture, Aquinas could not accept the Greek's argument for God's existence. For Aristotle, no cause is required by a cosmos that is at once eternal and organic, for organic things are precisely those things capable of moving themselves. Like Plato, whose Demiurge produced the soul of the world, Aristotle, although rejecting a world-soul, remained faithful to the ancient Greek tradition of regarding the whole universe as animated (Aristotle, 1941, *On the Generation of Animals* II, chapter 6, III, chapter 2, IV, chapter 10, *On the Heavens* I, chapter 4, II, chapters 1, 9, 12, 13, *On the Parts of Animals* III, chapter 8, IV, chapters 5, 10; see also Solmsen, 1960, pp. 93, 240, 287–303).

Furthermore, being an existentialist means that Aquinas' philosophy of being is one of existence rather than substance. This is often overlooked. Whitehead, for example, believed that the rejection of Aristotle's substance (subject) and attribute (predicate) propositional form also entailed a rejection of Aquinas. Jumping to such a conclusion, though, loses sight of those elements that are common to Aquinas and twentieth-century process philosophers. To illustrate, Aquinas subscribed to the Augustinian doctrine that, because the material world is in process, process must reflect God. This view is shared by Whitehead, for whom there is an essential relevance between God and historic processes. In Aquinas' case, process is found in the inner life of God (the Trinity) and in the development of the world, society, and the Church.

In sum, the Aristotelian universe is composed of substances, while the Italian's universe is not. Strictly speaking, not even God is a substance (Aquinas, 1894b, I, 3, 5, ad 1, I, 3, 6, ad 2). Expressed concretely, a real thing is a being, not a substance. Without its act of existing it would be nothing at all. A substance is real because of something other than its substantiality (matter and form, potency and act), namely, its existence. It follows that the foundation of individuality must be 'to be', not essence. Essence does not make a thing to be or to be one.

Aquinas' unique metaphysics reverberates throughout all areas of his thought. In epistemology, knowledge is described in terms of intentional existence, not in terms of clear and distinct ideas or in terms of immateriality. For Aquinas, everything outside the mind is 'physical', including angels and God. Everything intra-mental is 'intentional'. In the process of knowing we become the thing known in an intentional way; the thing exists in us. The essence of the thing outside the mind and the essence of the thing inside the mind are one and the same. What is different is their respective acts of existing. This does not mean that we know concepts rather than things. We do know extra-mental things, not just our own ideas. Concepts are transparent. We know by means of concepts. In fact, we never know the concept itself.

Aquinas also insists that truth is not discovered in clear and distinct ideas, but in the act of judgment, that act whereby we come into contact with existence in its dynamic immediacy ('esse' as a verb, not 'existentia' as a noun). Truth follows upon a thing's existence. Although in agreement with those such as Kant who hold that being, in its immediacy as a verb, cannot be conceptualized, Aquinas would not agree that what cannot be conceptualized must be unintelligible. On the contrary, existence is the root of all intelligibility. Non-existing essences account for nothing, because in themselves essences are nothing.

Moreover, Aquinas has a unique approach to the problem of universal predication. How can the same predicate apply to many different subjects in the same way? Jane is a human being, Jim is a human being, and so on. Aristotle's strength is in taking seriously the substantial unity of real things. This particular human being, for instance, possesses his own matter and form in his own right; he is not the shadow of a Platonic idea. However, Aristotle never did figure out how a form that is numerically singular, and that makes the thing to be what it is (for example, a human being), can exist outside the mind in more than one thing at the same time. Also, how can a form that is individuated extra-mentally be universal intra-mentally? Does a singular thing (for example, this man) possess the whole form, in which case no other singular thing can have it, or does the individual have only a part of the form, in which case the individual is not what it is?

Even worse, if the latter is the case, we would have to study each and every singular in order to piece together a knowledge of the species as a whole. This, of course, is impossible. Thus, if doing it is required for science, and we cannot do it, then science is impossible. This is the same problem (the problem of induction) faced by Hume many years later. How do we get from the some to the all? If we must count each part, and if there are too many parts to count, then we can never get from the some to the all. Consequently, since real science is always about the necessary and the universal, we can never have science.

With respect to our knowledge of the essence (nature) of something, Aristotle ended up placing all the forms in the lowest of the separated substances (the gods), which then becomes the one, separated, perpetually active intellect common to all men and responsible for bestowing ideas upon individual rational souls. This takes him right back into Plato's problem of trying to account for the participation of individuals in their respective forms in some non-metaphorical way. Solving this problem in a rational way requires the real distinction between essence and existence, something Aristotle did not have.

In the philosophy of human nature, using the real distinction between essence and existence, Aquinas was able to show the immortality of each human soul, a feat that could not be accomplished using Aristotle's principles. Although he bent over backwards trying to find a doctrine of immortality in the Greek, we can see clearly from our modern perspective that Aristotle despaired of ever discovering such a thing within his own philosophy. Aristotle states quite clearly that to wish for personal immortality is to wish for the impossible (Aristotle, 1941, *Nicomachean Ethics* III, chapter 2, *On the Soul* II, chapter 2; see also Centore, 1979, pp. 129, 152).

Nor was it necessary for Aquinas to teach that man's intellectual knowledge was ultimately derived from a separated intellect (the lowest of the gods). In regard to knowledge, it is true that abstraction plays a role in both thinkers, but with an important difference. While Aristotelian abstraction excludes matter, Thomistic abstraction includes it (Aristotle, 1941, *On the Soul* II, chapter 4; Aquinas, 1949, pp. 37–8).

In addition, Aquinas' notion of the human person as an incarnated intellectual spirit is a duplication of no Greek whatsoever. In a nutshell, Aquinas teaches that each human soul possesses its own individual act of existence. This act (to be) is then communicated to the body, thus individuating it. As a result, the soul is naturally immortal, even while the soul and its body form a unity (psychosomaticism) while alive on earth. The soul is both the form of the body and a substance in its own right. Although the soul depends upon the body to operate in the material world, it does not depend upon the body to exist. This is not a gratuitous assertion on Aquinas' part. His psychosomatic position is just one more application of the fundamental real distinction between essence and existence.

Aquinas' view of man, in a way, marks him as closer to Plato than to Aristotle. After death, is a human being still a human being? Yes. Even though the body is an essential part of your definition? Yes. Compare the situation of the element fire when removed from its normal place in the universe. Even though out of place, says Aquinas, it is still fire. By the same token, a fish out of water is still a fish. The soul deprived of its body, although it cannot operate in a material world, nevertheless remains a human soul. The person, however, is incomplete, and eagerly awaits the resurrection of its own body.

As might be expected, such a radically different interpretation of the human person in the area of philosophical psychology gives rise to a radically different view of ethical behaviour. With Aquinas, the norm of morality is the natural moral law, which is a participation in the divine law and ultimately a reflection of God himself. Aristotle has neither natural moral law nor the participation of mankind in the life of God. This gives a sense of final futility permeating Aristotelian ethics. For the Greek, only the old philosopher can attain some semblance of happiness, provided he and his friends (no women allowed) have lives long enough to contemplate the gods, enjoy good health, possess material wealth, have the ability to experience bodily pleasures, and can exercise a limited and secular virtue as members of the city-state. Aristotle's ethics are based on finding a happy medium between earthly extremes in order to live securely on earth. One should be neither rash nor a coward, and the like. When seen in its overall configuration, it is clear that Aristotle's system of morality is a secular humanism. For the Italian, in contrast, man's life is permeated with divine faith, hope, and love, for both females and males.

In two other areas of philosophy, namely, the philosophy of nature and the philosophy of science, we find the same inability to reduce Aquinas to Aristotle. In the philosophy of nature, while Aristotle predicated 'the natural' (the physical) of mutable things in contrast to immutable (metaphysical) things, Aquinas contrasted 'the physical' with 'the intentional', thereby extending the physical to the supernatural and the metaphysical to the material things of the world. In Aquinas' view, metaphysics begins with the plumbing in the basement. Because of the real distinction in all beings other than God, metaphysics covers everything created by God in any way.

Early on in his life it looked as if Aristotle was going in for induction. Aristotle's mature philosophy of science, however, wherein properties are deduced from known essences, also contrasts sharply with Aquinas' view, which rejects the notion that our scientific knowledge of things is primarily deductive. Certainly there is a place for logic and deductive reasoning, but this sort of activity cannot act as a substitute for careful observations concerning the natural world. This is because essences (substantial forms) simply cannot be known by the human intellect in any direct and certain way. We must work through the effects in order to reach the cause of the effects. We must, for instance, research the actions of things in order to find the specific difference telling one species apart from another in the same genus (Aquinas, 1949, p. 52, 1894b, I, 29, 1, ad 3).

Aristotle's identification of a thing's formal and final causes led his disciples to believe that the essence and properties of something could be known once the thing's purpose had been ascertained. So, although at first it looked as if Aristotle was on the path to experimental science, his return to a metaphysics of essences quickly killed off such a move. The conflicts among science, philosophy, and theology that ensued over the centuries because of this are familiar to everyone and need not be elaborated upon here. Aristotelian opposition to novelty was monumental. According to Aristotle, all essences continue unchanged forever, including those of organic species, thus making evolution impossible (Aristotle, 1941, *On the Soul* II, chapter 4; see also Centore, 2001, pp. 50–67).

In contrast to Aristotle, for those interested in natural science, Aquinas knew that actions, in all their concreteness, must be carefully examined in order to obtain some tentative idea of what the thing is. The only way to discover the nature of something is to actually examine it and the best sort of examination is to carefully observe the thing in action. This goes for whole classes of things as well as for individual things. If, for instance, you are interested in the nature of life, it does no good making a detailed list of a dead thing's parts. You must instead examine the living thing in action (Aquinas, 1894b, I, 32, 1, ad 2; see also Azar, 1989).

Aquinas' accomplishments are truly amazing, especially when contrasted with his contemporary Islamic thinkers. After an illustrious start in science and mathematics over a period of 400 years (800–1200), which included such brilliant mathematicians as Alhazen (?–1045), science and mathematics came to a halt in the Islamic world. Human beings can live without modern science but not without religion. After the greatest of the Islamic thinkers (Averroes) had failed to reconcile science and religion, the Islamic political and religious leaders had no choice but to suppress science in an effort to preserve religion and society. In contrast, in Europe, freed of Islamic religious control and enjoying the reconciliation of science and religion, science and mathematics flourished.

The conclusion is that Aquinas' existentialism is in fact very anti-Greek in its most fundamental orientation, that is, in its philosophy of being. With this fact firmly in mind, we are now in a position to understand Aquinas' uniquely existential core argument for the existence of God.

The God of Abraham, Isaac, and Jacob

The rebuttal to Hume is in Aquinas, not in Paley. For Aquinas, the only way to demonstrate the existence of God is from his effects. However, an objection states, there is no proportion between the infinite (God) and the finite (the world) and so we cannot prove the existence of God from the existence of the world. Aquinas' answer is that the objection is right in so far as it shows that we cannot form a concept of God as he is in himself. Nevertheless, we can know that God exists as the cause of the effect, even without knowing the cause in a perfect way (Aquinas, 1894b, I, 2, 2, ad 3). The same point is made later when he states that from the knowledge of sensible things the whole power of God cannot be known and neither can his essence be understood (Aquinas, 1894b, I, 12, 12). This statement is from an article that is part of the question concerning the names of God. For Aquinas, we can know that God exists, even though we cannot grasp from a knowledge of the natural universe (the effect) the full richness of God. This is plain common sense. Is an artist equivalent to one of his paintings?

Aquinas' core argument for the existence of God is found in his brief work *On Being and Essence*. Methodologically speaking, Aquinas' basic principle is that you cannot start off dealing only with abstractions (essences, ideas, concepts) and then, later on, switch over to something existential. An existential approach must be existential from the beginning. As we see throughout Aquinas' works, this also applies to proving God's existence. (On where in his works Aquinas proves the existence of God see Owens, 1963.)

In our ordinary life, our attention is always directed first and foremost to real things outside of our own mind. Our ordinary experience of the world around us tells us that we are a complex being with both senses and intellect. We know the world by means of our bodily sensations, while at the same time making intellectual judgments on what is happening around us. We are aware of two things simultaneously, both that something exists and that we are defining things by way of the judgments we make.

Building on this, as an ordinary part of our judgmental process, we know that things can be grouped into sets, classes, species, categories, kinds, and so on. To be intelligent is to think in terms of categories and relationships. We also know that one thing within a given species can never be the cause of the specific nature of another thing within that same species. For instance, a male and a female dog can bring into existence this particular puppy, but they cannot cause the existence of 'dogness' itself. This is because, first of all, the nature, essence, definition, or the 'what', of something cannot exist simply as a nature. It must exist either as a thing outside the mind or as an idea in the mind. In Aquinas' existential philosophy, how something exists is not determined by the nature itself. In a word, essences are existentially neutral. Realizing this, Aquinas also realizes that Anselm's definitional approach to God is impossible. Long before Kant, Thomas realized that no essence can bring itself into existence.

To be something outside the mind, something must be actualized by a real thing in the real world. A mere idea in the mind cannot do the job. Real children are produced by real parents, not possible parents; real paintings are made by real artists, not possible ones; real carpenters are needed to make real tables. There must be some already existing thing that can bring the new being into existence. Even in modern science, the scientist who creates a new virus, genetic structure, chemical compound, breed of animal, and so on must be real, as must be his material, equipment, and so on. In the real world, existence always precedes essence. This information gives us the first part of Aquinas' argument.

- Anything whose essence (nature) does not include its own existence is something dependent upon some other, already extra-mentally existing, thing external to itself for its existence.
- Every sensible thing is something whose essence does not include its own existence.
- Ergo, every sensible thing is dependent upon some other, already extra-mentally existing, thing external to itself for its existence.

The conclusion means that every sensible thing must be efficiently (existentially) caused by some other already existing thing that is both real and external to the thing caused. Whether or not the cause is also a sensible thing is another matter. There is no reason to assume that the cause must be sensible. All we know at this point is that, with respect to any being whose existence is accidental (contingent) to its actual extra-mental existence, there must be something other than the being in question that already really exists and upon which the being in question depends for its existence.

Moving on, we can now add to our chain of reasoning another link. Is it necessary to enumerate every last contingent thing in the universe in order to see that whatever is true of the very nature of any one sensible thing here and now is true of all sensible things taken together here and now? No. If existential dependency is true of the very nature of any one sensible thing here and now (the conclusion reached above), it must also be true of all sensible things taken together here and now.

- Whatever is true of the very nature of any one sensible thing here and now is true of all sensible things taken together.
- Existential dependency is true of the very nature of any one sensible thing here and now.
- Ergo, existential dependency is true of all sensible things taken together.

It is important to note here that this is not an unjustified jump from the part to the whole (the fallacy of composition). It refers to the very nature of each sensible thing, which means that all sensible beings are homogeneous with respect to both the accidental nature and the priority of the cause of their existence. There is no problem of induction (going from a few observed cases to all cases) here. Those who deny the reality of essences cannot understand this fact. As a result, neither can they understand science, which demands necessary and universal knowledge. Without essences, all significant scientific generalizations (for example, all ordinary water is analysable into hydrogen and oxygen) would commit the fallacy of composition. Those committed to a totally materialistic world must deny the existence of anything really common to individual things, thus locking themselves into the position of never being able to go from the some to the all in scientifically significant cases. For the realist, however, what is true of one molecule of water is true of all molecules of water, thus saving the rationality of science.

Aquinas' argument also has the advantage of sidestepping the old problem of the chicken and the egg, the wheel and the road. Even though we live in a world of constant change, the argument is not concerned with a long series of ancient events. Because Aquinas did not take existence for granted, he had to redefine contingency. Even if the world were eternal, he taught, it would still require a giver of existence. Contingency does not mean something time-dependent, as when we say that something is here today and gone tomorrow. Even if the chicken and egg series went back forever, it would still require a creator. Time alone does not explain anything. Anything that exists requires the constant activity of God to maintain it in existence. Things are liable to death and destruction, not because they exist in time, but because they are composites. Where there is a composite nature, decomposition is possible. For Aquinas, contingency means the existential dependency of beings, not a temporal sequence. When water, for instance, breaks down into hydrogen and oxygen, this shows the contingency of water, but it does not deny its dependence upon a cause in the first place. When a piece of paper burns it becomes something else. The paper is gone, replaced by ashes and the products of combustion. To understand Aquinas' existential way we must think vertically (existential dependency here and now) rather than horizontally (a series stretching back into the past).

Interestingly enough, on this score, Aquinas' argument is stronger today than it was in his own day. When the science of Aristotle reigned supreme in Europe, it was taken for granted that the universe was eternal. Today, however, with the Big Bang theory, we know that this is not the case. In addition, as described by Werner Heisenberg, although Aristotle's geocentric view of the universe, with its 47 to 55 gods moving around the concentric spheres, is gone forever, the old Greek's doctrine of matter and form (potency and act), in opposition to Descartes' formless matter and Newton's atoms, is making a comeback (Heisenberg, 1962).

Although he never anticipated modern astronomy, Aquinas was aware of the fact that, if it could be shown that the world had a beginning, then the existence of God would be much easier to accept. He poses a question about the beginning and duration of created things. He inquires, in the first article of the question, about whether or not the universe of creatures has always existed. He maintains that we cannot prove by reason alone that the universe had a beginning. Nevertheless:

> For the world leads to a knowledge of the divine creating power more evidently if it had not always existed than if it had always existed. This is the case because it is obvious that everything that comes into existence has a cause, whereas having a cause it not so obvious for something that has always existed. (Aquinas, 1894b, I, 46, 1)

We are now ready for the last segment of the proof. So far we have seen that all sensible things taken collectively here and now can be regarded as one existentially dependent being. We can now ask, what if the one existentially dependent being cannot account for its own existence?

- Any existentially dependent being that has completely exhausted every possible other already really existing external explanatory cause is caused by an existentially independent being.
- The universe as a whole is such.
- Ergo, the universe as a whole is caused by an existentially independent being.

As Aquinas saw very well, if all we had were existentially dependent beings, there would be no beings at all, at any time. A series of existential zeros, however long, still adds up to zero. Indeed, there would not even be time. This is obviously contrary to fact. Neither can we appeal to nothingness as a cause of anything. From nothing we get nothing. It cannot even be thought in any direct way. Appealing to nothingness would be the height of irrationality.

What, then, is the nature of this existentially independent being? It must be the biblical He Who Is. Recall that the real cause of a sensible being does not have to be a sensible thing. It is possible that the cause of the world is totally transcendent with respect to the world. The whole point of the argument is that the existentially independent being is a being whose essence is to exist. As such, he is absolutely unique. This is the very same being who gave his proper name to Moses. Thus the God of Revelation is the same as the God of reason (Exodus 3:14 and John 8:58).

A clear statement of Aquinas' proof shows that it is not a scientific design-type argument. Aristotle was a polytheist who knew neither creation from no previously existing matter nor God's providence over his creation. With respect to Paley, even though God is indeed the author of nature, Paley's notion of God is inferior to Aquinas' supreme being. Thomas' argument, expressed in a fashion parallel to Paley's, would be: A single existentially dependent being is to its efficient cause as the whole existentially dependent realm of beings is to its efficient cause. Such a cause can only be the unique Who Is. (For more on these themes, see Varghese, 2000b.)

Now and only now does it make sense to talk about creation, that is, a real creation rather than a rearrangement of pre-existing parts. God's proper name is not the author of nature, for God would still be God even if he had never created the least little thing. When God freely does choose to create, however, he gives what only God can give, which is existence. Everything depends on the act of existence, not the other way around. God creates beings, that is to say, things with both essence and existence. This means that the world has both essences (species, law and order, science) and individuality, that is, each thing with its own act of existing, diverse from every other act of existing. This emphasis on God as the unique cause of all being also turns out to be the special feature of Genesis in contrast to the many other similar stories circulating at the time in the Middle East.

Once this is understood many other points also become clear. First, both deism and pantheism must be rejected. God is not the world and neither is he absent from the world. He is in fact continuously present to everything and everyone (Aquinas, 1894b, I, 8). Next, the giver of being gives everything else of a positive nature. Evil, though, as a negation, is not caused by God.

It also explains why there can be several different ways to God. These are summarized by Aquinas at the beginning of his *Summa Theologiae* (1894b, I, 2, 3). In a constantly changing world, God is the being that does not change. In a world of efficient causes and effects, God is the uncaused cause; God is not the self-caused cause, which makes no sense in an existential context. In a world of things that might or might not be, God is the necessary being. In a world of good, better, and best, God is the cause of good. In a world of operations moving toward definite goals (teleology), God is the final cause of all existence and change. (On the five ways, see Gilson and Wippel, 2000.)

At the end of the day, therefore, we see that it is possible to harmonize science, philosophy, and theology. This, though, is not the end of the story. Aquinas was the last person in the world to look down on the simple faith of the uneducated person. He knew that knowledge alone does not guarantee sanctity. Satan is smarter than any human being. He knew that the most uneducated person can be a saint. Even children can die as martyrs for the faith. The New Commandment (John 13:34) is not to go off and acquire doctorates in science, philosophy, and theology. It is to love one another as God loves you. Faith, hope, and charity are the three great virtues, and the greatest of these is love.

If God Loves Me, Why Do I Suffer?

Sonnet 146

Poor soul, the centre of my sinful earth,
Behold these rebel powers that thee array.
Why dost thou pine within and suffer dearth,
Painting thy outward walls so costly gay?
Why so large a cost, having so short a lease,
Dost thou upon thy fading mansion spend?
Shall worms, inheritors of this excess,
Eat up thy charge? Is this thy body's end?
Then, soul, live thou upon thy servant's loss,
And let that pine to aggravate thy store.
Buy terms divine in selling hours of dross;
Within be fed, without be rich no more.
   So shall thou feed on Death, that feeds on men,
   And Death once dead, there's no more dying then.
                          William Shakespeare (1564–1616)

Both Plato and Aristotle were polytheists. For Plato, in descending order, there was the one-above-being and then being (the ideas). The ideas were divine but impersonal. Then there were the personal gods, namely, the Demiurge, the world-soul, the gods of the heavens, and individual human souls. In addition, there was the material world, which, given its geometric nature, can only be understood by means of mathematics. For Aristotle, the gods (between 47 and 55 of them) were the movers of the heavenly spheres, which moved in perfect circles. At the top of the hierarchy rested the absolutely unchanging self-thinking thought, the Prime Mover. The area of change in the universe was restricted to the area below the moon. At the centre of everything was the earth, which was spherical in shape and which did not move at all.

Neither of the two Greeks had any problems with the fact that there was a disunity of ultimate causes. For both Plato and Aristotle there were two separate sets of explanatory principles. Science and mathematics were impersonal and applied to the natural world. The gods, on the other hand, were personal and were used to satisfy personal needs, as well as being used in part to account for the operations of the universe. There was no need for a creator or for divine providence.

In sharp contrast, in Judao-Christianity, God is the one cause of everything that exists. There is a unity of ultimate cause. All science, philosophy, and religion depend on the same ultimate source. The Trinity is the inner life of God. If we look at Genesis, for instance, we see that the basic creation story is very much like others in the Middle East at the time, but with one big difference, namely, God is the absolute creator of everything that is. Moreover, continuing with Genesis,

1 man *qua* man was created to know, love, and serve God;
2 man is subordinate to God, ruler (not abuser) over all the earth and over all the subhuman creatures on it;
3 among humans, we are necessarily social and community-minded by nature.

With respect to creation, God is free to either not create or create. If God creates, he is free to make beings at any level of perfection he wishes, for example, angels, humans, chimpanzees, chickens, worms, and bugs. He is also free to either create them all at once or gradually over a long period of time, that is, there can be an unfolding or unrolling (evolution) of God's will. There was no time before creation, so it is meaningless to ask why God did not make the world sooner or later.

Now to the problem of good and evil, which is the same thing as asking about the nature of divine providence. Aquinas takes up this issue in his *Summa Theologiae*, Part I, Question 22 (1894b). The question is subdivided into four articles:

1 whether providence is suitable to God;
2 whether everything is guided by providence;
3 whether God is immediately concerned with everything;
4 whether God's concern destroys all freedom of action on the part of creatures.

In the first article, Aquinas defines any sort of providence as the intelligent ordering of things to an end. In the case of divine providence, it is the ordering of all things to one final goal, which is God himself. Because of his infinite goodness, God himself is the proper end of everything that has being. Moreover, because of his infinite wisdom, God is most suited to direct everything to himself as the chief exemplar of everything that he himself has created.

Moving on to the second article, it may be true that guiding things is suitable to God, but is it true that God in fact guides everything, from the birds flying through the air to the rain drops falling from the sky? Is God aware of the number of hairs on your head? True, if God were comparable to an earthly king, he would employ ministers to act as intermediaries between himself and his subjects. This occurs with earthly rulers, though, only because they are deficient in knowledge and power. Okay, but then how do we explain the fact that there are deficiencies in those things over which the ruler has power? Does this mean that either God is not all-powerful or that some things fall outside of divine providence?

Aquinas gives a fairly long answer to this objection. This objection would be fatal to Aquinas' position if God were operating on a small scale. On a large scale, however, the situation is different; the overall good of the whole scheme of things must be considered. A well-organized society, for instance, demands the existence of hierarchy in leadership, a division of labour, and different economic groupings. Likewise, a beautiful painting demands a variety of colours. So also in the material universe. What appears as a defect on the small scale can very well be beneficial when viewed as a part of the big picture.

With respect to biological creatures, for example, old ones die and new ones are born, thus allowing for both variety within the species and for the simultaneous existence of many different species. Far from telling against divine providence, this arrangement of things shows us God's infinite richness. A more static arrangement would be boring and unrevealing of God's richness. Do we really want a plastic-coated world in which everything remains fixed forever?

With respect to the hierarchy of nature, it is proper for superior creatures to use (not abuse) inferior creatures. A lion fulfils its place in nature by using the antelope for food. For their part, human beings use minerals, plants, and animals to serve their need for food, clothing, and shelter. In addition, with respect to human life, we must contend with the existence of free choice and sinfulness. Is the power of free choice a good thing? If so, then we must be prepared to accept the consequences, even if, on the small scale, some of the consequences are bad for us. Due to original sin, human beings have a propensity to act in destructive ways. Sinful individuals think that the whole universe revolves around them.

This, though, is only one side of the coin. In the constant battle between good and evil, the evil deeds of others are often the occasions for heroic deeds on the part of the saints. Without troubled lives there would be no great novels. In agreement with Augustine, Aquinas affirms that God would not allow the evil deeds of some people if he did not expect others to draw good out of evil. For instance, considering all of the jealousy, fighting, promiscuity, rape, and pain that is occasioned by the human sex drive, is sex as a means of reproduction for human beings really worth all the trouble it causes? Apparently it is. For all of its problems, sex also allows for many good things to happen in human lives. And so nothing escapes divine providence. In addition, human beings are gifted with the special providence of heaven and hell.

In the third article Aquinas asks about deism. Did God leave the daily operation of the universe in the care of lesser things, such as angels? Aquinas does not see this as impossible, but he does see it as unfitting to a loving God who counts the very hairs on your head. There is no contradiction between God's omnipotence and his delegating authority to creatures, which can also be creators to a limited degree. The difference is that creatures might easily be corrupted, whereas there is no danger of corruption in God. So, although it might be argued that it is better for us not to know evil, it cannot be said that God must not know evil for fear he will be corrupted. There is therefore no objection to God's providence over all things.

The fourth article of Question 22 then asks an obvious question. If God's providence is so complete, how can there be any freedom for anything? A completely deterministic world is fine for science, but what about for human beings? Aquinas says that if God creates something as necessary and unalterable then it is necessary and unalterable. In addition, though, God is free to create other sorts of things. If God creates something as contingent and variable then it is contingent and variable. Being contingent can mean that it need not be or that it need not happen. However, either way, necessary or contingent, God's providence is preserved. It is possible for something to be unpredictable for us, and yet still be under divine law. By the same token, God can delegate the power of free choice to some creatures and not to others. In either case, though, God is still required to preserve the creatures in their respective states of existence. In whatever way God creates something, God's power maintains it in that state.

We should not confuse God's knowing that something is happening and God's causing something to happen in such and such a way. A contingent event remains contingent, if that is the way God creates it to be. Said otherwise, the universe is so freely made by God that some events can happen by chance. A particular fox catching a particular rabbit at a particular time and place is a chance event. Chance, though, is not by any means opposed to science in a contradictory way. In fact, chance presupposes a fixed framework of scientific order, stability, and predictability.

Thus, your automobile accident, for instance, need not be deliberately caused by God as punishment for sin. There really is such a thing as bad luck. There is also such a thing as good luck. Likewise in the case of your death. Rather than being predetermined for a fixed time and place in history, the actual time and place of your death depends upon the interaction of a large number of contingent variables, many of which are within your power to control. Nevertheless, chance events remain a part of the divine guidance of the world, including our human life on earth.

What is chance anyway? In Book 4 of his *Physics* Aristotle distinguished between spontaneous events and chance events. He reserved the term chance event for the unintended action of an intelligent agent that imitated an intended action, as when two people, one of whom owes money to the other, happen to meet at the market place, thus allowing the debt to be paid. A spontaneous event was one that occurred within the realm of unintelligent nature, as when the wind blows a rock off a cliff, which kills someone below. Aquinas, however, blends the two sorts of events together.

Chance is the crossing of two or more independent chains of events, such as a fox going its way crossing the path of a rabbit going its way. A chance event imitates deliberate intention, even though the creatures involved, whether intelligent or unintelligent, do not in fact intend the event. In a similar way, evil is the lack of something that should be there, especially with respect to the orientation of the human will toward God. We are free to choose something other than God, even though it destroys us. Freedom does not mean the lack of determination; it means self-determination. Neither does freedom mean unpredictability. From our point of view, an unfree act may be unpredictable (a chance event for us), while a free act may be predictable, as for instance when I must will a certain means to an end if that means is the only one that can achieve that goal. None of this, though, is contrary to God's providence.

This world-view is something that thinkers such as Hume and Darwin did not understand. Both lived at a time when British intellectuals thought of God as the author of nature. How, though, can a perfect workman create an imperfect product? However, as Aquinas explains, God's power is in no way exhausted by the presently existing scheme of things. There is no need for the present world to be the best of all possible worlds. God's proper name is Who Is, not the great engineer in the clouds. Consequently, even though whatever he makes is good, God can still make something better. The number four, for instance, is just fine, but there can still be something better, even in the realm of numbers. In response to the objection that the currently existing world must be the best if we are to preserve God's goodness and perfection, Aquinas says that such a thing would decrease rather than increase God's power. Admittedly, given the present array of things, everything is arranged in a very good way. This, though, does not rule out God's power to make other things, or even to add something to the present world, so as to make it better. God is under no obligation to say everything he knows or to do everything he can (Aquinas, 1894b, I, 25, 6).

In summary, God is compatible with science, freedom, and evil. God's plan is both a map and a mystery; some questions are answered and some are not. As far as we can see, though, harmful natural events can be explained in terms of accidents taking place in an overwhelmingly orderly (scientific) world. Violent natural changes in themselves are not good or evil. What happens, though, when they affect us? Were the people of Pompeii fated from all eternity to die? No. Likewise, the fact that you had an automobile accident was not 'on the cards', that is, it was not necessarily preordained from all eternity by God.

Human-caused evil, on the other hand, can be explained in terms of the biblical doctrine of original sin and our God-given power of free choice. Moral evil is due to human failings. Whose fault is it that we spend our money on warfare, overeating, and prostitutes rather than on pure water? Pornography, for instance, is hate literature directed against all women. Whose fault is it that so much money is spent on such hate literature, that so many women cooperate in their own degradation, and that we are ruled by Hollywood, TV, cable and satellite companies, and playboy-type businesses? (Centore, 2000).

In naturalistic theism, which has natural physical law but no natural moral law, things such as cancer and warfare are as natural as anything else. The volcanic lava and the crude oil have as much right to be on the beach as do the turtles and the human swimmers. You have as much right to life as do the grass and the flowers, which is to say, you have no right to life at all. For pantheism, everything is holy. Warfare, violence, and destruction are as sacred as life. There is no such thing as pollution, either physical or moral.

Not so with Aquinas. In opposition to pantheism, including ecological feminism, as well as in opposition to deism, we would never know that there is a mismatch of the parts of nature and human relationships unless we know what the match-up should be. Cancer and war, for example, are unnatural to us. For Aquinas, this brings us back to YAHWEH. He Who Is created things for our good and demands our love and obedience. Yet, when we fail to do his will, he is always ready to forgive and welcome home the truly repentant sinner, especially if approached though the Second Person of the Holy Trinity, as when someone sincerely says, 'Lord Jesus Christ, Lamb of God, I trust in your mercy, have mercy on me, a sinner'.

As explained by the modern writer Jacques Maritain, in the beginning man was not subject to the usual physical problems of nature. It was only after original sin that man became subject to the conditions that are a normal part of the subhuman world. On the compatibility of God and moral evil, Maritain concludes:

> My idea is that in insisting to the very end on the dissymmetry between the line of good and the line of evil and on the essential importance of the perspective of non-being, these views permit us to break the iron-collar of antinomies in which we are apparently enclosed by this truth that all that we do which is good comes from God and all that we do which is evil comes from ourselves. (Maritain, 1966, p. 111)

Bibliography

Adams, R.M. (1966) *Nil: Episodes in the Literary Conquest of Void During the Nineteenth Century*, New York: Oxford University Press.
Adler, M.J. (2001) 'A Novel Mechanism for Evolution?', *Science* 294, 5 October: 53-4.
Anselm (1958) *Proslogium; Monologium; An Appendix in Behalf of the Fool by Gaunilon; and Cur Deus Homo*, trans. S.N. Deane, La Salle, IL: Open Court.
Aquinas, Thomas (1894a) *Summa Contra Gentiles*, Rome: Forzani et S.
Aquinas, Thomas (1894b) *Summa Theologiae*, Rome: Forzani et S.
Aquinas, Thomas (1929-47) *Commentary on the Four Books of Sentences of Peter Lombard*, 4 vols, ed. R.T. Mandonnet. Paris: Lethielleux.
Aquinas, Thomas (1949) *On Being and Essence*, ed. and trans. A. Maurer, Toronto, ON: Pontifical Institute of Medieval Studies.
Aquinas, Thomas (1997) *Aquinas on Creation*, trans. S.E. Baldner and W.E. Carroll, Toronto, ON: Pontifical Institute of Medieval Studies.
Aristotle (1941) *The Basic Works of Aristotle*, ed. R. McKeon, New York: Random House.
Augustine (1948) *Basic Writings of Saint Augustine*, 2 vols, ed. W.J. Oates, New York: Random House.
Ayer, A.J. (1946) *Language, Truth and Logic*, New York: Dover.
Ayer, A.J. (1978) *The Central Questions of Philosophy*, New York: Penguin.
Azar, L. (1989) *Man: Computer, Ape, or Angel?*, Hanover, MA: Christopher.
Bacon, F. (1883) *Bacon's Essays*, ed. H. Morley, New York: Hurst.
Ball, W.W.R. (1912) *A Short Account of the History of Mathematics*, London: Macmillan.
Behe, M.J. (1996) *Darwin's Black Box*, New York: Free Press.
Behe, M.J., Dembski, W.A. and Meyer, S.C. (2000) *Science and Evidence for Design in the Universe*, San Francisco, CA: Ignatius.
Bhagavad-Gita As It Is (1986) trans. A.C. Bhaktivedanta Swami Prabhupada, Sydney, Australia: The Bhaktivedanta Book Trust.
Boethius (1962) *The Consolation of Philosophy*, trans. R. Green, Indianapolis, IN: Bobbs-Merrill.
Bourke, V.J. (1965) *Aquinas' Search for Wisdom*, Milwaukee, WI: Bruce.
Boyce, M. (1975) *The History of Zoroastrianism*, Leiden, Holland: Brill.
Browne, J. (2002) *Charles Darwin: The Power of Place*, 2 vols, New York: Knopf.
Burkitt, F.C. (1925) *The Religion of the Manichees*, London: Cambridge University Press.

Camus, A. (1955) *The Myth of Sisyphus*, trans. J. O'Brien, New York: Random House.
Centore, F.F. (1970) 'Whitehead's Conception of God', *Philosophical Studies* 19: 149–71.
Centore, F.F. (1991) *Being and Becoming*, Westport, CT: Greenwood.
Centore, F.F. (2000) *Two Views of Virtue*, Westport, CT: Greenwood.
Centore, F.F. (2001) 'Faith and Biological Reductionism: Darwin as a Religious Reformer', in *Proceedings of the American Fellowship of Catholic Scholars: Science and Faith (1998)*, ed. G.V. Bradley and D. DeMarco, South Bend, IN: Saint Augustine's Press.
Chesterton, G.K. (1937) *Autobiography*, London: Hutchinson.
Chesterton, G.K. (1956) *Saint Thomas Aquinas: the Dumb Ox*, Garden City, NY: Doubleday.
Chroust, A.-H. (1978) 'Aristotle's Doctrine of the Uncreatedness and Indestructibility of the Universe', *The New Scholasticism* 52: 268–79.
Confucius (1955) *The Sayings of Confucius*, trans. J.R. Ware, New York: Mentor.
Copleston, F.C. (1947) *Arthur Schopenhauer: Philosopher of Pessimism*, London: Burns Oates and Washbourne.
Copleston, F.C. (1980) *Philosophies and Cultures*, New York: Oxford University Press.
Copleston, F.C. (1982) *Religion and the One: Philosophies East and West*, New York: Crossroad.
Darwin, C. (n.d.) *The Origin of Species; The Descent of Man; and Selection in Relation to Sex*, New York: Modern Library.
Darwin, C. (1990) *Concordance of Charles Darwin's Notebooks, 1836–1844*, ed. D.J. Weinshank, Ithaca, NY: Cornell University Press.
Descartes, R. (1901) *The Method, Meditations and Philosophy of Descartes*, trans. J. Veitch, Washington, DC: Dunne.
Descartes, R. (1960) *A Discourse on Method and Other Writings*, trans. A. Wollaston, Baltimore, MD: Penguin.
Desmond, A.J. and Moore, J.R. (1991) *Darwin: The Life of a Tormented Evolutionist*, New York: Norton.
Dostoyevsky, F. (1912) *The Brothers Karamazov*, trans. C. Garnett, New York: Grosset and Dunlap.
Dougherty, J.P. (2000) *Western Creed, Western Identity*, Washington, DC: Catholic University of America Press.
D'Souza, J. (1959) 'Christianity and Indian Tradition', *America* 102(3): 13–15.
Ferris, P. (1998) *Dr Freud: A Life*, Washington, DC: Counterpoint.
Fisher, S. and Greenberg, R.P. (1996) *Freud Scientifically Reappraised: Testing the Theories and Therapy*, New York: Wiley.
Fothergill, P.G. (1952) *Historical Aspects of Organic Evolution*, London: Hollis and Carter.
Freud, S. (1961) *Civilization and Its Discontents*, ed. and trans. J. Strachey, New York: Norton.

Freud, S. (1963) *A General Introduction to Psychoanalysis*, trans. J. Riviere, New York: Washington Square Press.
Freud, S. (1965) *New Introductory Lectures on Psychoanalysis*, ed. and trans. J. Strachey, New York: Norton.
Gadamer, H.-G. (1989) *Truth and Method*, trans. J. Weinsheimer and D.G. Marshall, New York: Crossroad.
Gard, R.A. (ed.) (1963) *Buddhism*, New York: Washington Square Press.
Gilman, S.L. (1993) *Freud, Race, and Gender*, Princeton, NJ: Princeton University Press.
Gilson, E. (1941) *God and Philosophy*, New Haven, CT: Yale University Press.
Gilson, E. (1952) *Being and Some Philosophers*, Toronto, ON: Pontifical Institute of Medieval Studies.
Gilson, E. (1956) *The Christian Philosophy of Saint Thomas Aquinas*, New York: Random House.
Gilson, E. (1963) *Elements of Christian Philosophy*, New York: Mentor-Omega.
Gruber, H.E. and Barrett, P.H. (1974) *Darwin on Man*, New York: Dutton.
Healey, E. (2001) *Emma Darwin*, London: Headline.
Hegel, G. (1967) *Hegel's Philosophy of Right*, trans. T.M. Knox, New York: Oxford University Press.
Hegel, G. (1975) *Hegel's Logic*, trans. W. Wallace, New York: Oxford University Press.
Hegel, G. (1984) *Hegel: The Letters*, ed. and trans. C. Butler and C. Seiler, Bloomington: Indiana University Press.
Heisenberg, W. (1962) *Physics and Philosophy*, New York: Harper.
Hirsch, D.H. (1991) *The Deconstruction of Literature: Criticism After Auschwitz*, Hanover, NH: Brown University Press.
Hume, D. (n.d.) *History of England*, 6 vols, London: Warne.
Hume, D. (1938) *An Enquiry Concerning the Principles of Morals*, La Salle, IL: Open Court.
Hume, D. (1947) *Dialogues Concerning Natural Religion*, ed. N.K. Smith, Indianapolis, IN: Bobbs-Merrill.
Hume, D. (1961) *A Treatise of Human Nature*, Garden City, NY: Doubleday.
Hume, D. (1962) *On Human Nature and the Understanding*, ed. A. Flew, New York: Collier.
James, W. (1963) *Psychology*, ed. A. Montagu, New York: Fawcett.
James, W. (1968) 'The Will to Believe', in *The Writings of William James*, ed. J.J. McDermott, New York: Modern Library.
Kant, I. (1920) *Kants Opus Postumum*, ed. E. Adickes, Berlin: Reuther und Reichard.
Kant, I. (1956) *The Critique of Practical Reason*, trans. L.W. Beck, Indianapolis, IN: Bobbs-Merrill.
Ker, I. (1990) *John Henry Newman: A Biography*, New York: Oxford University Press.

Knox, R.A. (1955) 'The Problem of Suffering', in *A Retreat for Lay People*, New York: Sheed and Ward.
Knox, R.A. (1958) *The Belief of Catholics*, Garden City, NY: Doubleday.
Knox, R.A. (1963a) 'The Sufferings of Christ', in *University Sermons of Ronald A. Knox*, ed. P. Caraman, Montreal, PQ: Palm.
Knox, R.A. (1963b) 'The Church and Human Progress', in *University Sermons of Ronald A. Knox*, ed. P. Caraman, Montreal, PQ: Palm.
Kreeft, P.J. (1968) *Making Sense Out of Suffering*, Ann Arbor, MI: Servant.
Kreeft, P.J.(1999) *A Refutation of Moral Relativism*, San Francisco: Ignatius.
Lauer, R.Z. (1961) *The Mind of Voltaire*, Westminster, MD: Newman.
Lehman, D. (1991) *Signs of the Times: Deconstruction and the Fall of Paul de Man*, New York: Poseidon.
Locke, J. (1876) 'Elements of Natural Philosophy', in *Locke's Philosophical Works*, 2 vols, ed. J.A. Saint John, London: George Bell, vol. 2.
Lunn, A. and Knox, R.A. (1958) *Difficulties*, London: Eyre and Spottiswoode.
Maritain, J. (1944) *The Dream of Descartes*, trans. M.L. Andison, New York: Philosophical Library.
Maritain, J. (1966) *God and the Permission of Evil*, trans. J.W. Evans, Milwaukee, WI: Bruce.
Matthews, S. (2001) *Reason, Community, and Religious Tradition: Anselm's Argument and the Friars*, Burlington, VT: Ashgate.
Mosse, G.L. (1978) *Toward the Final Solution: A History of European Racism*, New York: Fertig.
Mossner, E.C. (1954) *The Life of David Hume*, London: Nelson.
Myers, G.E. (1986) *William James: His Life and Thought*, New Haven, CT: Yale University Press.
Newman, J.H. (1927) *Apologia Pro Vita Sua*, London: Longmans Green.
Newman, J.H. (1959) *The Idea of a University*, Garden City, NY: Doubleday.
Newman, J.H. (1985) *An Essay in Aid of a Grammar of Assent*, ed. I. Ker, New York: Oxford University Press.
Newton, I. (1950) *Newton's Theological Manuscripts*, ed. H. McLachlan, Liverpool, UK: Liverpool University Press.
Nietzsche, F.W. (1968) *The Will to Power*, ed. and trans. W. Kaufmann, New York: Vintage.
Nietzsche, F.W. (1974) *The Gay Science*, trans. W. Kaufmann, New York: Vintage.
Nietzsche, F.W. (1982) *The Portable Nietzsche*, ed. and trans. W. Kaufmann, New York: Penguin.
Nietzsche, F.W. (1987) *Beyond Good and Evil*, trans. R.J. Hollingdale, New York: Penguin.
Paley, W. (1819) *Natural Theology*, Hallowell, UK: Goodale.
Oates, W.J. (ed.) (1940) *The Stoic and Epicurean Philosophers*, New York: Modern Library.
Owens, J. (1963) *An Elementary Christian Metaphysics*, Milwaukee, WI: Bruce.

Pascal, B. (1941) *Pensées and Provincial Letters*, trans. W.F. Trotter and T. M'Crie, New York: Modern Library, section 139.
Peacocke, A. (1985) 'Biological Evolution and Christian Theology, Yesterday and Today', in *Darwinism and Divinity: Essays on Evolution and Religious Belief*, ed. J. Durant, Oxford, UK: Basil Blackwell.
Pinkard, T. (2000) *Hegel: A Biography*, New York: Oxford University Press.
Plato (1963) *The Collected Dialogues of Plato*, eds E. Hamilton and H. Cairns, New York: Pantheon.
Prichard, H.A. (1970) *Knowledge and Perception*, New York: Oxford University Press.
Pyle, A. (1997) *Atomism and Its Critics*, Bristol, UK: Thoemmes.
Raby, P. (2001) *Alfred Russel Wallace: A Life*, Princeton, NJ: Princeton University Press.
Rees, M. (2001) *Our Cosmic Habitat*, Princeton, NJ: Princeton University Press.
Russell, B. (1967) *Why I am not a Christian and Other Essays on Religion and Related Subjects*, ed. P. Edwards, London: Unwin.
Sartre, J.-P. (1982) *Existentialism is a Humanism*, trans. P. Mairet, London: Methuen.
Schopenhauer, A. (1958) *The World as Will and Presentation*, 2 vols, trans. E.F.J. Payne, Clinton, MA: Falcon's Wing Press.
Schopenhauer, A. (1970) *Essays and Aphorisms*, ed. and trans. R.J. Hollingdale, Baltimore, MD: Penguin.
Secord, J.A. (2001) *Victorian Sensation: The Extraordinary Publication, Reception, and Secret Authorship of Vestiges*, Chicago, IL: University of Chicago Press.
Sih, P.K.T. (1952) *From Confucius to Christ*, New York: Sheed and Ward.
Skinner, B.F. (1974) *About Behaviorism*, New York: Random House.
Solmsen, F. (1960) *Aristotle's System of the Physical World*, Ithaca, NY: Cornell University Press.
Stern, K. (1961) *The Third Revolution: A Study of Psychiatry and Religion*, Garden City, NY: Doubleday.
Strick, J.E. (2000) *Sparks of Life: Darwinism and the Victorian Debates over Spontaneous Generation*, Cambridge, MA: Harvard University Press.
Torrell, J.-P. (1996) *Saint Thomas Aquinas*, trans. R. Royal, Washington, DC: Catholic University of America Press.
Vaihinger, H. (1952) *The Philosophy of 'As If'*, trans. C.K. Ogden, London: Routledge and Kegan Paul.
Varghese, R.A. (2000a) *God-Sent*, New York: Crossroad, Introduction.
Varghese, R.A. (ed.) (2000b) *Theos, Anthropos, Christos: A Compendium of Modern Philosophical Theology*, New York: Peter Lang.
Vecchierello, H. (1934) *Einstein and Relativity; Le Maitre and the Expanding Universe*, Paterson, NJ: Saint Anthony Guild Press.
Vitz, P.C. (2000) 'The Psychology of Atheism', in *Theos, Anthropos, Christos: A Compendium of Modern Philosophical Theology*, ed. R.A. Varghese, New York: Peter Lang.

Voltaire (1961) *Philosophical Letters*, trans. E. Dilworth, Indianapolis, IN: Bobbs-Merrill.
Vrooman, J.R. (1970) *Rene Descartes*: A Biography, New York: Putnam's.
Weisheipl, J.A. (1974) *Friar Thomas D'Aquino: His Life, Thought, and Work*, Garden City, NY: Doubleday.
Weisheipl, J.A. (ed.) (1979) *Albertus Magnus and Science*, Toronto, ON: Pontifical Institute of Medieval Studies.
Whitehead, A.N. (1958) *The Function of Reason*, Boston, MA: Beacon.
Whitehead, A.N. (1960) *Process and Reality*, New York: Harper.
Whitehead, A.N. (1969) *Religion in the Making*, New York: Meridian.
Wilson, E.O. (1998) *Consilience: The Unity of Knowledge*, New York: Knopf.
Wippel, J.F. (2000) *The Metaphysical Thought of Thomas Aquinas: From Finite Being to Uncreated Being*, Washington, DC: Catholic University of America Press.

Index

Absolute, the, and Hegel 91–2
Adams, Robert Martin 98
Adeodatus 76
Agassiz, Louis 64
agnosticism
  as atheism 12
  origins of term 11
Ahriman 36
Ahura Mazda 36
Al-Qaeda 38
Alaric the Visigoth 76
Albertus Magnus 160
Albigensians 37, 166
Alexander the Great 37
Alexander III (Pope) 72
Alexander IV (Pope) 161
Alexander VI (Pope) 72
Alhazen 179
Allen, Ethan 4, 43
Ambrose, St 76
American Revolution, and Deism 43
analytic geometry, Descartes 83, 84
Anselm of Canterbury, St
  on existence of God 72–4
  life 71–2
  works
    Cur Deus Homo 71
    Monologium 71
    Proslogium 71, 72
anthropic principle 127
appearances, deceptiveness of 4
Aquinas, Thomas, St 1, 58, 74, 79, 151
  and Aristotle 170–71
  on essence 174–5
  on existence of God 175–6, 180–84, 186–9
  and existentialism 176
  life 160–65
  on morality 178
  philosophy 169–80
  on providence 186
  works
    Commentary on the Sentences 161–2, 163, 173
    Compendium of Theology 163
    Disputed Questions on the Power of God 162
    Disputed Questions on Truth 162
    An Exposition of Boethius' De Trinitate 162
    On Being and Essence 161, 180
    On the Reasonableness of the Faith 162
    Summa Contra Gentiles 162
    Summa Theologiae 163, 184, 186
Arians 76
Aristotle 40, 168–9, 174
  and Aquinas 170–71
  gods 185
  works
    Categories 78
    Metaphysics 1, 171, 172, 173, 176
    Nichomachean Ethics 41
    On the Soul 171
    Perihermeneias 78
    Physics 40, 172, 188
    Posterior Analytics 78
    Prior Analytics 78
    Refutations of the Sophists 78
    Topics 78
Arnauld, Antoine 85
  On Frequent Communion 48
Arnold, Matthew, *Dover Beach* 25
Arrian
  Discourses of Epictetus 32
  on education 32
as-if approach
  existence of God 45–68
  and risk 46
Ashoka 29

Assassins 37
atheism
    agnosticism as 12
    and Epicureanism 33
    and evil 12–13, 79–80
    Kant on 62–3
    Sartre on 20
Augustine, St
    on existence of God 77–8
    life 75–6
    works
        Against the Academics 76
        The City of God 77
        Confessions 75, 76, 77
        list 76
        The Nature of the Good 77
        On the Trinity 77
authenticity, personal 20–21
Averroes 173, 180
Avesta 36
Avicenna 172–3
Ayer, Alfred Jules 12, 68

Bacon, Francis
    Of Atheism 118
    On the Non-Existence of Magic 162
    Opus Majus 162
Bagavad-Gita 27
Ball, W.W.R. 82
Bayle, Pierre 54
Beauvoir, Simone de, *The Second Sex* 7
Beckett, Samuel, *Waiting for Godot* 1
Beeckman, Isaac 83
Beethoven, Ludwig van 90
Benedict XI (Pope) 164
Bentham, Jeremy 122
Bentley, Richard 120
Berulle, Pierre de 83
Big Bang theory 110
Boethius
    life 78
    works
        The Consolation of Philosophy 21, 79
        On the Holy Trinity 79
        On the Person and Dual Nature of Christ 79
        On the Six Days of Creation 79
Bogomils 37

Boniface VIII (Pope) 166
boredom, Schopenhauer on 98–9
Bourdin, Pierre 85
Brahmans 27
Bridget of Sweden, St 166
Bruer, Josef, *Studies in Hysteria* 107
Buddha 30
Buddhism
    Eight-Fold Path 29–30
    Four Noble Truths 29–30
    origins 29
    Pure Land 30
    salvation 29
    traditions 30
Buffon, Georges 125

Camus, Albert 19
capitalism 36
caste system, Hinduism 27–8
Cathari 37
Catherine the Great 43
Catherine of Siena, St 166
Chambers, Robert, *Vestiges of the Natural History of Creation* 126
chance, and freedom 188–9
Charcot, Jean Martin 107
Charles V (Holy Roman Emperor) 167
Chesterton, Gilbert Keith 94
    Autobiography 137
Christina of Sweden (Queen) 86
Church of the New Jerusalem 63
Clausius, Rudolf 55
Clement IV (Pope) 162
Clement VII (Pope) 167
Clement XI (Pope) 72
Conduitt, John 119, 120
Confucianism 38–9
    Five Classics 38
    Five Relationships 38
    Four Classics 38
    Li 38
    Negative Golden Rule 38
Council of Trent (1545–63) 165
craving, and suffering 29
Crusades, The 165
crutch theory, religion 4–5, 112
cultural relativism, and existence of God 5–10
Cusanus, Nicolaus 117

Dalai Lama 30
Dante Alighieri 164
Darius I (King of Persia) 37
Darwin, Charles 42
   evolutionary theory 140–48
   on existence of God 146–8
   life 137–9
   on morality 148–52
   Paley, influence of 122
   works
      The Descent of Man... 64, 140, 143, 144, 145, 148, 149, 151
      Origin of Species 141, 142, 143
      Selection in Relation to Sex 140, 151
Darwin, Erasmus 137, 138
Darwin, Robert Waring 137
Darwinism, and Deism 42–3
death, Pascal on 48–50
deconstructionism, literature 9
Deism 42–3
   and the American Revolution 43
   and Darwinism 42–3
   Voltaire 54, 56–9
Deists 43
Descartes, René 42
   analytic geometry 83, 84
   on existence of God 87–90
   inquiry method 86–8
   life 81–6
   on optics 84
   scepticism 84
   works
      Compendium of Music 83
      The Dioptics 84
      Discourse on Method 84
      Geometry 84
      Meditations on First Philosophy 84, 85, 88, 89, 90
      The Meteors 84
      On Man... 86
      The Passions of the Soul 86
      Principles of Philosophy 85
      Rules for the Direction of the Mind 83
      The Search After Truth 83
      The World 83
Dickens, Charles, *A Tale of Two Cities* 142
Dickinson, Emily, poem on belief 66
Diderot, Denis 43, 129
Dominic, St 168
Donatists 76
Doomsday Book 71
Dostoyevsky, Fyodor, *The Brothers Karamazov* 88
Dryden, John, *The Hind and the Panther* 119
duty, Kant on 63

Eddy, Mary Baker 155
education, Arrian on 32
Eight-Fold Path, Buddhism 29–30
Elizabeth Stuart of Bohemia, Princess 85
Enlightenment, European 54
entropy 55
Epictetus 32
Epicureanism 32–3
   and atheism 33
Epicurus 134
   Letter to Herodotus 131
   life 32
Erasmus, Desiderius 117
essence
   Aquinas on 174–5
   existence, difference 175
evil
   and atheism 12–13, 79–80
   definition 21
   and existence of God 21, 187, 189–90
   and good 22–3, 186
   and moral relativism 12
   Paley on 126
   Whitehead on 154
evolutionary theory, Darwin 140–48
existence, essence, difference 175
existentialism
   and Aquinas 176
   and Sartre 20

faith 14
   and understanding 72
feminism, and nature 7–8
Feuerbach, Ludwig 5
Fichte, Johann G. 90
for-real approach, existence of God 69–190

Four Noble Truths, Buddhism 29–30
Fox, William 138
Francis of Assisi, St 168
Francis I (King of France) 167
Franklin, Benjamin 43
Frederick II (Holy Roman Emperor) 55, 59, 159–60, 165
free will 187–8
freedom, and chance 188–9
French Revolution 56
Freud, Sigmund
  on existence of God 113–15
  life 106–7
  Oedipus Complex 107
  on religion 109–13
  works
    Civilization and Its Discontents 108
    The Ego and the Id 108
    The Future of an Illusion 108
    A General Introduction to Psychoanalysis 107
    The Interpretation of Dreams 107
    Moses and Monotheism 108, 113
    New Introductory Lectures on Psychoanalysis 108, 109
    Studies in Hysteria 107
    Totem and Taboo 108, 113
Froude, Richard Hurrell 100

Gadamer, Hans-Georg 6, 9
Galileo Galilei 118
Galton, Francis 138
Gassendi, Pierre 85
Gaunilon, *Book in Behalf of the Fool* 74
Gibbens, Alice 65
Gibbon, Edward 42
Gilson, Etienne 40–41, 169–70
God
  existence
    Anselm of Canterbury on 72–4
    Aquinas on 175–6, 180–84, 186–9
    arguments for 2
    as-if approach 45–68
    Augustine on 77–8
    Boethius on 79–81
    and cultural relativism 5–10
    Darwin on 146–8
    Descartes on 87–90
    and evil 21, 187, 189–90
    for-real approach 69–190
    Freud on 113–15
    god-of-the-gaps theory 42
    Hegel on 93–6
    Hume on 130–37
    in Judao-Christianity 185–6
    Kant on 61–2
    Newman on 102–6
    Newton on 120–22
    non-arguments 2–10
    Paley on 123–7
    Pascal's Wager 51–3
    Whitehead on 153–7
    William James on 67
  experience of 1
god-of-the-gaps theory, existence of God 42
gods
  Aristotle 185
  Greece 39–40
  Plato 185
  Rome 40
good
  definition 22
  and evil 22–3, 186
Gray, Asa 144
Greece, gods 39–40
Gregory IX (Pope) 160, 166
Gregory VII (Pope) 166
Gregory X (Pope) 163
Groote, Geert 117
Guillotin, Joseph 56

Halley, Edmund 120
happiness formula 26, 31, 35
Harvey, William 86
Hegel, Georg
  and the Absolute 91–2
  on existence of God 93–6
  and Hinduism 91
  life 90–91
  and Non-Being 92–3
  and Pseudo-liberty 94–6
  works
    Encyclopedia of the Philosophical Sciences 91
    Phenomenology of the Spirit 90
    Philosophy of Right 91
    Science of Logic 91

Heidegger, Martin 6
  and Nazism 9
Henry VIII (King of England) 167
Henslow, John Stevens 138
Heraclitus 40
Herford, Lord 129
Herodotus 36
Hill, Joe, poem on religion 5
Hinayana Tradition 30
Hinduism
  caste system 27–8
  deities 27
  and Hegel 91
  sacred writings 26
  salvation 27
  untouchables 28
Hirsch, David H. 9
Hitler, Adolf 20
  and Darwin 145–6
Hobbes, Thomas 85
Hooke, Robert 119, 120
Hugo, Victor 42
Hume, David 1, 33, 167
  on existence of God 130–37
  life 128–30
  on morality 135–7
  Paley, critique 131–2
  works
    Dialogues Concerning Natural Religion 128, 132, 135
    Enquiry Concerning Human Understanding 60, 134
    Enquiry Concerning the Principles of Morals 128, 129, 134
    History of England 129
    Political Discourses 128
    A Treatise of Human Nature... 128, 135
Hunt, William Morris 64
Huxley, Thomas Henry 11, 143
  Evolution and Ethics 145
Huygens, Christiaan 85

Ibsen, Henrik, *Hedda Gabbler* 98
impersonal, vs personal 41
Innocent III (Pope) 159, 160
Innocent IV (Pope) 161
Innocent V (Pope) 164
Innocent X (Pope) 48

Inquisition, establishment 166

James, Henry 63
James, William
  on existence of God 67
  life 63, 64
  Pragmatism 65, 66–7
  works
    Essays in Radical Empiricism 65
    Human Immortality 65
    The Meaning of Truth 65
    A Pluralistic Universe 65
    Pragmatism... 65
    Principles of Psychology 65
    Psychology: Briefer Course 65, 66
    Some Problems of Philosophy 65
    A Study in Human Nature 65
    The Varieties of Religious Experience... 65, 67
    The Will to Believe 66
Jansen, Cornelis, *Augustinus* 48
Jansenists 47, 48
Jefferson, Thomas 43
Jesus Christ
  imitation of 17
  as mediator 51
  suffering 16
John Lackland (King of England) 159
John XXII (Pope) 165
John-Paul II (Pope) 6
Johnson, Samuel 138
Justinian I (Byzantine Emperor) 79

Kafka, Franz, *The Trial* 99
Kant, Immanuel
  on atheism 62–3
  on duty 63
  on existence of God 61–2
  life 59–60
  works
    Anthropology from a Pragmatic Viewpoint 60
    The Contest of the Faculties 60
    The Critique of Judgment 60
    The Critique of Practical Reason 60, 61
    The Critique of Pure Reason 60, 61
    The Foundations of the Metaphysics of Morals 60

Metaphysics of Ethics 60
On the Real Advances in Metaphysics... 60
The Only Possible Foundation... 60
A Prolegomena to Any Future Metaphysics 60
Religion Within the Bounds of Reason Alone 60
karma 27
Kaufmann, Walter Arnold 15
Keble, John 100
Kempis, Thomas of, *Imitation of Christ* 117
Kepler, Johan 119
Kierkegaard, Søren 91, 166
Kingsley, Charles 101
　When All the World is Young 23
Knox, Ronald Arbuthnott 25, 166, 169
Kung Fu-Tzu 38

Lamarck, Jean Baptiste 138
　Philosophical Zoology 125
Lanfranc 71
Langton, Stephen 159
Lao-Tzu 39
Lauer, Rosemary Z. 56
Lavoisier, Antoine 56
Le Maître, Georges Henri, Abbé 110
Lehman, David 9
Leibniz, Gottfried Wilhelm von 55, 119
Li, Confucianism 38
Lincoln, Abraham 43
literature, deconstructionism 9
Locke, John 54, 57, 59, 120
loneliness 41
Louis IX (King of France) 161
love, and sex 151
Lunn, Arnold 166
Luther, Martin 117
Lyell, Charles, *Principles of Geology* 138

Mahayana Tradition 30
Maimonides, Moses 174
　Guide for the Perplexed 170
　Mishnah Torah 170
Malebranche, Nicolas 83
Malthus, Thomas 126
　An Essay on the Principle of Population 138

Man, Paul de 9
Manes (Mani) 37
Manichaeism 37–8, 75
　destructiveness 38
　duality 37
　spread 37
Marco Polo 164
Marcuse, Herbert 9, 145
Maritain, Jacques 9, 190
Marx, Karl
　and Darwin 145
　and religion 5, 109–10
Master of Darkness 37
Master of Light 37
Mersenne, Marin 84
Mill, John Stuart 131
　On Liberty 142
Mithraism 37
Mivart, Saint George Jackson, *On the Genesis of Species* 143
Monica, St 75
Montaigne, Michel de 84
Montanists 76
Monteverdi, Claudio 81
Moore, Thomas
　poem on God 75
　The Last Rose of Summer 41
moral relativism, and evil 12
morality
　Aquinas on 178
　Darwin on 148–52
　Hume on 135–7
Mussolini, Benito, and Darwin 145

Napoleon Bonaparte 42, 56
natural theology, origins 1
naturalistic theism 25–33, 117–18, 189
　Schopenhauer on 97
nature
　and feminism 7–8
　hierarchy of 187
Nazism
　and Heidegger 9
　and Nietzsche 16
Negative Golden Rule, Confucianism 38
Newman, John Henry
　on existence of God 102–6
　influences on 106
　life 100–102

on original sin 50–51
works
  An Essay in Aid of a Grammar of Assent 102
  An Essay on the Development of Christian Doctrine 101
  Apologia Pro Vita Sua... 101–2
  The Arians of the Fourth Century 100
  Discourses on University Education 101
  The Idea of a University 101, 102, 143
  Lectures and Essays on University Subjects 101
  On the Present Position of Catholics in England 101
Newton, Isaac
  on existence of God 120–22
  inventions 118
  life 118–20
  works
    Mathematical Principles of Natural Philosophy 119, 120–21
    On Motion 119
    Opticks 120
    Theological Manuscripts 121
Nicaean Creed 76
Nietzsche, Elisabeth, *The Life of Nietzsche* 15
Nietzsche, Friedrich Wilhelm
  life 14
  and Nazism 16
  and religion 15, 17–18
  style 16
  and the superman 18–19
  and Wagner 14–15
  works
    Beyond Good and Evil 15
    Dawn 15
    Ecce Homo 15
    Human, All Too Human 15
    The Anti-Christ 15
    The Birth of Tragedy... 15
    The Complete Works 15
    The Corruption of Wagner 15
    The Decline of the Gods 15, 18
    The Gay Science 15
    The Genealogy of Morals 15
    The Will to Power 15, 16
    Thus Spoke Zarathustra 15
    Untimely Meditations 15
nihilism 16
nirvana 30, 31
Non-Being, and Hegel 92–3

Oedipus Complex, Freud 107
optics, Descartes on 84
original sin
  Newman on 50–51
  Pascal on 50–51
Ormuzd 36
Orwell, George, *1984* 95
Otto the Great (Holy Roman Emperor) 165
Otto, Nikolaus 65

Paganism 39–42
Paine, Thomas 43
Paley, William
  Darwin, influence on 122
  on evil 126
  on existence of God 123–7
  Hume, critique by 131–2
  life 122
  works
    Horae Paulinae... 122
    Natural Theology... 122, 123
    The Principles of Moral and Political Philosophy 122
    A View of the Evidence of Christianity 122
pantheism *see* naturalistic theism
Parmenides 40, 92, 171
Pascal, Blaise
  on death 48–50
  on existence of God 47–53, 66
  life 47
  on original sin 50–51
  works
    Essay on Conic Sections 47
    Pensées 51
    Provincial Letters 47
    Thoughts on Religion 47
  Voltaire on 56–7
Pascal's Principle 47
Pascal's Wager, and existence of God 51–3

Paschal II (Pope) 71
Paul III (Pope) 167
Paulicians 37
Pelagians 76
Perier, Gilberte 47
personal, vs impersonal 41
Peter the Great (King of Russia) 59
Peter the Lombard, *Sentences* 161
Peter the Venerable 162
Petrarch, Francesco 117
Philip IV (King of France) 166
Piazzi, Giuseppe 90
Pius V (Pope) 165
Pius XI (Pope) 101
Pius XII (Pope) 3–4
Plato 40, 171, 174
   gods 185
   Phaedo 171
   Symposium 77
   The Laws 1
Plotinus 76, 171
   Enneads 77
Plutarch 36
polytheism 36–42
Pope, Alexander 129
post-modernism, and truth 5–6
Pragmatism, William James 65, 66–7
Priestley, Joseph 138
providence
   Aquinas on 186
   divine 187–9
Pseudo-liberty, and Hegel 94–6
Psychical Research, Society for 65
Pure Land, Buddhism 30

Radewyns, Florens 117
reason, and religion 117–18
religion
   crutch theory 4–5, 112
   diversity 42
   Freud on 109–13
   and Marx 5, 109–10
   and Nietzsche 15, 17–18
   origin 111–12
   and reason 117–18
   and science 1–2
Renaissance, The 117
Renouvier, Charles 64
reproduction, and sex 152
risk, and as-if approach 46
Rome
   gods 40
   sack by Visigoths 76
Rousseau, Jean-Jacques 42, 55, 129, 138
Royal Society of London 118–19
Russell, Bertrand 13–14
   Principia Mathematica 153

Saint Clair, General 128
salvation
   Buddhism 29
   Hinduism 27
Sartre, Jean-Paul
   on atheism 20
   existentialism 20
   works
      Being and Nothingness 7, 20
      Existentialism is a Humanism 7
scepticism, Descartes 84
Schelling, Friedrich W.J. von 90
Schopenhauer, Arthur
   on boredom 98–9
   life 96
   on pantheism 97
   works
      The Four-Fold Root of Sufficient Reason 96–7
      On Will in Nature 97
      Parerga and Paralipomena 97
      The World as Will and Idea 96, 97, 99
Schultz, Franz Albert 59
science
   determinism 5
   and religion 1–2
   Whitehead on 153
Sedgwick, Adam 138, 143
sex
   and love 151
   and reproduction 152
Shakespeare, William, sonnet on the soul 185
Shang Ti 38
Shinshu Buddhism 30
Siddhartha Gautama 29
Skinner, B.F. 111
Smith, Adam 129

Snellius, Willebrord 84
Sorbonne, Robert de 161
Spinoza, Baruch 91, 92
Stern, Karl 113
Stoicism 31–2
    meaning 31
    origins 32
Strabo 36
Strauss, Leo 9
Suárez, Francis 59
suffering
    and craving 29
    Jesus Christ 16
supernaturalistic theism 35–43
Swedenborg, Emanuel 63–4
Symmachus 78

Taoism 39
Tennyson, Alfred, *In Memoriam A.H.H.* 139, 141–2
Teresa of Avila, St 113
Thales 40
Theodoric the Great 78
Thirty Years' War (1618–48) 83
Tindal, Matthew, *Christianity as Old as the Creation...* 42
Toland, John
    Christianity not Mysterious 42
    Pantheisticon 42
tradition, function 6
truth, and post-modernism 5–6
Twain, Mark 65

understanding, and faith 72
uniformitarianism 138–9
universe, expanding 110
untouchables, Hinduism 28
Upanishads 26–7
Urban II (Pope) 71
Urban IV (Pope) 162
Urban V (Pope) 164
Urban VIII (Pope) 83

Vaihinger, Hans 62–3
Vatican Council II (1962–65) 165
Vitz, Paul C. 107
Voetius, Gisbertus 85
Voltaire 42, 119
    Deism 54, 56–9
    life 54–5
    on Pascal 56–7
    works
        An Essay on the General History... 55
        Candide 55
        For and Against 54
        The Henriad 54
        The Lisbon Disaster 55
        The Metaphysics of Sir Isaac Newton... 55
        Oedipus 54
        The Philosophical Dictionary 55
        Philosophical Letters 55, 56, 57, 58
        Treatise on Metaphysics 54, 56

Wagner, Richard, and Nietzsche 14–15
Wallace, Alfred Russel 142
Warburton, William 129
Washington, George 43
Watt, James 138
Wedgwood, Emma 139
Wedgwood, Josiah 138
Wedgwood, Susannah 138
Whitehead, Alfred North
    on evil 154
    and existence of God 153–7
    life 152–3
    on science 153
    works
        list 153
        Principia Mathematica 153
        Process and Reality... 155
        Religion in the Making 153, 154, 173
Wilberforce, Samuel 143
Wilberforce, William 143
Wilhelm IV, Friedrich (King of Prussia) 14
William the Conqueror 71
William II (King of England) 71
William of Saint Amour 161
Wilson, Edward Osborne 108
Wolff, Christian von, influence 59
Wordsworth, William, *The World is Too Much With Us* 39

Yin-Yang 39

Zen Buddhism 30
Zeno of Citium 32

Zoroaster 36
Zoroastrianism 36–7